False Prophets

False Prophets

Studies on Authoritarianism

Communication in Society, Volume 3

LEO LOWENTHAL

Routledge
Taylor & Francis Group

LONDON AND NEW YORK

First published 1987 by Transaction Publishers

Published 2017 by Routledge
2 Park Square, Milton Park, Abingdon, Oxon OX14 4RN
711 Third Avenue, New York, NY 10017, USA

Routledge is an imprint of the Taylor & Francis Group, an informa business

Library of Congress Catalog Number: 86-30899

Library of Congress Cataloging in Publication Data

Lowenthal, Leo.
   False prophets.
   (Communication in society; v. 3)
   Bibliography: p.
   Includes index.
1. Authoritarianism. 2. Authority. 3. Prejudices.
I. Title. II. Series: Lowenthal, Leo. Communication in society; v. 3
HM271.L68   1987   303.3'6
ISBN 0-88738-136-7   86-30899

ISBN-13: 978-1-4128-5701-7 (pbk)

YEA, THEY ARE PROPHETS OF
THE DECEIT OF THEIR OWN HEART.

Jer. 23:26

Contents

Acknowledgments

Part IV as well as the Excursus and the Afterword were translated from German into English, especially for this volume, by Theodor R. Weeks to whom I am very grateful. I also acknowledge with profound gratitude numerous editorial suggestions of Susanne Hoppmann-Lo-wenthal.

Thanks is also due to the Institute of Advanced Study at Berlin (Wissenschaftskolleg zu Berlin) which extended generous support for the technical preparation of the manuscript of this volume.

Foreword

Ideologies and ideological manifestations may be measured, or they may be understood as qualities, as meaningful structural units. Both techniques of content analysis lead the scientist to insights into the roots of social problems, in this case, of group prejudice and discrimination. This book by Leo Lowenthal and Norbert Guterman is confined to qualitative analysis. Not the frequency of the ideas, formulas, and devices to be found in agitational material, but the meaning of demagogy, of its techniques and appeals, its arguments and its personalities, is the theme.

Although the study employs many psychoanalytical concepts, in fact it is devoted not so much to the private physiognomy of the agitator as to the psychological content and significance of the agitator's behavior. It seeks to cast light on the inner, and often unconscious, mechanisms at which agitation is directed. But all this must be understood sociologically. Though the demagogue plays upon psychological predispositions with psychological weapons, the predispositions themselves and the aims striven for are socially created.

It is only the highly developed social situation that sets our demagogue apart from numerous predecessors back through the centuries and millennia. Demagogy makes its appearance whenever a democratic society is threatened with internal destruction. In a general sense, its function has always been the same: to lead the masses toward goals that run counter to their basic interests. And this function accounts for the irrationality of demagogy; the psychological techniques it employs have a definite social basis.

Today, under the conditions of a highly industrialized society, consumption is largely determined by production even in the field of ideologies. Attitudes and reactive behavior are often "manufactured." The people do not "choose" them freely but accept them under the pressure of power, real or imaginary. Study of the people themselves therefore does not suffice. The nature of the stimuli must be studied along with the reactions if we are to grasp the true significance of the phenomena of mass behavior. Otherwise, one might erroneously attribute to an underlying frame of public mind what may in fact be the product of calculated techniques of communication.

None of the specific techniques of agitation can be judged outside their political and social contexts. Their specific significance as a means of antidemocratic mass manipulation lies solely within the structural unity of the pattern this book seeks to formulate.

It is notable, for example, that the contemporary agitator, the expert propagandist who has assumed the role of leader, dwells incessantly on his own person. He portrays himself as both leader and common man. By suggesting that he too is a victim of sinister social forces, by displaying his own weakness as it were, he helps conceal from his followers the very possibility of independent thinking and autonomous decision. He sets the pattern for that most contemporary phenomenon, the deindividualized, incoherent, and fully malleable personality structure into which antidemocratic forces seek to transform man.

The content of present-day demagogy is obviously empty, accidental, and entirely subordinate to manipulative considerations. Our home-grown agitators, in the absence of an American tradition of nationalistic aggressiveness, created an artificial fusion with Italian and German fascist notions. They have also borrowed from certain forms of religious revivalism, without regard to any specific content, forms that exploit such rigid stereotypes as the distinction between the "damned" and the "saved." The modern American agitator has put these old-fashioned techniques to very good use.

"Good use?" the reader may well ask with some incredulity. American hatemongers are at present at a low point in influence and prestige. Even at the peak of their strength before the war, they failed to build a unified organization or to win substantial financial backing.

This is true, of course. But because the emphasis of the book is on the *meaning* of the phenomena under analysis, the agitator should be studied in the light of his *potential* effectiveness within the context of present-day society and its dynamics, rather than in terms of his immediate effectiveness. Although overt anti-Semitic agitation is at an ebb, it is important to study its content and techniques as examples of modern mass manipulation in its most sinister form.

This volume does not exaggerate the immediate importance of American demogogy, nor does it pretend to offer a photographic picture of the political realities of the day. Instead, it places under the microscope certain phenomena that may seem negligible at first sight, and by thus enlarging the most extreme and apparently unrealistic manifestations of antidemocratic behavior, it gains diagnostic insight into the latent threat against democracy.

Max Horkheimer

Preface

Before and during the past war Americans were amazed to find that there existed in their midst a number of individuals who strikingly resembled the local Nazi *führers* of the 1920s in Germany. Most of them openly expressed admiration for Hitler and Mussolini, were rabidly anti-Semitic, and indulged in intensive vituperation of our national leaders. In addition, most of them headed small "movements" and published periodicals. They all made frequent political speeches, and some gave comfort and aid to our enemies.

It is this type of self-appointed popular spokesperson that is designated by the term agitator in the present study. No attempt has been made here to cover the history of political agitation in all its aspects or to analyze other forms of contemporary propagandistic manipulation of popular psychology, indigenous or imported.

The conventional image of the American agitator is that of an American copy of a foreign model. He is usually thought of as a crackpot whose appeals and goals derive neither from domestic conditions nor from native attitudes. Seen thus as a kind of foreign agent, the agitator has usually been fought by the method of exposure. His nefarious purposes and affiliations as well as the obvious internal inconsistencies in his statements have often been pointed out. Underlying this view of the agitator—and its attendant strategy of exposure—is the assumption that he can succeed in enlisting public support only through deception, his utterances serving merely to camouflage his true aims. Expose his tricks it is held, and you reduce him to helplessness.[1]

In this study of American agitation we have tried to demonstrate that the conventional image of the agitator is not a faithful portrait, that it differs from the picture that emerges from a careful study of his texts. These texts serve as the sole basis of the present study, but because we believe that the agitator often relies upon unconscious mechanisms to build instruments for manipulating his audience, we have tried to probe beneath the manifest content of his speeches and writings to disinter their latent content.

We have sought to extract what is common in the various agitational texts; on the whole, we have ignored the differences. From a mass of writings and speeches by this country's notorious agitators we have drawn the most significant characteristics of the different types of those who are sophisticated and intellectual in their approach as well as of those who are naive and primitive; of those who come from industrial areas and of those who come from rural areas. In the overwhelming majority of instances, the quotations used in this book can easily be found as recurrent themes in the agitational material.

The idea of studying agitation as a surface manifestation of deeper social and psychological currents was conceived by Max Horkheimer, director of the Institute of Social Research. The institute has conducted research along these lines since 1940 through pilot studies by Theodor W. Adorno, Leo Lowenthal, and Paul W. Massing. The present study, based partly upon these previous investigations, was undertaken in cooperation with the Department of Scientific Research of the American Jewish Committee, to whom the authors are indebted for continued encouragement and interest. Although they have drawn freely upon the earlier studies of the institute on the subject, especially that of Adorno, the authors take full responsibility for their interpretations and conclusions. Obviously, only a certain degree of probability can be claimed for conclusions about latent content. A merely textual analysis cannot determine with precision which of several possible meanings an audience might ascribe to a given theme. We recognize that our interpretations cannot claim to represent actual audience reactions. Rather, our purpose here has been to establish hypotheses on possible reactions. We believe that this approach may pave the way for an empirical exploration of the psychology of the agitator and for field work on his actual effects upon audiences. Methodologically, this study is frankly experimental; it touches a field that has been hardly explored.[2]

We wish to express our appreciation and thanks to associates and friends who were unsparing of their time and effort in helping us with this book. To Dr. Adorno, Professor Edward N. Barnhart of the University of California, Dr. Horkheimer, Dr. Paul Massing, Professors Paul F. Lazarsfeld, Robert K. Merton, and C. Wright Mills of Columbia University, and Professor Hans Speier of the Rand Corporation, who were kind enough to read the entire draft, we are deeply grateful for their comments and constructive criticism. Dr. Ernst Kris of the New School of Social Research, Dr. S. Kracauer, Miss Thelma Herman, Dr. Herta Herzog, and Joseph Klapper, gave us valuable suggestions on methodological and sociological problems.

In the selection of the representative agitators and the quoted texts, various organizations prominent in the task of combating antidemocratic propaganda have given us generous assistance. We wish to express special thanks to Leon Lewis of Los Angeles and to Miss Ellen Posner of the Library of Jewish Information in New York for their making source material available. Mrs. Edith Kriss of the Institute of Social Research showed exceptional devotion in the complicated and thankless task of organizing voluminous files of material. To Irving Howe we owe much for his help in preparing the final manuscript.

Leo Lowenthal
Norbert Guterman

Institute of Social Research
December, 1948

Notes

1. A pioneering exception is the study *The Fine Art of Propaganda* (edited by Alfred McClung Lee and Elizabeth Briant Lee, New York. 1939, and published under the auspices of the Institute for Propaganda Analysis). The authors sensed the need for a content analysis of agitational output and succeeded in isolating a number of central rhetorical devices used by the agitator. Another interesting study along these lines is "The Technique of Propaganda for Reaction: Gerald L. K. Smith's Radio Speeches" by Morris Janowitz *(Public Opinion Quarterly,* 1944, pp. 84–93).

2. Cf. Max Horkheimer, "Egoismus und Freiheitsbewegung." *Zeitschrift für Sozialforschung 5* (1936): 161–234. This study on the psychological background of various liberation movements in modern history has set the historical frame of reference for our book.

Part I

Prophets of Deceit:
A Study of the Techniques of
the American Agitator

(with Norbert Guterman)

1

The Themes of Agitation

The Agitator Speaks

When will the plain, ordinary, sincere, sheeplike people of America awaken to the fact that their common affairs are being arranged and run for them by aliens, Communists, crackpots, refugees, renegades, Socialists, termites, and traitors? These alien enemies of America are like the parasitic insect which lays his egg inside the cocoon of a butterfly, devours the larvae and, when the cocoon opens, instead of a butterfly we find a pest, a parasite.

Oh, this is a clever scheme and if the American people don't get busy and fight it the whole vicious thing will be slipped over on you without your knowing what hit you. A comprehensive and carefully planned conspiracy, directed by a powerfully organized clique, and operating through official and semiofficial channels, has been in continuous existence since the days of Nimrod of Babylon, and is the ever lurking enemy of the people's liberty. Remember at all times that the tactics employed by these usurpers of Christian liberties will be to create horror and panic by exhibitions of maximum brutalities. (How would you like to have the bloodstream of your baby, or your son, or daughter, or wife polluted by dried blood collected from Jews, Negroes, and criminals?) It will be only ordinary sense at the first announcements of trouble for all householders to have several large receptacles for storing drinking water on their premises so that ravages of thirst may not add to the general ordeal.

Hitler and Hitlerism are the creatures of Jewry and Judaism. The merciless programs of abuse which certain Jews and their satellites work upon people who are not in full agreement with them create terrible reactions. I am not justifying the reactions and I am not condoning the reactions; I am merely explaining them. Have the Jews forgotten that the more they organize materially against their opponents, the more assaults will increase and the closer they are to persecution?

3

Remember, these Jews expect to show no mercy to Christians. What is to prevent Jewish gangsters from doing damage to synagogues on purpose so as to create apparent justification for retaliation—in which Christian Americans, who know too much and have displayed too much courage, would be picked up dead in or near synagogues?

We know what the stuffed shirts and reactionaries will say. They will say we are crackpots. They will say that this program will appeal only to the lunatic fringe. But surely it is not anti-Semitism to seek the truth. Or is it?

What's wrong? I'll tell you what is wrong. We have robbed man of his liberty. We have imprisoned him behind the iron bars of bureaucratic persecution. We have taunted the American businessman until he is afraid to sign his name to a pay check for fear he is violating some bureaucratic rule that will call for the surrender of a bond, the appearance before a committee, the persecution before some Washington board, or even imprisonment itself.

While we have dissipated and persecuted management, we have stood idly by and watched a gang of racketeers, radicals, and conspirators regiment our workers in the name of organized labor into a dues-paying conspiracy designed in Moscow to recruit workers for what they hope would become the American Red Revolution.

We are going to take this government out of the hands of these city-slickers and give it back to the people that still believe that 2 and 2 is 4, that God is in his heaven and the Bible is the Word. Down must come those who live in luxury, the laws that have protected the favored few, and those politicians who are disloyal to the voters!

Whenever a legislative body meets, liberties of the people are endangered by subtle and active interests. Lust for power, financial and political, is the ever-lurking enemy of the people's liberty. There is a deserved odium resting upon the word "liberal." Whether applied to Religion, Morals, or Politics, "Liberalism" is destructive of all fundamental values. In matters pertaining to Religion. Liberalism leads to Atheism. In Morals, it leads to Nudism. In Politics, it leads to Anarchy. In the framework of a democracy the great mass of decent people do not realize what is going on when their interests are betrayed. This is a day to return to the high road, to the main road that leads to the preservation of our democracy and to the traditions of our republic.

Alien-minded plutocrats roll in wealth, bathe in liquor, surround themselves with the seduced daughters of America, and cooperate in all schemes to build up pro-Communist and anti-Christian sentiment.

America, the vain—America, the proud—America, the nation of gluttons and spenders and drinkers. When Harry Hopkins got married, Mr. Baruch arranged the party. There were seven kinds of meat served—twenty-two kinds of food, and it had cost Barney Baruch $122 a plate; and they drank of the vintage of '26. You talk about the drunken orgies of history—we expect Capone to live like that, but as long as I am a Christian soul, I will not be governed by a man like that. That's what they do not want me to say. That's why I am such a bad man. Because I say what you all want to say and haven't got the guts to say.

We leaders are risking our lives to write a new page in American history. We propose without further ado, without equivocation, without any silly sentimentality sometimes known as Tolerance, to emasculate the debauchers within the social body and reestablish America on a basis where this spoliation can never again he repeated. I am attempting to speak one hundred times between the sixth of August and the fifteenth of September. This would be physically impossible for most men but thanks to the temperate and Christian life of my mother and father, I have been given a strong body and strong constitution. Even so, there will he nights that I will drop to the bed almost like a dead man, I will be so fatigued and exhausted. But I'll never throw mud at my opponent . . . I am led by the ethics and morals of Christ.

We are coming to the crossroads where we must decide whether we are going to preserve law and order and decency or whether we are going to be sold down the river to these Red traitors who are undermining America.

This meeting is not a lecture course, it is not an open forum . . . we are making history here today. This is a crusade. I don't know how we can carry on without money. All we want is money from enthusiastic friends.[1]

Background for Seduction

The agitator's harangue may appear simply as the raving of a maniac—and may be ignored as such. Yet speeches and articles that voice essentially the same ideas and are couched in similar language do attract steady audiences in this country, if, for the time being, only small ones. What are the social and psychological implications of such materials?

American agitation is in a fluid stage. Some agitators have occasionally come fairly close to the national political scene. Acting on the assumption that the United States was nearing a grave crisis, they have tried to build a mass movement—with most notable success during the years of the New Deal and shortly before U.S. entry into the war. But by and large this has been the exception.

Far more numerous are those less conspicuous agitators who are active locally and who, far from evoking the image of a leader worshipped by masses of followers, rather suggest a quack medicine salesperson. Their activity has many characteristics of a psychological racket: they play on vague fears or expectations of a radical change. Some of these agitators hardly seem to take their own ideas seriously, and it is likely that their aim is merely to make a living by publishing a paper or holding meetings.[2] What they give their admission-paying audience is a kind of act—something between a tragic recital and a clownish pantomime-rather than a political speech. Discussion of political topics invariably serves them as an occasion for vague and violent vituperation and often seemingly irrelevant personal abuse. The line between ambitious politician and small-time peddler of discontent is hard to draw, for there are many intermediary types. What is important, however, is that American agitation finds itself in a preliminary stage in which movement and racket may blend.

Whatever the differences among American agitators, they all belong to the same species. Even the unforewarned listener or reader is immediately struck by the unmistakable similarity of their content and tone. A careful examination of agitational speeches and writings shows that this similarity is not accidental but based on a unifying pattern—on certain recurrent motifs, *the constants of agitation.* Because these are not explicitly stated as such, the agitation analyst's first task is to isolate them. This, then, is the basic task of the present study: to discover the social and psychological strains of agitation by means of isolating and describing its fundamental themes.

As differentiated from propagandistic slogans, agitational themes directly reflect the audience's predispositions. The agitator does not confront his audience from the outside; he seems rather like someone arising from its midst to express its innermost thoughts. He works, so to speak, from inside the audience, stirring up what lies dormant there.

The themes are presented with a frivolous air. The agitator's statements are often ambiguous and unserious. It is difficult to pin him down to anything and he gives the impression that he is deliberately playacting. He seems to be trying to leave himself a margin of uncertainty, a possibility of retreat in case any of his improvisations fall flat. He does not commit himself, for he is willing, temporarily at least, to juggle his notions and test his powers. Moving in a twilight zone between the respectable and the forbidden, he is ready to use any device, from jokes to double-talk to wild extravagances.

This apparent unseriousness is, however, concerned with very serious matters. In his relationship to the audience the agitator tries to establish a tentative understanding that will lead to nothing less than seduction. There is a sort of unconscious complicity or collaboration between him and the listeners; as in cases of individual seduction, neither partner is entirely passive, and it is not always clear who initiates the seduction. In seduction there operates not only mistaken notions or errors of judgment that are the result of ruses but also, and predominantly, psychological factors that reflect the deep conscious and unconscious involvement of both parties. This relationship is present in all the themes of agitation.

When the serpent suggests to Eve that she eat the forbidden fruit, Eve knows that she would thereby be violating God's commandment. The serpent does not present an idea completely alien to her; he plays rather upon her latent desire to do the forbidden, which is, in turn, based on her inner rebellion against the commandment.

Working on the Audience

Agitation may be viewed as a specific type of public activity and the agitator as a specific type of "advocate of social change," a concept that will serve us as a convenient frame of reference.

The immediate cause of the activity of an "advocate of social change" is a social condition that a section of the population feels to be iniquitous or frustrating. This discontent he articulates by pointing out its presumed causes. He proposes to defeat the social groups held responsible for perpetuating the social condition that gives rise to discontent. Finally, he promotes a movement capable of achieving this objective, and he proposes himself as its leader.

Here, then, are the four general categories under which the output of any "advocate of social change" can be classified: Discontent; the Opponent; the Movement; and the Leader. Significant variations in the categories can be used to isolate subclasses; an especially useful division is to break down "advocate of social change" into "reformer" or "revolutionary," depending on whether the discontent is seen as circumscribed in area or as involving the whole social structure.

Unlike the usual advocate of social change, the agitator, while exploiting a state of discontent, does not try to define the nature of that discontent by means of rational concepts. Rather, he increases the audience members' disorientation by destroying all rational guideposts and by proposing that they instead adopt seemingly spontaneous modes of behavior. The opponent he singles out has no discernibly rational features. His movement is diffuse and vague, and he does not appeal to any well-defined social group. He lays claim to leadership not because he understands the situation better than others but because he has suffered more than they have. The general purpose of his activity, be it conscious or not, is to modify the spontaneous attitudes of his listeners so that they become passively receptive to his personal influence.

It is quite obvious that the agitator does not fit into the reformer type; his grievances are not circumscribed but, on the contrary, take in every area of social life. Nor does he address himself to any distinct social group, as does the reformer; except for the small minority he brands as enemies, every American is his potential follower.

Yet he does not fit into the revolutionary group, either. Although the discontent he articulates takes in all spheres of social life, he never suggests that in his view the causes of this discontent are inherent in and inseparable from the basic social setup. He refers vaguely to the inadequacies and iniquities of the existing social structure, but he does not hold it ultimately responsible for social ills, as does the revolutionary.

He always suggests that what is necessary is the elimination of people rather than a change in poitical structure. Whatever poitical changes may be involved in the process of getting rid of the enemy he sees as a means rather than an end. The enemy is represented as acting, so to speak, directly on his victims without the intermediary of a social form, such as capitalism is defined to be in socialist theory. For instance, although agitational literature contains frequent references to unemployment, one cannot find in it a discussion of the economic causes of unemployment. The agitator lays responsibility on an unvarying set of enemies, whose evil character or sheer malice is at the bottom of social maladjustment.

> Sometimes, these internationalists [a few international financiers] are not even interested in price or profit. They use their monopoly control to determine the living standards of peoples. They would rather see unemployment, closed factories and mines, and widespread poverty, if they might see the fulfillment of their own secret plans.[3]

Unlike the reformer or revolutionary the agitator makes no effort to trace social dissatisfaction to a clearly definable cause. The whole idea of objective cause tends to recede into the background, leaving only on one end the subjective feeling of dissatisfaction and on the other the personal enemy held responsible for it. As a result, his reference to an objective situation seems less the basis of a complaint than a vehicle for a complaint rooted in other, less visible causes.

This impression is confirmed when we observe with what facility the agitator picks up issues from current political discussions and uses them for his own purposes. Throughout the past sixteen years, despite the extraordinary changes witnessed in American life, the agitator kept grumbling and vituperating in the same basic tone. Unlike political parties, he never had to change his "general line." When unemployment was of general concern, he grumbled about that; when the government instituted public works to relieve unemployment, he joined those who inveighed against boondoggling.

Sensational news items supply him with occasions for branding the evil character of the enemy:

> The death of General George S. Patton, Jr., remains a mystery. He was a careful driver. He admonished all who drove for him to drive carefully.
>
> He was known to be wise and cautious in traffic. He was killed by a truck that charged into him from a side road.
>
> He opposed the Morgenthau Plan. He was against the liquidation of the German race merely because they were Germans. He refused to be dominated and bulldozed by revengeful Jews. He had promised to blow off the lid if he ever returned to the United States. Some people doubt if his death was an accident.[4]

His imagination does not shy away from obvious incongruities:

> Suppose—that the Third International had issued secret formulae and technical instructions to a handpicked personnel of the Communist Party in all countries . . .
>
> Do you remember a couple of years ago that a mysterious gas cloud of drifting death fell upon northern France and Belgium and floated across the channel and up the Thames even to London itself? . . .
>
> Do you know that even in Free America at the present moment, stark and violent Death waits upon the footsteps of men who know such facts and give them effectively to the public?[5]

It should by now be clear tht the agitator is neither a reformer nor a revolutionary. His complaints do refer to social reality but not in terms of rational concepts. When the reformer and revolutionary articulate the original complaint, they supplant predominating emotional by intellectual elements. The relationship between complaint and experience in agitation is rather indirect and nonexplicit.

The reformer and revolutionary generalize the audience's rudimentary attitudes into a heightened awareness of its predicament. The original complaints become sublimated and socialized. The direction and psychological effects of the agitator's activity are radically different. The energy spent by the reformer and revolutionary to lift the audience's ideas and emotions to a higher plane of awareness is used by the agitator to exaggerate and intensify the irrational elements in the original complaint.

The following incident illustrates the difference between the two approaches. In a crowded New York bus a woman complained loudly that she was choking, that she was pushed and squeezed by other passengers, and added that "something should be done about it." (*A typical inarticulate complaint.*) A second passenger observed: "Yes, it's terrible. The bus company should assign more busses to this route. If we did something about it, we might get results." (*The solution of a reformer or revolutionary. The inarticulate expression of the complainant is translated into an objective issue—in this case "the faulty organization of the transportation services that can be remedied by appropriate collective action."*) But then a third passenger angrily declared: "This has nothing to do with the bus company. It's all those foreigners who don't even speak good English. They should be sent back where they came from." (*The solution of the agitator who translates the original complaint not into an issue for action against an established authority but into the theme of the vicious foreigners.*)

In contradistinction to all other programs of social change, the explicit content of agitational material is in the last analysis incidental—it is like the manifest content of dreams. The primary function of the agitator's words is to release reactions of gratification or frustration whose total effect is to make the audience subservient to his personal leadership.

It is true that the agitator sometimes appears to introduce concepts that were not originally present in the audience's complaints. But these are not the result of an objective analysis. When the agitator denounces government bureaucrats for the privations of wartime rationing, he does so not because he has discovered any causal relationship between the two but rather because he knows that there is a potential resentment against bureaucrats for reasons that have nothing to do with rationing. The appearance of an intellectual distance between the agitator and the audience is deceptive: instead of opposing the "natural" current, the agitator lets himself be carried by it. He neglects to distinguish between the insignificant and the significant; no complaint, no resentment is too small for the agitator's attention. What he generalizes is not an intellectual perception; what he produces is not the intellectual awareness of the predicament but an aggravation of the emotion itself.

Instead of building an objective correlate of his audience's dissatisfaction, the agitator tends to present it through a fantastic and extraordinary image, which is an enlargement of the audience's own projections. The agitator's solutions may seem incongruous and morally shocking, but they are always facile, simple, and final, like daydreams. Instead of the specific effort the reformer and revolutionary demand, the agitator seems to require only the willingness to relinquish inhibitions. And instead of helping his followers to sublimate the original emotion, the agitator gives them permission to indulge in anticipatory fantasies in which they violently discharge those emotions against alleged enemies.

Sometimes this hostility takes on paranoiac overtones. The change of the shape of traffic lights in New York City, for instance, may inspire the following remarks:

> What a shock it must be to the descendants of the STAR OF DAVID to see *all* traffic signal lights in the Five Boroughs of Greater New York being changed, for the duration, from the full red and green circular light, about 6 inches in diameter, now to show a RED OR GREEN CROSS, for or against traffic. This change is made in the DIMOUT idea, but the use of the CROSS is the work of our Engineering Department of the N.Y. Police, so the Jews can be reminded that this is a Christian Nation.[6]

The reformer or revolutionary concentrates on an analysis of the situation and tends to ignore irrational or subconscious elements. But the agitator appeals primarily to irrational or subconscious elements at the expense of the rational and analytical.

Notes

1. The speech is a composite of actual statements made by American agitators. Except for the punctuation, everything—words, thoughts, appeals—is all theirs.
2. Compare the excellent study by J. V. Martin, "A Gentleman from Indiana," *Harper's Magazine,* (January 1947): 66.

3. SJ, Sept. 8, 1941.
4. CF, Feb., 1946.
5. Pelley, *Official Despatch: Silver Shirts of America Are Mobilizing to Protect* YOUR *Life!*, p. 2.
6. AID, June 15, 1942, p. 3.

2

Social Malaise

The first and most natural task that confronts a student of any movement of social change is to locate the cause of the movement in a specific condition of discontent. In most instances the solution of this problem presents no difficulties at all—in fact, the advocate of social change himself devotes a great part of his energy to articulating this cause. When we examine agitation, however we face an entirely different situation. That the agitator wants to exploit existing discontent is obvious enough; he seems always to be addressing people who are smarting under the harshest injustice and whose patience has been strained to the breaking point. But whenever the investigator scans the texts of agitation and, on the basis of experience in studying other kinds of social movements, tries to discover what is the discontent it articulates, he is consistently disappointed.

The difficulty is not that agitation fails to provide the investigator with answers but, rather, that it answers a question he did not ask: whenever he asks *what,* he is answered as if he had asked *who.* He finds numerous vituperative and indignant references to enemies, but nowhere can he find a clearly defined objective condition from which the agitator's audience presumably suffers. At best, agitation provides the investigator with contradictory or inconsistent references to such alleged conditions. Unless we decide that the agitator is simply a lunatic, we must assume that although a sense of discontent exists, he, unlike other advocates of social change, is either unable or unwilling to state it explicitly. Hence, the agitation analyst faces the task of himself explicating the state of discontent to which the agitator refers.

A Catalogue of Grievances

Even a cursory glance at agitational material shows that any attempt to analyze it by methods that help discover the purposes of the revolutionary or the reformer could lead only to an impasse. If we try to

13

classify the agitator's complaints in terms of the simplest categories, we obtain approximately the following picture:

1. *Economic Grievances.* The agitator roams freely over every area of economic life. He may begin anywhere at all. Too much help is being extended to foreign nations. "If we have any money to offer for nothing, or to loan, or to give away, we had better give it to our own first. Of course, that is old fashioned."[1]

   Not only are foreigners taking our money, they also threaten our jobs. "People born in America have to commit suicide because they have nothing to eat while refugees get their jobs."[2]

   Behind such injustices stand "the International Bankers, who devised and control our money system, [and] are guilty of giving us unsound money."[3]

   Such situations constitute a danger to the American way of life, for "what is more likely to follow many years of Nudeal communistic confiscatory taxation, wool-less, metal-less, auto-less regimentation and planned scarcities than our finally becoming stripped by necessity to Nudism?"[4]

2. *Political Grievances.* International commitments by the United States government jeopardize political liberties. "Like Russia, the United States is suffering from the scourge of internationalism."[5] The American people are warned: "Be not duped by the internationalists who dwell amongst us."[6]

   Of course, it is only reasonable that "treaties and agreements . . . shall be reached with other nations, but. . . we want no world court and no world congress made up of a few Orientals and a few Russians and a few Europeans and a few British . . . to make laws for us to obey. . . ."[7]

   From within, this country is threatened by radicalism, which prepares strikes that are "dress rehearsals for a forthcoming general strike that is meant to paralyze the Nation. . . ."[8]

   We face both the danger of a "Soviet America . . . where . . . an Austrian-born Felix Frankfurter presides over an unending 'Moscow trial'. . . ."[9] and the rule of "tyrannical bureaucrats" who if they "could have their way completely" would institute a "dictatorship in America as merciless as anything on earth."[10]

3. *Cultural Grievances.* The agitator is greatly disturbed because the media of public information are in the hands of enemies of the nation. ". . . The Hollywood motion picture industry is being exploited by Russian Jewish Communists determined to inject their materialistic propaganda into the fresh young minds of our children."[11] Hollywood is "largely dominated by aliens who have appropriated to their own use the inventions and discoveries of native citizens and who now specialize in speculation, indecency and foreign propaganda."[12]

   "The American press will never be free" until control "is removed from racial, religious and economic pressure groups."[13]

4. *Moral Grievances.* The enemies of the agitator are notoriously lax in morals: they engage in luxury consumption, they are a "crowd of Marxists, refugees, left-wing internationalists who enjoy the cream of the country and want the rest of us to go on milkless, butterless, cheeseless days while they guzzle champagne."[14]

    And what is most galling of all is that "we gentiles are suckers," for "while we were praying they had their hands in our pockets."[15]

Emotional Substratum

This list of diffuse complaints could be lengthened indefinitely; it should be sufficient to indicate that the grievances the agitator voices do not refer to any clearly delineated material or moral condition. The only constant elements discernible in this mass of grievances are references to certain emotions or emotional complexes. These may be roughly divided as follows.

Distrust

The agitator plays on his audience's suspicions of all social phenomena impinging on its life in ways it does not understand. Foreign refugees cash in on the "gullibility" of Americans, whom he warns not to be "duped" by internationalists. Strewn through the output of the agitator are such words as *hoax, corrupt, insincere, duped, manipulate.*

Dependence

The agitator seems to assume that he is addressing people who suffer from a sense of helplessness and passivity. He plays on the ambivalent nature of this complex, which on the one hand reflects a protest against manipulation and on the other hand a wish to be protected, to belong to a strong organization or be led by a strong leader.

Exclusion

The agitator suggests that there is an abundance of material and spiritual goods, but that the people do not get what they are entitled to. The American taxpayer's money is used to help everyone but him. "We feed foreigners,"[16] the agitator complains, while we neglect our own millions of unemployed.

Anxiety

This complex manifests itself in a general premonition of disasters to come, a prominent part of which seems to be the middle-class fear of a dislocation of its life by revolutionary action, and the middle-class suspicion that the moral mainstays of social life are being undermined. The agitator speaks of "the darkest hour in American history"[17] and graphically describes a pervasive sense of fear and insecurity:

> This afternoon America is caught in the throes of fear, apprehension and concern. Men are afraid . . . to vote, afraid not to vote. . . . Our population has been caught by the ague and chills of uncertainty. Unless these uncertainties can be removed, unless these fears can be destroyed, we shall never have prosperity again.[18]

Disillusionment

This complex is seen in such remarks as the agitator's characterization of politics as "make-believe, pretense, pretext, sham, fraud, deception, dishonesty, falsehood, hypocrisy."[19] In fact, "whenever a legislative body meets, liberties of the people are endangered by subtle and active interests."[20] Ideological slogans inspire resentment: "Democracy A Misnomer, A Trick Word Used by Jew and Communistic Internationalists to Confuse and Befuddle American Citizens."[21] Values and ideals are enemy weapons, covering up the machinations of sinister powers that, "taking advantage of the mass ignorance of our people, accomplish their purposes under the cloak of humanitarianism and justice."[22]

The Individual in Crisis

The analyst of agitation now faces the problem: Are these merely fleeting, insubstantial, purely accidental, and personal emotions blown up by the agitator into genuine complaints, or are they themselves a constant rooted in the social structure? The answer seems unavoidable: These feelings cannot be dismissed as either accidental or imposed, they are basic to modern society. Distrust, dependence, exclusion, anxiety, and disillusionment blend together to form a fundamental condition of modern life: malaise.

When we define the discontent utilized by agitation as malaise, we are, so to speak, on our own, for we cannot justify this definition by explicit references to agitational statements. It is a hypothesis, but it is a highly plausible one because its only alternative would be to see the maze of agitational statements as a lunatic product beyond analysis. Moreover, it helps to account for certain recurrent characteristics of agitation: its diffuseness, its pseudospontaneity, its flexibility in utilizing a variety of grievances, and its substitution of a personal enemy for an objective condition.

The agitator does not spin his grumblings out of thin air. The modern individual's sense of isolation, his so-called spiritual homelessness, his bewilderment in the face of the seemingly impersonal forces of which he feels himself a helpless victim, his weakening sense of values—all these motifs often recur in modern sociological writings. This malaise reflects the stresses imposed on the individual by the profound transformations taking place in our economic and social structure—the replacement of the class of small independent producers by gigantic industrial bureaucracies, the decay of the patriarchal family, the breakdown of primary personal ties between individuals in an increasingly mechanized world, the compartmentalization and atomization of group life, and the substitution of mass culture for traditional patterns.

These objective causes have been operating for a long time with steadily increasing intensity. They are ubiquitous and apparently permanent, yet they are difficult to grasp because they are only indirectly related to specific hardships or frustrations. Their accumulated psychological effect is something akin to a chronic disturbance, an habitual and not clearly defined malaise that seems to acquire a life of its own and that the victim cannot trace to any known source.

On the plane of immediate awareness, the malaise seems to originate in the individual's own depths and is experienced by him as an apparently isolated and purely psychic or spiritual crisis. It enhances his sense of antagonism toward the rest of the world. The groups in our society that are at present most susceptible to agitation seem to experience this malaise with particular acuteness, perhaps precisely because they do not confront social coercion in its more direct forms.

Although malaise actually reflects social reality, it also veils and distorts it. Malaise is neither an illusion of the audience nor a mere imposition by the agitator; it is a psychological symptom of an oppressive situation. The agitator does not try to diagnose the relationship of this symptom to the underlying social situation. Instead he tricks his audience into accepting the very situation that produced its malaise. Under the guise of a protest against the oppressive situation, the agitator binds his audience to it. Because this pseudoprotest never produces a genuine solution, it merely leads the audience to seek permanent relief from a permanent predicament by means of irrational outbursts. The agitator does not create the malaise, but he aggravates and fixates it because he bars the path to overcoming it.

Those afflicted by the malaise ascribe social evil not to an unjust or obsolete form of society or to a poor organization of an adequate society

but, rather, to activities of individuals or groups motivated by innate impulses. For the agitator, these impulses are biological in nature, they function beyond and above history. Jews, for instance, are evil—a "fact" that the agitator simply takes for granted as an inherent condition that requires no explanation or development. Abstract intellectual theories do not seem to the masses as immediately "real" as their own emotional reactions. It is for this reason that the emotions expressed in agitation appear to function as an independent force, which exists prior to the articulation of any particular issue, is expressed by this articulation, and continues to exist after it.

Malaise can be compared to a skin disease. The patient who suffers from such a disease has an instinctive urge to scratch his skin. If he follows the orders of a competent doctor, he will refrain from scratching and seek a cure for the cause of his itch. But if he succumbs to his unreflective reaction, he will scratch all the more vigorously. This irrational exercise of self-violence will give him a certain kind of relief, but it will at the same time increase his need to scratch and will in no way cure his disease. The agitator says keep scratching.

The agitator exploits not primarily the feelings generated by specific hardships or frustrations, but more fundamentally those diffuse feelings of malaise that pervade all modern life. The malaise that is experienced as an internal psychic condition can, however, be explained only by the social process in its totality. Such an explanation, following the classical method of articulating causes of discontent in universal and verifiable terms and then proposing definite methods to remove them, is beyond the resources of the agitator.

Here the agitator turns to account what might appear his greatest disadvantage: his inability to relate the discontent to an obvious causal base. Although most other political movements promise a cure for a specific, and therefore limited, social ailment, the modern agitator, because he himself indirectly voices the malaise, can give the impression that he aims to cure some chronic, ultimate condition. And so, he insinuates, while others fumble with the symptoms, he attacks the very roots of the disease in that he voices the totality of modern feeling.

Because the malaise originates in the deepest layers of the individual psyche, it can appear to be an expression of frustrated spontaneity and essential spiritual needs. The agitator, implicitly working on this assumption, thus claims in effect that he represents the most general interests of society, while his opponents, who concern themselves with such limited, specific matters as housing or unemployment or wages, represent only selfish class interests. He can excoriate the others for their seemingly materialistic attitude because he, on the contrary, has at heart only the nation and the race.

He can thus identify himself with any symbol suggesting spiritual spontaneity and, by extension, with any symbol suggesting that he strives to gratify suppressed instinctual impulses. He can appear as the enemy of those unjust constraints of civilization that operate on a deeper, more intimate level than those imposed by social institutions, and he can represent himself as a romantic defender of ancient traditions that today are being trampled by modern industrialism.

This alleged spirituality is vague enough to include or exclude anything at all, to be dissociated from history and to be associated with the most primitive biological instincts. In its name the agitator can appeal to the Promethean energies of sacrifice and promise to satisfy the essential needs for participation in communal life, for spiritual security, spontaneity, sincerity, and independence. He can easily switch from money and unemployment to spiritual matters.

> There is something deeper, more substantial which has been removed from the foundation of our national life than the mere loss of money and loss of jobs. . . . Charity means seeking first the kingdom of God and His justice rather than seeking banks filled with gold.[23]

Malaise is a consequence of the depersonalization and permanent insecurity of modern life. Yet it has never been felt among people so strongly as in the past few decades. The inchoate protest, the sense of disenchantment, and the vague complaints and forebodings that are already perceptible in late-nineteenth-century art and literature have been diffused into general consciousness. There they function as a kind of vulgarized romanticism, a *Weltschmerz in perpetuum*, a sickly sense of disturbance that is subterranean but explosive. The intermittent and unexpected acts of violence on the part of the individual and the similar acts of violence to which whole nations can be brought are indices of this underground torment. Vaguely sensing that something has gone astray in modern life but also strongly convinced that he lacks the power to right whatever is wrong (even if it were possible to discover what is wrong), the individual lives in a sort of eternal adolescent uneasiness.

The agitator gravitates toward malaise like a fly to dung. He does not blink its existence as so many liberals do; he finds no comfort in the illusion that this is the best of all possible worlds. On the contrary, he grovels in it, he relishes it, he distorts and deepens and exaggerates the malaise to the point where it becomes almost a paranoiac relationship to the external world. Once the agitator's audience has been driven to this paranoiac point, it is ripe for his ministrations.

The prevalence of malaise in recent decades is reflected in growing doubt with relation to those universal beliefs that bound Western society together.[24] Religion, the central chord of Western society, is today often justified even by its most zealous defenders on grounds of expediency. Religion is proposed not as a transcendent revelation of the nature of man and the world, but as a means of weathering the storms of life, or of deepening one's spiritual experience, or of preserving social order, or of warding off anxiety. Its claim to acceptance is that it offers spiritual comfort. A similar development may be found in morality. There are today no commonly accepted—commonly accepted as a matter of course and beyond the need for discussion—moral values. Such a pragmatic maxim as "honesty is the best policy" is itself striking evidence of the disintegration of moral axioms. And much the same is also true for economic concepts; the businessman still believes in fair competition, but in his "dream life . . . the sure fix is replacing the open market."[25]

As a result, the old beliefs, even when preserved as ritualistic fetishes, have become so hollow that they cannot serve as spurs to conscience or internalized sources of authority. Now authority stands openly as a coercive force and against it is arrayed a phalanx of repressed impulses that storm the gates of the psyche seeking outlets of gratification.

When, for whatever reasons, direct expression of feelings is inhibited. they are projected through some apparently unrelated materials. We may accordingly assume that if the audience is not aware of the causes of the malaise, this is due not only to the inherent complexity of these causes but chiefly to unconscious inhibitions, which probably originate in a reluctance to struggle against seemingly superior forces. So the agitator sanctions immediate resentments and seemingly paves the way for the relief of the malaise through discharge of the audience's aggressive impulses, but simultaneously he perpetuates the malaise by blocking the way toward real understanding of its cause.

All such utilizations of malaise are possible only on condition that the audience does not become aware of its roots in modern society. The malaise remains in the background of agitation, the raw material of which is supplied by the audience's stereotyped projections of the malaise. Instead of trying to go back to their sources, to treat them as symptoms of a bad condition, the agitator treats them as needs that he promises to satisfy. He is therefore not burdened with the task of correcting the audience's inadequate ideas; on the contrary, he can let himself be carried along by its "natural" current.

Notes

1.   CF, Feb. 1946. p. 710.
2.   Phelps, Los Angeles, Dec. 23, 1940, radio.
3.   CF, Oct., 1944, p. 454.
4.   RTL, Mar. 27, 1942, p. 11.
5.   DEF, Aug., 1939, p. 4.
6.   Coughlin, Speech on March 26, 1939, reprinted in *Why Leave Our Own*, p. 161.
7.   CF, Oct.–Nov., 1942, p. 8.
8.   AP, Nov., 1945, p. 5.
9.   Kamp, *Vote CIO . . . and Get a Soviet America*, p. 64.
10. CF, June 1942, p. 9.
11. Smith. *Letter*, "The Battle of Babylon," July, 1945, p. 2.
12. AP, Aug., 1944, p. 1.
13. SJ, Sept. 11, 1939, p. 13.
14. SJ, July 21, 1941, p. 11.
15. Charles White, New York, July 18, 1940, street corner.
16. Phelps, Los Angeles, July 27, 1940, radio.
17. Smith, Detroit, April 9, 1942, meeting.
18. Smith, *Why Is America Afraid?*
19. AP, Sept. 1944, p. 2.
20. SJ, Jan. 15, 1940, p. 19.
21. X, February 17, 1945, p. 1.
22. SJ, June 6, 1938, p. 5.
23. Coughlin, *Father Coghlin's Radio Discourses*, pp. 236–237.
24. Cf. Max Horkheimer, *Eclipse of Reason,* (New York: Oxford University Press, 1947).
25. C. Wright Mills, "The Competitive Personality," *Partisan Review* 13, no. 4 (1946): 436.

3

A Hostile World

The agitator articulates the themes of his writings and speeches as if they referred to specific and genuine issues arising from current social problems. He tries to appear as a bona fide advocate of social change, but in effect he merely manipulates and modifies those of the audience's feelings that reflect the malaise. He crystallizes and hardens these feelings and distorts the objective situation. In the themes related to discontent the audience's vague, inarticulate distrust becomes fixated as the stereotype of perpetual dupery; its sense of dependence serves to foster the belief that it is the object of a permanent conspiracy; its sense of exclusion is externalized into the image of forbidden fruits; its disillusionment is transformed into the complete renunciation of values and ideals; and its anxiety is both repressed and magnified into the perpetual expectation of apocalyptic doom.

Theme 1: The Eternal Dupes

Every form of persuasion implies an effort to convert or seduce and presupposes an initial intellectual or emotional distance between the speaker and the listener. The leader of a movement must first convince his audience that its ideas are inadequate for coping with the situation that produces its discontent. He cannot win adherents without in a sense humiliating them, that is, suggesting that they are inferior in knowledge, strength, or courage and that they need him more than he needs them.

In intellectual communication—for example, the activity of a teacher in relation to his students—the aim is to nullify the distance altogether. In the activity of a reformer or revolutionary, there is a similar tendency to decrease initial distances. The adherent's humiliation is at least in theory only temporary, for the leader always suggests that in the end the ignorant will become enlightened, the moderately informed citizen will acquire a higher social consciousness, and the timid follower will share in the leader's courage.

In agitation, this humiliation is permanent. In establishing the inferiority of his prospective followers, the agitator claims superior knowledge, which, he implies, he has obtained by virtue of his special position and abilities. The audience is inferior not because it is temporarily "unenlightened" but because it is composed of "dupes" and "suckers." Throughout his utterances there can be found many unflattering references to potential followers. The agitator speaks of striking workers as "just plain ordinary sincere sheeplike Americans."[1] When he refers to the "bemused" people taken in by the New Dealer's "hoax"[2] or of the "deluded innocents,"[3] his tone is relatively mild. It changes to worry when he speaks about the "gullibility of Americans"[4] and the "mass ignorance of our people" of which the "powers of anti-Christianity" take advantage.[5] When he deplores the fact that the "blind populace" is being led into the "horrible ditch of war" by blind leaders,[6] the agitator adopts a tone of regret. And when he calls his potential followers "sappy Gentiles"[7] or "dumb Americans,"[8] the agitator becomes stingingly indignant.

He intimates that the unenlightened condition of his audience is hopeless and permanent, is something the audience itself cannot remedy. He warns his audience that it needs his guidance in the bewildering situation in which it finds itself, but he offers it no way to escape its bewilderment by its own intellectual efforts. He enhances his listeners' sense of distrust by reminding them that they are ruled by "remote control" and that they are exposed to constant sinister manipulations. They are cheated all along the line, in rationing, in war, through the press and the movies.

He not only denounces Communist slogans as "catch-phrases to obtain power over . . . dupes"[9] but also brands preparedness against the Axis as a pretext for inflicting a hoax "on a long-suffering people in the name of and behind the cruel mask of 'defense.'"[10] Against such unscrupulous tactics, the "plain ordinary sincere sheeplike" people are helpless; they are always the victims, the eternal dupes.

The effectiveness of such frank and unflattering talk should not be underestimated. It must not be forgotten that the agitator banks on an audience composed of "dupes," people who bear the world a grudge because they feel it has cheated them, and who are therefore insecure, dependent, and bewildered. The agitator is referring to a common life experience. From childhood on, people are burdened by a repression of instinctual drives imposed on them by civilization in the name of its values. To live up to these values, they must constantly deny themselves and make sacrifices, for which the only solace is the promise that ultimately they will be rewarded. But in the lives of most people there occurs a moment, usually near middle age, when they realize that their dreams have remained and will remain unfulfilled. This realization gives way to a painful inner conflict, which may be resolved in several ways. The shock of disillusionment may be absorbed internally: the individual attributes responsibility to himself, to his real or imaginary inadequacies, lack of industriousness or thriftiness, inferior natural endowment, or even to insufficiently sincere adherence to the unfulfilled ideals. Or he seeks consolation in the promises of religion, transferring the realization of the ideals to the beyond. Or again he may draw some satisfaction from the fact of disillusionment itself, by becoming, as so many aging persons do, a "cynic," and flaunting that attitude with a kind of malicious pleasure. One way or another, the conflict or at least the acute awareness of it can be repressed, but the smooth operation of such repression depends upon the hold ideals or values have on the individual. In the past the values were unassailable, and if they were not realized, the fault was due to one's inadequacy. Today the hold of values is weakened, while the pressure of reality has grown greater. And precisely because values are now questioned, the fury of disillusionment can be turned against them.

The individual's growing belief that the values are fictitious adds the motive of humiliation to that of disillusionment. He has sacrificed his life, his "real" life, which comes to be defined precisely as the life denied by the ideal, for the sake of mere nothings. He is confirmed in such feelings by the everyday experience that ruthlessness and unscrupulous pursuit of material advantage are more profitable than rigid adherence to moral principles. All his life he has been a sucker, cheated by the values he accepted and those who preached them.

By calling his followers suckers and telling them they must follow him if they are no longer to be cheated, the agitator promises that he will take care of them and "think" for them. Those who chafe under an authority they distrust and whose motives they cannot understand, are now to be subjected to the promptings of an agitator who will sanction their spontaneous resentments and seem to gratify their deepest wishes.

The agitator thereby tends to destroy the common social rule that imposes optimistic stereotypes ("I feel fine"; Everything is OK") on human intercourse. In a society of independent producers this rule helped to smooth the mechanism of free competition by eliminating any possible intrusion of pity or self-pity. It also helped to preserve the sanctity of the individual by keeping his inner life concealed from his neighbor's curiosity. To pour out one's troubles in public was considered a mark of bad taste and vulgarity. Social life, of which the dominant image was the impersonal marketplace, was a neutral arena in which everyone was supposed to feel equally at ease. Unless he wanted to become an object of charity, the individual's intimate problems were not exposed to the group. The agitator breaks down these folkways; he seems to say, "let us be honest, let us admit we are disillusioned, ignorant and cheated." Such an invitation can only be welcomed by people who feel that they have always been "misunderstood." Hence, by reversing the optimistic stereotypes of liberal society, the agitator makes the feeling of acknowledged failure seem respectable.

Because in the eyes of the audience the whole world has become suspicious and estranged, it yearns for facile certainties and is ready to put its fate in the hands of someone who confirms it in its helplessness. "It is high time for Americans to get wise," says the agitator.[11] Yet those who have got wise to all the tricks are just the ones who are deceived by the most primitive ruse. The investment swindler knows that his easiest victims are to be found among those who have learned to distrust respectable banking establishments. Even while he tells his listeners that they are a group of fools, the agitator lays claim to their confidence—for how could someone who warns and insults them possibly want to cheat them? His bad manners become a guaranty of his sincerity. They can trust him, for he does not flatter them, and because they are unable by themselves to "pierce the sham of propaganda,"[12] their only possible course of action is to join his movement. "Better find out whom you can trust—now."[13]

On the one hand the agitator brands his followers as suckers, harping on the suffering they have endured in their unsuccessful lives and thereby satisfying their latent masochism. On the other hand, he transforms this very humiliation into something to be proud of, a mark of the new elite he will eventually elevate. By projecting the responsibility for it on an unscrupulous and immoral enemy, he offers his followers a means of warding off in advance all future humiliations. The humiliation is simultaneously deepened and surrounded by a halo.

While the agitator thus frees the audience from its burdensome obligation of understanding its plight, he gives it a feeling that it is at last facing the true facts of existence. Yes, they are suckers, but now they know it. And what is more, they do not have to be inhibited about their intellectual inferiority; they can admit it openly; their leader encourages them to do so. Ordinarily intellectual inferiority results in exclusion from the company of the successful, but in the relationship between agitator and audience, this is reversed: the agitator seems to be especially interested in the little man who has not made the grade. Though he does not give his listeners the feeling of having attained intellectual insight or of being accepted as demarcated individuals, he does make it possible for them to feel at ease in their common inferiority.

Theme 2: Conspiracy

The dupe is pictured not merely as cheated but as cheated systematically, consistently, and perpetually. Nor is his inability to overcome his bewilderment and helplessness surprising, for he is the victim of a *"comprehensive and carefully-planned political conspiracy."*[14]

In nurturing the idea of a permanent conspiracy directed against the eternal dupes, the agitator plays upon and enlarges the tendency among people who suffer from a sense of failure to ascribe their misfortunes to secret enemy machinations. The dismissed employee, the jilted lover, the disgruntled soldier deprived of a promotion, the student who fails an examination, the small grocer driven out of business by a chain competitor—any of these may be inclined to blame mysterious persecutors motivated by obscure grudges. However, the tendency of frustrated people to imagine themselves the targets of powerful enemies need not necessarily lead to paranoia. Often enough such suspicions are not devoid of objective justification in a world where the individual's sphere of action is increasingly restricted by anonymous social forces. Our daily existence actually is influenced by tremendous developments whose causes are difficult to grasp. Hence many people are anxious to learn what is happening behind the scenes.

When the agitator tells his listeners that they are "pushed" or "kicked" around and are victimized by bankers and bureaucrats, he exploits feelings that they already have. Such stereotypes as "Wall Street machinations," "monopolist conspiracies," or "international spies" are present, however, not as well-defined ideas but as tentative suspicions about the meaning of complex phenomena. As inadequate reflections of reality, they might serve as starting points for analysis of the economic and political situations.

The agitator proceeds in exactly the opposite way. He refers to popular stereotypes only to encourage the vague resentments they reflect. He uses them not as springboards for analysis but rather as "analyses" themselves—the world is complicated because there are groups whose

27

purpose it is to make it complicated. On a social scale he stirs his audience to reactions similar to those of paranoia on an individual scale, and his primary means of doing this is by indefinitely extending the concept of conspiracy.

Where others might speak of the ultimate implications of a political program, he sees a deliberate plot: the New Deal is nothing but "good Marxian sabotage to break down the existing order."[15] British War Relief is "sponsored by same internationalists who got us into World War I."[16] The B'nai Brith is "a worldwide spy and pressure system"[17] that has "unlimited funds" and "maintains its own Gestapo."[18] Economic crises are contrived by "a small but powerful, well-organized and well-financed minority."[19] Even such a trivial occurrence as a polemical attack on a senator is sufficient for the agitator to evoke a "secret society" for "smearing of individual members of the senate."[20] Phrases like the "Hidden Hand"[21] or "International Invisible Government"[22] appear in his writings and speeches again and again.

Any organization the agitator conceives as hostile to his aims he includes in the conspiracy. He speaks of it as seeking "to destroy . . . the American way of life,"[23] and calls on "all Christians to stand together" because a conspiracy is afoot "to ruin the Church."[24] Similarly, "class hatred is created by lies and *conflicting explanations,* all helping to create *confusion* and to conceal *the real authors* of the devilish plans for the destruction of Christian or Western civilization."[25]

This inflation of the notion of conspiracy not only serves as a diversion from attempts to investigate social processes but also blurs the identity of the groups designated as conspirators. The very stereotypes that once referred more or less definitely to social oligarchies now refer to gigantic but undefined secret international plots. The term *octopus,* once used by Frank Norris in a novel about railroad magnates, now becomes diffused into the "international invisible government."[26]

In this transformation of a circumscribed group of magnates into mysterious invisible rulers, the process of blurring reality by encouraging paranoiac tendencies is clearly evident. As compensation, the idea of conspiracy acquires a sensational and thrilling connotation, and all the problems of modern life are centered in a comfortingly simple, if vague and mysterious, cause. This systematization of conspiracies into one grandiose plot is declared by the agitator to be "obvious even to a dullard," for

> all this step-by-step bungling—this amazing unity of deception, internal sabotage, and gross incompetence in the leaders of Britain, France

and even of the United States—is not an accident. It is, rather, indicative of a central directing influence—a World Government group."[27]

There is no telling how far this conspiracy may extend. In fact, it has been going on since time immemorial.

> The doctrine of ruling by force from hidden sources, and this secret group, ruled over Babylon of Nimrod, Egypt, Babylon of Nebuchadnezzar, Medio-Persia, Greece and Rome. And this same secret society became the Jacobins of the French Revolution and placed Napoleon in power in Europe and when Russia and then England overthrew him (see Dumas' works), they moved into Germany where they became known as Communists, from whence they overthrew Russia, and produced the bastard children, Fascism and Nazism.[28]

These fantastic images seem, first of all, to satisfy the audience's craving for an explanation of its sufferings. In that sense the agitator seems to continue the work of the muckrakers by courageously revealing why the powers that rule the world wish to remain hidden. But by dealing, as it were, with the audience's notions at their face value, by exaggerating to the point of the fantastic its suspicions that it is the toy of anonymous forces, and by pointing to mysterious individuals rather than analyzing social forces, the agitator in effect cheats his audience of its curiosity. Instead of diagnosing an illness, he explains it as the result of an evil spirit's viciousness, for the conspirators are not pictured as motivated by any rational purpose but, rather, by a gratuitous will to destruction:

> My informant tells me that the bloodless revolution is being brought about through a planned policy of destructionism—a destructionism which pretends to alleviate suffering, poverty, unemployment and hunger . . . a destructionism which eventually aims at bankrupting the nation and thereby bringing about repudiation of debts and the overthrow of government.[29]

And this conspiracy is directed at the very vitals of the people—in fact, if the people are to survive, they must act immediately to destroy this conspiracy, for "the intriguers have taken us so far down their alley that we have lost our time honored powers of resistance. More than a palliative is needed at this critical juncture."[30]

Here we see how the paranoiac brooding and the projection of conspiracies end with suggestions for acts of violence. Because the very term *conspiracy* has connotations of illegality and treason, the conspirators are pictured as acting in lawless fashion and with complete impunity. This implies that existing laws and institutions cannot cope with them and that extraordinary measures are needed.

Theme 3: Forbidden Fruit

If the agitator's audience is composed of eternal dupes who have always been the prey of an ubiquitous conspiracy, the agitator will presumably emphasize all the good things of life that the "others" enjoy but the audience does not. Here, as in almost all other themes, it might appear that the agitator is following the beaten track of revolutionaries, by advocating redistribution of social wealth.

Actually, he manages to steer clear of such explosive implication. True, he refers to the alleged good life led by those he calls the enemies. But he associates enjoyment of private pleasure with vice and luxurious excess. He is eloquent in describing the carefree existence of "alien-minded plutocrats" who "roll in wealth, bathe in liquor, surround themselves with the seduced daughters of America."[31] But he is equally eloquent in denouncing indulgence in materialistic pleasures: "America, the vain—America, the proud—America, the nation of gluttons and spenders and drinkers. A nation whose population has deserted the church and in many instances, debauched the home."[32]

The debauch of "alien-minded plutocrats" is condemned in the following moral reflections: "Drunkenness became just a humorous, though effective way of getting relaxation. Adultery became just a method of showing sincerity of affection and a usual part of comradeship between good friends of opposite sex."[33]

The agitator evokes a bizarre vision of oversized, luxurious homes, where alcohol flows and swimming pools abound. Children play in nurseries while adults revel in game rooms, nightclubs, racetracks, and bedrooms. "The sweet and simple things of life" are "discarded, absent, forgotten."[34] This perverse and adulterous life is branded as un-American, characteristic of foreigners and refugees who squander fabulous fortunes when they are not busy stealing jobs from Americans. "With hundreds of thousands of Jews running away from war bringing wealth here and making themselves obnoxious in 'hot spots' and vice resorts with their lavish spending."[35]

Such a way of life is also un-Christian, enjoyed by "Oriental erotics" of whom American Christians are the "unwary hosts."[36] These "erotics" debauch "youth for the purpose of wrecking Gentile morale."[37] Uncannily and scarily, "all this is being done by an invisible power. Rape and the evasion of income taxes plays a big part in all this."[38]

The very presence of material comfort is viewed with suspicion and implicitly condemned by the agitator. Among the accusations leveled against President Roosevelt is the fact that he was "born in the lap of luxury" and "never made a payroll in his life."[39] Often the agitator whets the appetite of his followers with detailed descriptions of the luxuries of the enemy while arousing their moral disgust at such corrupt practices.

> When Harry Hopkins got married, Baruch gave a party for the "Palace Guard" at the Carlton Hotel, where you need $100.00 before you can rent a room; and pay $2 before you can order a cup of coffee. But Mr. Baruch arranged the party, and they were all there: Harry Hopkins, the bride, Mr. Nelson, Mr. Henderson. There were seven kinds of meat served—twenty-two kinds of food, and it had cost Barney Baruch $122 a plate; and they drank of the vintage of '26. Now, I am no connoisseur of champagne. McCullough of the Post-Dispatch says it is $20.00 a quart—and if I had a quart of that I might get a good story in the Post-Dispatch tomorrow. [Laughter.] But there isn't any more of that, I understand, now because of the war with France. There was $2000 served of that drink. There was precious perfume at $40 a tiny vial to each woman there. You talk about the drunken orgies of history—we expect Capone to live like that, but as long as I am a Christian soul, I will not be governed by a man like that.[40]

Even while the agitator seems to be furiously voicing the claims of his audience for a greater share of social wealth, he is actually suppressing their claims. Even while he offers, he actually denies enjoyment of the good things of life. Enjoyment of wealth means debauch and vice—hence wealth is a forbidden fruit. Moreover, the agitator portrays it in such fantastic terms that the common man cannot even dream of acquiring it but must content himself with the "sweet and simple things of life."

Rather than offering suggestions for a greater utilization of productive facilities or a more just distribution of the social product, the agitator encourages resentment against the excesses of luxury. Appealing to puritanical attitudes the agitator condemns indulgence not in order to propose the elimination of poverty but, rather, to exasperate his followers' feelings of envy while simultaneously arousing their sense of guilt at being envious. He activates revolutionary sentiment but directs it against the caricature he has himself drawn of human aspirations for pleasure. The violent language in which he castigates those who enjoy the "cream" of this country while the rest go "milkless" is thus ultimately directed against the audience's own desires. Even when the agitator denounces the "society world of snobbery and fraud" and shouts "Down must come those who live in luxury!"[41] he is not proposing to the audience a way for it to increase its share of wealth and pleasure. When the golden calf is destroyed and its worshippers dispersed, his followers may still expect nothing for themselves—they have been taught by the agitator to distrust their own aspirations to comfort. The image of abundance is dangled before them but is never accessible. All that can result for the follower is an inner exacerbation of his resentments. If the agitator cannot promise his adherents a greater share of the good things of life, he can suggest that the good life consists in something else, the gratification of repressed impulses; and that if they are obedient to him they will be offered the luxurious sinners as sacrificial prey.

Theme 4: Disaffection

An important aspect of the malaise is a growing sense of disillusionment with ideals, values, and institutions. The agitator skilfully works on this disillusionment by simultaneously damning and praising the accepted ideologists. On the one hand, he likes to give the impression that, like most other advocates of social change, he is against certain social conditions because they violate universally accepted values. On the other hand, he often concurs in and reinforces his audience's suspicion about those values.

He speaks as a champion of democracy and Christianity and protests that he is "merely defending the Bill of Rights."[42] He invokes the "Christian doctrine of human liberty"[43] and extols "American individualism" and "free enterprise."[44] He is the guardian of "the Bible, the Christian Faith, American institutions and the Constitution."[45]

Yet, when confronted with his audience's moral confusion, he implies that he shares neither the conservative's total acceptance of existing values and institutions nor the "naive idealism of the liberals."[46] He knows that the "two-party system is a sham"[47] and "democracy" a "trick word."[48] "In fact, justice matters more than democracy."[49] And "Liberaliam—in politics—leads to Anarchy."[50]

It can of course be maintained that the first group of statements is merely camouflage for the second. To some extent this is probably true, but it is hardly likely that the audience is fooled into taking the agitator for a sincere champion of democracy. It is much more likely that the agitator who utilizes democratic stereotypes is quite aware that his words ring hollow: he does not intend to be taken literally. In view of his known sympathy for European fascism, the agitator's use of democratic phrases serves to create the impression that the difference between fascism and democracy is not as important as it is made out to be—or more accurately, that it is not at all what really matters. The agitator constantly seeks to blur this difference. In reality, he declares, he is "no more a fascist than Abraham Lincoln and Teddie Roosevelt";[51] he is called one merely because he is one of the "individualists who still believe in Constitutional government."[52] To muddy the waters further, he hurls the accusation of fascism against those who have come to symbolize opposition to fascism. He consistently denounces the New Deal as an effort to introduce totalitarianism into the United States, and declare that "Roosevelt got his technique from Hitler and the Jews."[53]

In bandying the two antithetical concepts of democracy and fascism in such a way that the clear distinction between them is obliterated, the agitator seems to act on the premise that his audience's loyalties are uncertain. He therefore seems bent not on concealing but on flaunting his cynicism, the effect of which is to sanction and fixate his audience's disillusionment. It is characteristic of the agitator's whole approach that he confirms his adherents' disillusionment by both his affirmations and negations, for in the way they are expressed by him both bar any possible surmounting of the disillusionment. In the way he points to the traditional as the great ideal, the agitator discourages a serious critique of existing values; in the way he debunks existing values, he makes impossible any sincere attempt to realize them more effectively in practice.

This dual assault on the value system, which runs like a thread through agitational material, is, so to speak, the one occasion when the agitator comes to grips with opposing arguments. It is part of his general desecration of the idea of truth as such. Underlying the agitator's rejection of those values by which it is possible to distinguish democracy from its opposite is the implication that in the present world, where the masses are eternal dupes and the victims of a perennial conspiracy, everything must give way to the urge for self-survival. The distinction between truth and lies is accordingly inconsequential; both are neutral means to be used according to their helpfulness to his cause.

That the agitator's preachments profoundly contradict ideals such as democracy, equality, and justice, that are commonly held to be universal does not seem to bother him, for he capitalizes on the general sense of disillusionment among his adherents by articulating their suspicion that the enemy's ideals are mere camouflage for social coercion. Instead of sifting the valuable aspects of the ideal from the way it may be misused, he junks both. All that is left then for him—and this is what he takes great pains to imply to his audience—is an idealless use of force against the troublemaking enemy. His doctrine thus consists in drawing the ultimate consequences of a totally amoral opportunism, as discussed below.

Unseriousness

The agitator's ambiguous approach to values is often revealed in an undercurrent of unseriousness in his statements, the effect of which is to dismiss ideals as mere bunk, hogwash, lies. Take his attitude toward the law, for example. There are too many laws and regulations behind which are hidden "the gossamers of un-Americanism."[54] What is more, "any '*law*' is alien fodder to Anglo-Saxons."[55] As against "inspired" laws he champions "individualism."[56] Yet the agitator simultaneously poses as a champion of legality, denouncing the "rulings" of the New Deal as "illegal."

These apparently conflicting views are synthesized in statements that express more fundamentally the agitator's genuine attitude toward law:

> Will the United States be required to remunerate Jews for their losses in a war with Hitler's Germany, a war that the Jews, themselves, promoted? Would it not be nearer to equity, nearer to measure for measure if the Jews were required to compensate non-interventionists and political "isolationists" for their loss of life and treasure?[57]

What is serious in these statements is their very lack of seriousness. Going beyond the revelation that law can be a cloak for brute force, the agitator shows here that brute force need hardly be clothed at all, for instead of being discarded as a sham, legality is now exploited as a blatant gesture of defiance. Behind such statements is the outlook that led the Nazi regime to "fine" the German Jews $400,000,000 when a Polish Jew killed a German embassy clerk in Paris. That a legal justification was given to such a step was not primarily, as it might seem, a concession to hypocrisy or prejudice; on the contrary, it was simply a means of emphasizing the complete arbitrariness of the operation.

Transformation of meaning

The agitator twists the meaning of basic ideals in such a way that he infuses them with his own content. He celebrates "the instrument of the American ballot, which instrument makes all men equal in the affairs of their government"[58] while simultaneously calling for extralegal measures: "I am talking about cleaning America. Let me tell you how to do it. General Franco found one way."[59]

The agitator transforms democracy from a system that guarantees minority rights into one that merely affirms the privileged status of the majority. Persecution of minorities is thus within the rights of the majority and any attempt to limit the exercise of this "right" is interpreted as persecution of the majority by the minority. Such an interpretation of democracy results in its negation: "Do the Jews clamor for democracy only because a democracy is too weak to resist their encroachments? . . . If it is, then a lot of us will want to be done with democracy."[60]

The agitator submits religion to the same kind of treatment. He stresses the particularistic connotations of religion by suggesting that Christianity is an exclusive creed, a kind of tribal fetish, endowed with primitive attributes of clannishness and violence. He denounces "the false premise that all, and particularly Jews, are 'brothers'—to the Christian. . . . The Jew, religious or otherwise, is today as always against Christ, therefore *not* a 'brother.' ABC stuff!"[61]

In the presence of demonic powers, the foremost feature of Christianity is "a militant routing of evil in high places by humble followers of Christ."[62] The church thus becomes a tabloid version of *ecclesia militans*. The agitator suggests that "for America to pray" and "for America to fight" are the same thing,[63] and he does not hesitate to recommend putting "prayers across . . . at the point of a gun"[64] or building "barricades to protect the principles of the Prince of Peace."[65] The agitator thus appears as a policeman of virtue, a sergeant defending the ideal, a corporal fighting for truth. "Unite in dropping prayer-bombs upon the camp of the enemy"[66] and exercise justice as a member of a "Social Justice platoon."[67]

This transformation of values into their opposites receives its final twist when the agitator declares: "If Smith is America's No. 1 Fascist (anti-Semite) as Judeo-Reds proclaim, then, according to New Testament, Christ must be World's greatest Anti-Semite!"[68]

Anti-Universality

The agitator explicitly rejects the ideal of universality. This rejection is evidenced, for instance, in his attitude toward tolerance, which he brands as "silly sentimentality"[69] and "non-Christian,"[70] as contrary to self-interest and a weakness that must be eradicated for the sake of survival.

> TOLERANCE—A numerous group of alien and native rascals shout "tolerance" but with their own foul tongues, they would lap up the blood of their own critics.[71]

As though realizing that tolerance is a cultural luxury for those in power who may preach and violate it with equal impunity, and that it reflects the social weakness of those out of power, the agitator uses the caption "None but the Strong Can be Magnanimous."[72] He implies that tolerance is opposed to truth, and when involking the concept of truth, he almost always associates it with violence. He claims that he is persecuted and threatened with death if he dares speak the truth, and then directly identifies it with the application of force: "The Cross and The Flag' speaks the truth. We have arrived at the hour when we must have more two-fisted talking and real action."[73]

Truth is further equated with intolerance in anti-Semitism: "When telling the truth about Jewish organizations or leaders is punished as a crime by our courts—what becomes of the four freedoms of the Gentile majority in the USA?"[74]

The agitator applies a similar technique to the concepts of the brotherhood, humanitarianism, universal justice: all are shown to be contrary to the crudest requirements of self-interest. "'Racial equality,' 'social equality,' and 'natural equality' are absurd concepts, either in biology or common sense, and nobody knows this better than Jews who are ballyhooing such concepts."[75]

Through these three devices—unseriousness, transformation of values, and negation of universalism—the agitator tries to convince his audience that ideals and values are merely misleading advertising slogans, used to defraud the dupes.

Theme 5: Charade of Doom

The possibility of total disaster is invoked by many advocates of social change as a contrast to their solutions. The reformer or revolutionary helps his audience visualize this possibility as a definite obstacle to be removed (capitalist society or antiunion employers or nationalism); although he evokes visions of catastrophe and, to some extent, exploits existing fears, he summons the audience to work toward an achievable utopia rather than to flee from imminent danger.

In agitation, however, the positive alternative to the threat of disaster is either totally lacking or suggested only in the vaguest form as a return to "the good old days." The agitator presents the threatening chaos as unavoidable and inexorable. By elaborating present dangers—and in our time he has abundant material to draw upon—he may seem bent on making his audience realize the urgency of the situation. In fact he achieves the opposite by associating these dangers with trivial ideas or grotesque fantasies. Just as through the theme of disaffection he cheats his audience out of intellectual curiosity, so does he cheat it out of fear as a possible stimulus to organized social thought and action.

Through the exploitation of the fear of impending chaos, the agitator succeeds in appearing as a radical who will have no truck with mere fragmentary reforms while he simultaneously steers his adherents wide of any suggestion of a basic social reorganization. He equates the threat to profits with the impending chaos:

> If we lose this fight, if the American worker bends his knee to Lewis, Browder, and Stalin, in the Middlewest tonight, this will be just the beginning. Then comes the destruction of profits. When profits go, wages go; when wages go, jobs go. Then comes chaos, revolution, confiscation, and the breakdown of our beautiful, free American system.[76]

The postwar strikes are interpreted as "a pretext for ushering in a new political and social order in the image of Karl Marx, Leon Trotsky, Prof. Harold J. Laski and the House of Rothschild."[77]

In the above passages the agitator embroiders on the usual conservative stereotypes. He goes further in playing on the middle-class fear of revolution, as associated with material discomfort and confiscation of private property:

> CIO and radical AF of L unions . . . can, and will, when "Der Tag" (sometime prior to 1941) is decided upon by the Hidden Hand, plunge cities into darkness, shut off water, gas, phone, telegraph, radio, food, and transportation generally, so that in terror imposed by fear, thirst, and starvation, the weakkneed NEW DEAL politicians, businessmen, and labor leaders in most large cities are expected to surrender to Anti-Christ dictatorship.[78]

Where the agitator diverges from the conservative politician, however, is in tying the threat of chaos not only to such relatively serious matters as strikes but also to circumstantial minor causes of discontent, such as food or tire shortages, which he represents as the deliberate work of liberals and radicals. The revolution is imminent whether or not there are strikes. War taxation is not merely a burden but a conspiracy to strip us down to the point of hunger and starvation and bankruptcy where our taxes will cost us our homes."[79]

In thrusting before his audience the terrors of the impending doom, the agitator often paints it in terms of sexual connotations:

> After all, what is more likely to follow many years of Nudeal communistic confiscatory taxation, wool-less, metal-less, auto-less regimentation and planned scarcities than our finally becoming stripped by necessity to Nudism.[80]

> The world is moving rapidly toward chaos, which will mean revolution, waves of sadism, murder, rape, incest, conflagration, atom bomb conflicts, annihilation of whole populations.[81]

It may be conjectured that by his references to rape, incest, and plunder, the agitator evokes sadistic fantasies that add a connotation of promise to the warning: his followers may vaguely hope that when the deluge comes they, too, may be allowed to perform the acts that are attributed to the enemy.

The fear of specific dangers, such as the threat of inflation or war, is drowned in gloating visions of universal chaos: "We approach our day of doom under the guidance of the most incompetent and Satanic array of rascals ever assembled by any government in the history of the world."[82]

Fear is no longer used as a psychological signal pointing to the existence of specific dangers; like the Conspiracy it becomes ubiquitous and eternal.

> History follows same pattern for Satan uses same tactics, and same kind of people. . . . Under Satanic guidance all activities of man are being forced into roads leading to chaos and destruction.[83]

Whatever associations the audience may have had with concretely experienced causes of apprehension are dissolved by the blaring alarum of threatening catastrophe. Confronted with such an inexorable fate, the audience can feel only complete impotence.

> No matter to what extent the Roosevelt dynasty betrays the common man in America, or what atrocious crimes it commits, or how low it sinks in ethics, morals and common decency, nothing will be done about it now and probably nothing can be done. The disease must run its course, the cycle must complete itself.[84]

The audience's unpleasurable reactions are here offset by the fact that its subordinate social role is vindicated by being placed in a historical perspective: individual and personal failures are subsumed under the national, international or even cosmic failure. Though the agitator's adherent has lost the dignity of a man participating in constructive activities on his own initiative, he is compensated by a kind of tragic dignity that raises his insignificant personal defeat to the status of an historical event.

By being spread over a larger surface, the original fear becomes thinner, less urgent and compelling, but it acquires an enhanced imaginative reality. Fear is transformed into a morbid nihilistic expectation, perhaps even hope, of total destruction.

The actual reasons for despair are utilized to indulge in a charade of despair, and as though to emphasize this, the agitator does not hesitate to introduce motifs of outright grotesqueness in his prophecies. He spices real threats with the vision of a deadly onslaught on the human race planned by celestial and earthly powers:

> Already restricted crop production due to Internationalists' schemes plus storms, floods, attacks by insects, etc., this year points to what may be expected in years 1943, 1944, and 1945, in which scientists say we will be plagued with the coldest summers and winters in history.[85]

As a consequence of this piling of mock horrors onto real ones, the listeners are encouraged to follow the path of least resistance intellectually. To understand the causes of their frustrations they need no longer cope with such complicated problems as tax laws, unions, governmental policies, the organization of the credit system, etc. All these bewildering matters have been reduced to a common denominator: they are nothing but various aspects of the essentially ruthless setup of the world, symptoms of one big, horrid overwhelming, superhuman or subhuman elemental phenomenon. Inability to meet resourcefully a bread-and-butter situation may produce a feeling of inferiority, but such a feeling is out of place when one is faced with a dilemma arising from cosmic causes. What else can one do but leave the understanding of such a confrontation to the available spiritual elite?

This conscious reliance on the wisdom of the great is probably furthered by unconscious regressive tendencies. The explanation of everyday mischances in terms of uncanny world catastrophes revitalizes and reinforces the heritage of infantile anxieties. The unconscious finds in the agitator's interpretations a replica of its own primitive reactions to the outside world; the listener plays the role of the little child responding to the warning that bogeys may come for him.

Something that is feared on one level of personality is often desired on another. This seems especially true for the peculiarly fascinating experience of catastrophe. The gospel of doom relieves the individual of responsibility for struggling with his problems; one cannot resist an erupting volcano. The agitator's listeners are told in effect that between their limited capacities and the tremendous forces that threaten them there is an ineradicable disproportion. As a result, everything goes. A man involved in catastrophe feels justified in departing from established moral codes if it, means saving his life. The idea of catastrophe contains a welcome stimulus to the listeners' destructive instinctual urges.

It is not difficult for the agitator's adherents to take the further step of projecting disaster onto the imaginary enemy. This is a process akin to that unconscious transference that permits the average man to assume that accidents or sudden fatalities are more likely to strike some unknown man rather than him. Thus the agitator offers his followers, who either are or believe themselves persecuted, a method of relieving their feeling of social inferiority by indulging in fantasies in which other people—those they envy or dislike—suffer annihilation.

The agitator expresses the unconscious wish of the dissatisfied to drag all other persons down to their own level of insignificance. Since "we" are down and out and have no chance to escape catastrophe, "we" do not want anyone else to be spared this fate. Freed from the inhibitions of conscience by the agitator's evocation of inevitable doom, his listeners can give gratifying play to fantasies arising from repressed destructive impulses. Because the agitator has used actual threats of catastrophe to construct a fantasy-threat that bars positive satisfactions to his adherents, they seem driven to seek the compensation of gratifying the death instinct: "The whole world will go down with us." For the unconscious, the threatened apocalypse, which might have been the stimulus to action to ward off social dangers, here becomes the "solution" itself.

Notes

1. CF, Feb., 1948, p. 714.
2. Smith, New York, Oct. 20, 1936, meeting.
3. Sanctuary, *The New Deal is Marxian Sabotage*, p. 1.
4. SJ, Dec. 8, 1941, p. 15.
5. SJ, June 6, 1938, p. 5.
6. SJ, Sept. 15, 1941, p. 3.
7. LIB, Mar. 21, 1940, p. 9.

8.   AID, Jan. 27, 1941, p. 3.
9.   Sanctuary, *The New Deal is Marxian Sabotage*, p. 1.
10.   Mote, Cleveland, July 2, 1942, meeting.
11.   SJ, July 21, 1941, p. 11.
12.   SJ, Nov. 17, 1941, p. 9.
13.   AID, July 3, 1938, p. 1.
14.   Mote, *Testimony before the U.S. Senate Committee on Military Affairs*, June 30, 1941, p. 6.
15.   Sanctuary, *The New Deal is Marxian Sabotage*, p. 1.
16.   AID, Nov. 18, 1940, p. 3.
17.   AID, Apr. 28, 1941, p. 4.
18.   Kamp, *Native Nazi Purge Plot*, p. 56.
19.   AP, June, 1945, p. 3.
20.   CF, June, 1942, p. 4.
21.   Hudson, passim.
22.   Winrod, passim.
23.   Kamp, *Native Nazi Purge Plot*, p. 6.
24.   Smith, Detroit, May 11, 1943, meeting.
25.   Sanctuary, *The New Deal is Marxian Sabotage*, p. 2.
26.   DEF, Feb., 1941, p. 7.
27.   SJ, Nov. 17, 1941, p. 9.
28.   DEF, Mar., 1939, p. 13.
29.   SJ, June 6, 1938, p. 5.
30.   Sanctuary, *Tearing Away the Veils*, p. 47.
31.   Smith. *Letter,* "Kill Him! Kill Him! Kill Him!" Aug., 1945, p. 2.
32.   CF, Aug., 1942, p. 12.
33.   Phelps, *An Appeal to Americans*, pp. 15, 16.
34.   Phelps, *An Appeal to Americans*, p. 16.
35.   AID, Jan. 6, 1941, p. 3.
36.   CF, Aug., 1945, p. 609.
37.   LIB, May 7, 1940, p. 12.
38.   Phelps, Los Angeles, Aug. 4, 1940, radio.
39.   Pelley, *What You Should Know About The Pelley Publications*, p. 2.
40.   Smith, St. Louis, March 25, 1944, meeting.
41.   Phelps, Los Angeles, Aug. 18, 1940 and Oct. 1, 1940, radio.
42.   CF, July, 1942, p. 12.
43.   SJ, Mar. 4, 1940, p. 19.
44.   Kamp, *Famine in America*, p. 50.
45.   DEF, Jan., 1940, p. 14.
46.   Smith, Detroit, Mar. 22, 1943, meeting.
47.   Smith, Detroit, Mar. 19, 1943, meeting.
48.   X, Feb. 17, 1945, p. 1.
49.   Coughlin, Speech on March 26, 1939, reprinted in *Why Leave Our Own*, p. 161.
50.   DEF, Sept. 1935.
51.   Smith, New York, Oct. 20, 1936, meeting.
52.   Kamp, *With Lotions of Love . . .*, p. 4.
53.   AP, Oct., 1945, p. 13.

54. SJ, Jan. 15, 1940, p. 19.
55. AP, Nov. 1945, p. 12.
56. Kamp, *Famine in America*, p. 50.
57. AP, Jan., 1945, p. 11.
58. Smith, "The Next President of the United States," radio address, p. 4.
59. McWilliams, New York, July 29, 1940, street corner.
60. AP, Jan., 1945, p. 11.
61. AID, May 5, 1941, p. 1.
62. AID, July 17, 1939, p. 3.
63. Smith, "The Next President of the United States," radio address, p. 4.
64. quoted in: A. B. Magil, *The Truth about Father Coughlin*, New York, no date, p. 14 (date of lecture referred to: January 22, 1934.)
65. Coughlin, Speech on March 26, 1939, reprinted in *Why Leave Our Own*, p. 161.
66. DEF, Feb., 1940, p. 4.
67. SJ, June 13, 1938, p. 3.
68. AID, Sept. 19, 1945, p. 4.
69. LIB, Oct. 14, 1933, p. 11.
70. Phelps, *An Appeal to Americans*, p. 16.
71. AP, Aug., 1944, p. 1.
72. LIB, Dec. 23, 1933, p. 8.
73. CF, May, 1942, p. 16.
74. PTB, Jan., 1943, p. 4.
75. AP, Apr., 1945, p. 14.
76. Smith, *Mice or Men*, radio address in 1939, p. 4.
77. AP, Nov., 1945, p. 5.
78. AID, July 3, 1938, p. 1.
79. Smith, Detroit, Feb. 7, 1943, meeting.
80. RTL, Mar. 27, 1942, p. 11.
81. CF, Feb., 1946, p. 702.
82. DEF, Nov., 1941, p. 30.
83. AID, June 2, 1942, p. 3.
84. AP, Jan., 1945, p. 3.
85. AID, July 1, 1942, p. 1.

4

The Ruthless Enemy

Like all advocates of social change, the agitator finds the enemy responsible for his followers' sufferings. But although in other movements defeat of the enemy is a means to an end (a new society or a reformed society of one sort or another), in agitation it is an end in itself. The enemy is conceived not as a group that stands in the way of achieving a certain objective but as a superoppressor, a quasi-biological archdevil of absolute evil and destructiveness. He is irreconcilable, an alien body in society that has no useful productive function. Not even in theory is he amenable to persuasion. There is no bridge that the enemy can cross for repentance. He is there forever, evil for the sake of evil.

The agitator finds the raw material for such a portrait in the existing stereotypes of hostility. His targets are innumerable. After naming them as the "communists," "the Nazis, the Fascists and the Japs," "the (so-called) Friends of Democracy," "the Internationalists," "the New Deal Bureaucrats," "Walter Winchell," and "Communist and pro-Communist journals," he remarks that "the above list does not include all of our enemies. We could name one hundred more classifications of foes, but the ones listed indicate the type of opposition we face. WE ARE PROUD OF OUR ENEMIES. IT IS AN HONOR TO BE HATED BY SUCH PERSONS AND ORGANIZATIONS."[1] However, the agitator makes an effort to integrate the diffuse hostilities of his audience into a definite image, which we shall now try to define.

For purposes of analysis, the agitator's portrait of the enemy is divided into three parts: the political appearance, the psychological substratum, and the pseudoreality reference, the Jew. Chapters 4, 5, and 6 discuss each of these versions.

Theme 6: The Reds

The agitator makes use of all the familiar antiradical stereotypes. He speaks of the "beast of Bolshevism, the desecrator of the divine, the killer of Christians,"[2] and warns his audience that:

> like a Bubonic plague, Bolshevism moves across the face of the earth, burning churches, slaughtering the ministers of God, ridiculing the things we hold sacred, referring to religion as the opiate of the people, breeding discontent.[3]

Yet the agitator's position as one who wishes to produce the impression of being the most vocal enemy of revolution is not without ambiguity, for the radicals are not merely his enemies, they are also his competitors. Like them he aims at enlisting mass support, and like them he promises not the partial palliatives of the reformist but a definitive solution of the problems that harass his audience.

The agitator must therefore establish the inferiority and unreliability of his radical rivals while simultaneously reassuring the earth's mighty that the passion aroused by his invective will not be turned against them. That is why his denunciations of communism are so virulent: he must show that he hates the enemies of private property more than do its wealthiest exponents.

Whenever he can, the agitator uses the language and ideas of what is currently respectable to show that he is a loyal and trustworthy citizen. No better example of this can be seen than in the way he seizes on the prevalent fear of communism to twist it for his own purposes. Many of his statements about the "reds" are indistinguishable from what a bona fide conservative, or even liberal, might say about communism. But when they are examined in the context of the agitator's total output, they are seen as utilized by him in a unique approach. This approach is marked by three features.

1. *For the agitator, the revolution may come tomorrow:* He never discusses or analyzes the particular stage of development at which the radical movement may be at any given time; he makes no effort to distinguish between various kinds of radical movements, revolutionary or reformist, extreme or mild; he does not differentiate between the different tactics used by these radical movements. All are lumped together into an undifferentiated revolutionary threat. This threat is not located in any specific movement or event or possible development; it is simply reduced to the danger of immediate revolutionary violence.

His imagery of communism is drawn from civil war situations, violent seizure of power by armed minorities amidst an orgy of blood and violence. In fact, the revolution may happen any minute:

> Only hope is for Congress to awaken in time. Present Judeo-Red inspired-directed-financed strikes are part of Bolshevik revolutionary technique to sabotage our economy and facilitate *Reign of Terror* coincident with outbreak of World War III.[4]

The agitator's concept of communism is infinitely extendable. Adopting the air of someone "in the know," the agitator tells his listeners that groups holding actual political or economic power are linked to communism. At the same time its threat is used to satisfy a craving for fantastic and gruesome stories. The agitator suggests a principle of systematization for an almost paranoiac state of mind: "Confusion out of mouths of columnists, ambassadors, bishops, courts, politicians, yet same RED THREAD tieing all together."[5]

The extent of this danger can be seen when it is realized that "with Communists drinking tea in the White House and 2,850 of them on the payroll of the United States . . . the time has come for America to wake up and act."[6] Under such circumstances, suggests the agitator, it seems almost impossible to expect the government to act, and no other way is available but the spontaneous rising of the people.

2. *He blurs the specific nature of the communist threat by identifying it with general forebodings of impending doom:* Behind communism are "international outfits," and whether they plan a revolution or a world union, the same force is at work: "Certain international outfits attempting to rob us of our national sovereignty, promote us into supergovernment, or make us part of an international Communist revolution, or take us back into the British Empire."[7]

The agitator blurs the distinction between communism and other ideologies distasteful to him by denying the very reality of communism: "There is no 'Communism' in the world and none is intended now or at any time in the future. It is a vast dupery."[8] It is as though "front" organizations are the dupes of communism, and communism itself is also a "front" for something else. This stigmatization of communism as a kind of dupery divests it of any ideological significance and extends its meaning to the point where it is completely vague. For the agitator, such an extension is a powerful device: it enables him to suggest that communism is merely a label to conceal sordid activities, and that consequently anyone whom the agitator considers sordid may be called a communist.

3. *He associates the communists with the Jews:* "Those who support . . . Communism will not escape our opposition even though they seek sanctuary under the banner of their advertised race or religion and cry aloud that they are the objects of unjust attack."[9]

The identification of the communist with the Jew is well known, but the use to which this identification is put by the agitator is not. When the agitator describes communists as Jews, he transforms them from a group of people who might presumably be converted to his side into a group forever irreconcilable.

He also introduces the connotation that the enemy is weak. To fight Stalin may be a formidable job, but once his advisers are identified as those Jews who "seek sanctuary under the banner of their race or religion," they are easy prey. The very fact that they complain of being "the objects of unjust attacks" shows this to be true. In this way the communist bogey is tremendously inflated only to be debunked, and the fears whipped up by references to its power are unmasked as ridiculous. The communist leadership is entirely Jewish: "Who Are the Leaders in Communism—JEWS? Can you name even one Irishman, Dutchman, Italian, Greek, or a German who are big Communist leaders?"[10] And for this very reason communism is weak:

> The weak point of the Communist Party lies in its almost 100% Jewish leadership. There are a few 'Gentile-fronts'—Foster, Browder, etc.—but from Comintern Representative down to local leader practically all authority and responsibility is in the hands of the Jews.[11]

The communist who had been portrayed as a wolf turns out in the end to be a disguised Jewish sheep who must be mercilessly punished by the other sheep as a means of exorcising their fears.

Theme 7: The Plutocrats

The agitator denounces both the radicals and those who are denounced by the radicals. It might be supposed that the primary purpose of his attacks on the wealthy is to reassure his followers of his radicalism. But closer scrutiny of agitational texts shows this purpose to be only an incidental part of a wider scheme.

Superficially, such attacks remind the audience of liberal and populist polemics against big business monopolies. In their private lives these financiers engage in terrible debauchery; in their public lives they are conspirators gratifying their lust for power. They cause war: "No one who is without an understanding of money and banking can have the slightest knowledge of what this European war is about."[12] They "have been waxing fat on the money of sucker stockholders."[13] This country is divided between "the billionaire bankers and their crowd on one side and the bulk of the American people on the other."[14]

Hence it might appear that the agitator adopts the ideas and language of the communists. In explaining the causes of the recent war, he seems to echo their declaration that it was provoked by imperialism:

> The battle of Singapore is a battle for Kuhn, Loeb and Company and J. P. Morgan Company. . . . Hundreds of thousands of American and English boys, possibly, will sacrifice their lives to save Malaya—and incidentally to preserve the investments from which profits are wrenched from the natives of Malaya to swell the purses of international bankers.[15]

But this debunking is only preparatory to a subtle, almost imperceptible twist: the attention of the audience is concentrated not on capitalism but on the bankers.

For all his articulation of spontaneous motives of anger, the agitator is remarkably consistent in avoiding any specific references to giant trusts in manufacture, transportation, and public utilities. But the agitator does attack the leading industries of communication; he seems to feel that they are his most immediate competitors. "You go to double feature shows and what you see is propaganda. About the only time you ever get any real meat is when you hear Gerald Smith."[16] When he does occasionally mention industrial enterprises, such as "mining facilities," he hastens to add that these are controlled by a "few international financiers" who insist on "laying down their own rules of production."[17] When enumerating his targets, he places "special interest, feudal lords, slave owners and imperialists" beside "international bankers," but he always manages to suggest that the main enemy is the "system of finance":

> They want an imperialistic combination which will exploit the whole world, its natural resources and its people, and ultimately make of all people imperialistic slaves to be taxed and killed in battle, at will, for the preservation of their system of finance and imperialistic greed.[18]

47

In sermonizing thus against "Mammon," the agitator seems to be exploiting traditional associations: Christ casting the money changers from the Temple. But his real motives are modern, even ultramodern, and he seems quite aware of this. He indicates this when he says:

> Let us be realists and recognize that our destiny is confined to our America. It is not woven with the destinies of the empires abroad. By fighting for them we are fighting for neither peace nor democracy, but for the perpetuation of an obsolete financial slavery operated and controlled by the Sassoons, the Montefiores, the Rothschilds, the Samuels.[19]

The key word in this quotation is "obsolete." Using the old populist image of the banker who manipulates gold, the agitator seems quite oblivious of the fact that in recent decades banks and industrial capital have merged into gigantic combines, but in fact he encourages the ruling powers to weed out from their ranks useless survivals of earlier decades: domination must be streamlined to be strengthened. The banker, here as almost everywhere else in agitation, identified with the Jew, is the symbol of outmoded methods of indirect domination. The banker is also an attractive target for the agitator's audience, which tends to seek personifications of the anonymous causes of financial loss.

The agitator is here following the stereotype that identifies economic power with financial power. Now that the banker or financier, an habitual object of hatred, has lost much of the power he had in the nineteenth century, this hatred can be more openly expressed. When the Nazis distinguished between productive and predatory capital, which they stigmatized as Jewish, they effectively exploited the distinction between economic and financial power.

To the audience the financier is especially hateful because he seems to enjoy life and luxury without holding, as does the industrialist, any actual commanding power. The omnipotent banker seems also to be identified with—to be, in fact, an enlarged symbol of—the middleman, who, in the eyes of the audience, is often responsible for economic processes that actually occur in the sphere of production. The middleman, like the banker, is thought of as particularly predatory; the industrialist is conceived as the apostle of initiative, ingenuity, and efficiency.

As though worried that his audience might misunderstand his intentions and extend his attack on the bankers to the groups he wishes to spare, the agitator hastens to add that "if the time has arrived for us to issue a democratic disclaimer against international banking, we will not accept in its stead international Communism."[20] In fact, he is opposed to capitalism only because he wants to destroy communism, which "can not be eliminated until capitalism with its usurious money system is removed, lock, stock and barrel, from our social lives."[21] Here again the phrase "with its usurious money system" indicates how strategically obsolete his characterization of capitalism is.

On an agitational plane, he is committed to a fight on two fronts: against communism and against "usurious" capitalism. He avoids the strategic drawbacks of such a fight by a bold imaginative construction: the identification of communism with capitalism. The exponents of revolution are equated with the exponents of plutocratic exploitation. At the same time, the agitator shows how much he hates the capitalists when he calls them communists. That there are obvious logical objections to the notion of a capitalistic group plotting the destruction of the system from which its profits are derived does not bother the agitator. He has several theories at hand to explain this phenomenon. In one of them, communism is represented as a tool of financial interests that aim to establish fascism:

> Communism—Special bait dangled before a large segment of the population that has been frustrated economically by international bankers but which, nevertheless, is promoted by international bankers to create a revolutionary background for the establishment of the Servile State, i.e., Fascism or Nazism.[22]

A variant theory is that communism and capitalism are both weapons in the hands of a third party: "Unrepentant capitalism and conniving Communism—the right and left hands of internationalist imperialism—have littered our fair land with un-American activities."[23]

But the agitator's preferred method of establishing the connection between capitalism and communism is by suggesting that "atheistic Communism" was "originally spawned in Jewish capitalism and Jewish intellectualism."[24] The most striking formulation of this theory traces all modern isms back to a common Jewish ancestor:

> One must remove the causes to get rid of recurring effects . . . we are concerned with liquidating the causes which created the concept of Hitlerism in the minds of men. These causes run back from Stalin to Lenin; from Lenin to Marx; from Marx to the Rothschilds; from

the Rothschilds to the Bank of England; from the Bank of England to the pack of usurers who transubstantiated a vice into a virtue in the sixteenth century.[25]

Here we see the essential purposes of the amalgamation of communism and capitalism: by being thrown together, they cancel each other's ideological and functional characteristics and can be made to appear a tool of a racial enemy—the Jew. Furthermore, the joint disavowal of "unrepentant" capitalism and communism suggests the possibility of a third system to replace them:

> An objective analysis shows that the German people could not have hoped to free their homes, churches, schools and institutions from the Red menace, without also breaking through the web of Jewish Capitalism which had been created around them. Necessity is the mother of Invention, so they established an economic system peculiarly their own, divorced from the international Jewish banking fraternity. *This fact sent a chill over the internationalists.*[26]

It is perhaps this very incongruity, amounting almost to uncanniness, of the idea of the "communist banker" that attracts the audience as a simple explanation of bewildering real situations. The agitator's attack on the banker who enjoys life seems to play up to the audience's resentments of the banker's enjoyments of the "forbidden fruit." And because the agitator's articulation of malaise contains a strong undercurrent of appeals to violence, the destruction of the "communist banker" seems, in anticipation at least, great fun to his audience.

The uncanniness of this combination of bankers and communists suggests a psychoanalytical interpretation. The banker who enjoys the forbidden fruit and preaches abstinence to others, who rolls in gold while he wants others to be thrifty, is a father image, object of ambivalent Oedipal emotions. The unnatural "marriage" of banker and communist seems "natural" to the unconscious, which in a sense considers every marriage forbidden because the mother grants the father sexual rights denied to the child. In this case, the marriage is particularly scandalous. The agitator's theory of communism "spawned" by capitalism or of the Jew who begets both, suggests that their marriage is incestuous. The banker and communist who enjoy one another and deprive the helpless child in the name of the incest taboo are hypocrites of the worst sort.

In the process of agitation the attachment to the father becomes diverted to the agitator himself functioning as a substitute father image who reminds his listeners of the incestuous marriage and confirms the scandalousness of incestuous relationships. At the same time he mobilizes resentment against both parents who deny sexual gratification to the follower and force him to look for it elsewhere, in a community of "brothers." These psychoanalytical connotations of the image of the communist banker are in accord with its political function of suggesting the inevitability of a fascist solution: psychoanalytically fascism has been viewed as a revolt of the "brothers" against parental authority.

We may then sum up agitation material on the theme of the plutocrat in the following propositions:

- When the agitator attacks capitalism, he rails not against social institution, but a group of evil individuals.
- These individuals he identifies as manipulative financiers, thereby appealing to the political emotions of an outlived era, usually the populist era in which the banker was seen as the great enemy.
- By identifying the banker as the enemy and by restricting his denunciations to finance, the agitator leaves free from attack the crucial area of modern capitalist production.
- The agitator reconciles his denunciations of communism and capitalism by constructing the "communist banker," the Jew, who utilizes both communism and "usurious" capitalism for his own ends.

Theme 8: The Corrupt Government

When the agitator criticizes the government, he behaves like any other spokesman for a party out of office, but he differs from the reformer in the verbal violence of his attacks. And unlike the revolutionary, he limits his denunciations to the personnel of the government; he does not attack its basic structure.

The New Deal proved to be a particularly convenient target for the agitator. By denouncing governmental agencies, he could pose as an enemy of regimentation:

> Those men who are sent to Washington to protect the welfare of their friends and neighbors, to follow the orders of the common masses for whom they have agreed to be servants, then fail to work for the welfare of their friends and neighbors, and to carry out their orders, should be punished as all traitors and breakers of faith should be punished.[27]

The agitator hints that he cannot expose the "vast bloc of lawless usurpers" who "have moved into positions of power"[28] as vigorously as he would wish. "You know today we cannot use free speech in America. . . .

A man gets up here to talk Americanism and they have a hundred lights on him. . . . Sure, an American can't talk today."[29] But the agitator is able to talk boldly about not surrendering "my Americanism to Samuel Dickstein or anyone else"[30] precisely because he knows that a liberal-minded administration will continue to grant him the opportunity to voice his opinions.

When the Nazis denounced the German Republic for its inability to cope with economic problems and its failure to break the *diktat* of Versailles, they benefited from a condition of acute crisis in which the breakdown of liberal government had become apparent to the masses. Much the same thing was true of the situation in which the Italian Fascists seized power. In both countries, moreover, there had been powerful socialist movements that for several decades had persuaded masses of people, especially the workers, that the governments were not "theirs" but were instruments of their exploiters. Both the Nazis and the Fascists capitalized on this general suspicion of established government by derailing the attitudes of "class consciousness" off the socialist tracks.

The situation in the United States is somewhat different. Here there is no long-established antigovernmental or anticapitalist tradition that the agitator can exploit. The influence of the various radical groups is and has been negligible, and even the populist rebellion, whose tradition the agitator tries at many points to utilize, was mainly against specific abuses of various financial groupings rather than against the government as such. In the United States there is no prevalent feeling among the masses that the government is not "theirs." Whatever complaints the bulk of the American people may have are formulated in terms of remedying a specific situation ("bureaucrats," "the trusts," "anti-labor Congressmen." "socialistic New Dealers"). Such complaints do not, however, constitute a rejection of the social or political status quo. For the agitator this is a very considerable handicap and as a result he must exercise a certain amount of care in the way he denounces the government. He stresses that Washington is the arena of a perpetual struggle for power between the forces of disintegration and national unity: "Washington is full of tricksters with whom it is very difficult for some of our most patriotic representatives to cope."[31]

Portraying the administration as influenced by agents of financial interests, the agitator suggests that it only pretends to represent the people as a whole: "The President, thereupon, appointed a committee to investigate the rubber situation, headed by Bernard Baruch, who for years has been known as a 'Wall Street fixer.' Someone has well said—Why should we appoint the Devil to investigate Hell?"[32]

But no matter how severe his denunciations of individual members of the government, he praises the nation's "capable executives" or "foremost business executives and managers" and urges them to "resist the aggressions of political bureaucrats."[33] He suggests that the social forces that hold actual economic power in this country do not exercise the influence they should, while the influence of the "tyrannical bureaucrats" in the government is "out of all proportion to the influence they exert among the people."[34]

The agitator is interested in suggesting, however, that at least as now practiced, representative government in this country is a sham, and that the actual rulers are secret groups. In this respect he benefits from a widespread present-day feeling that major decisions do not originate with the elected representatives but with lobbies catering to special interests. The audience may thus believe that he is revealing the true state of affairs by naming the groups he dislikes as the manipulators of the government. "We have a set of bureaucrats in power in Washington who are working for certain foreign monopolies and certain banking interests when they should be working for the people of the United States."[35] He confirms suspicions that "big financiers get tips of contracts before they are given out by the government, enabling them to buy stocks."[36]

The administration is accused of aiming at the confiscation of all privately owned property and the agitator is "amazed at the lack of courage exhibited in America by its foremost business executives and managers to resist the aggressions of political bureaucrats and revolutionists in Washington."[37] Such seemingly trivial remarks serve in effect to glorify the direct rule of economic power groups at the expense of representative government.

The agitator can play on the inchoate suspicions of his audience that vague impersonal and irresistible powers determine the destiny of the nation. He fans the traditional American distrust of bureaucracy and centralization and interprets the New Deal's attempts to regulate big business as the first steps in the establishment of a dictatorship:

> Roosevelt State Capitalism is not to be pursued under constitutional forms. The wealth is *not* to be supervised by capable executives of the people who have created it individually, that high and low may profit. These Americans, victims of Reaction in government, are

> simply to relinquish their massed increments into the hands of a perpetual political oligarchy whose fiat is to be unalterable and whose omnipotence is sacrosanct.[38]

Such criticism directed against individuals who supposedly insinuate themselves into high posts, can have wide popular appeal: the listener is free to apply the stigma of vicious abuse of power to every official who is for any reason whatever an object of his resentment. The agitator's attacks further a preexisting ambivalent attitude toward institutionalized authority. Officials are pilloried while at the same time respect for authority is maintained by the eulogy of established institutions.

Theme 9: The Foreigner

In the agitator's portrait of the enemy, foreignness is a prominent trait. The plutocrat or banker is "international"; the administration is dominated by "international monopolies." Because foreign encirclement would hardly seem a plausible danger to the United States, the agitator warns against the dangers of foreign entanglements. And he finds a replica of the Nazi motif of living space in the immigrant population. He denounces plans to let new immigrants enter this country:

> Once landed on our shores, they would immediately start muscling Americans out of their jobs and their businesses. These "pioneers" would not develop new farms, mines, and enterprises, as did our forefathers. They haven't the intestinal stamina to pioneer; they would take, by their gold-usury-squeeze methods, what has been built by Americans.[39]

In the above portrait the alien seems to be a dangerous competitor, a predatory element associated with "international" bankers, but he is simultaneously associated with communism:

> From the four corners of this earth, foreigners came to our country to monopolize our resources. They are wolves in sheep's clothing, wise in the ways of propaganda and crime . . . the countries across the seas have sent crafty propagandists, who are destroying everything through subversive agitation.[40]

As against this banker-communist foreigner, the agitator evokes the image of the "good old days" when aliens with "their foreign isms were not busy working among the American people."[41] The alien is thus connected with the disturbing aspects of contemporary life, while the nostalgic image of the "good old days" suggests a pristine and uncontaminated era of security.

Overshadowing such immediate political implications is the agitator's stress on the foreigner's intrinsic differences from the native. Because he is endowed with immutable characteristics, the foreigner is essentially unassimilable. Aliens not only are responsible for "atheism, mental and moral decay, vulgarity, communism, imperialism . . . intolerance, snobbery, treason, treachery, dishonesty"[42] but they bring with them asocial characteristics that no amount of exposure to clean American air can purge:

> When he [the foreigner] comes to American or grows up in America, he carries the cheating, double dealing, ugly spirit of some Asiatics and Europeans in his heart and nourishes that ugly spirit by reflecting it in his social, political, fraternal and business affairs.[43]

While stressing how much of a danger aliens are because they "cleverly" divide "the American people . . . into groups,"[44] the agitator identifies them with Jews, a device that reassures those among his listeners who may themselves be among the millions of foreign-born or descendants of foreign-born that he intends no harm against them. The concept of the foreigner is narrowed down to those who "inevitably bear a characteristic racial stamp."[45] The agitator declares that "we don't care whether you come from Italy or Czechoslovakia . . . from Ireland or Wyoming. . . . Are you Christian and are you Aryan?"[46]

We see here an interesting development of the agitator's stereotype of the foreigner: from a specific external political threat to the country's economy, the foreigner is transformed into the perennial stranger characterized by irreducible qualities of foreignness. When the agitator arouses fear of communism, resentment against the government, and envy of financiers, he is largely referring to the audience's conscious experience; but when he arouses hostility against the stranger, the agitator seems to be reaching for a deeper layer of the psyche. In the agitational image of the enemy, the foreigner tends to be transformed from a specific dangerous but tangible power into an uncanny, irreconcilable extrahuman or subhuman being. This role of the foreigner in the agitator's total image of the enemy is explicitly seen in his references to the refugee.

The Refugee

For the agitator, the refugee is the most fearsome version of the foreigner. The very weakness, the very plight of the refugees is an argument against them for "*they fled from the wrath of the treacherously outraged peoples of those nations,* as they may one day flee as well from the wrath of a finally aroused populace in America."[47] The refugee becomes identified with the parasite who seeks dupes to do his dirty work.

> A "Refugee" is a member of the male sex who comes boo-hooing to the United States because he's "too cowardly" to fight like "real men" do, in Europe. He would establish himself in business or profession while the "real men" fight for HIS liberty.[48]

The refugee not only refuses to do dirty work but threatens the economic security of native Americans:

> According to the admission of our State Department, 580,000 Refugees had been admitted to the United States up to January, 1944, mostly on temporary permits. These Refugees have swarmed into positions formerly held by American professional men now absent on account of the war and constitute a serious threat of postwar unemployment for native Americans. . . .
>
> If there are hungry to be fed abroad, let the spirit of Christ stimulate us to export our surpluses instead of destroying them. It is not necessary or desirable that Refugees be brought to America to be fed.[49]

And the final identification of the refugee with the image of the enemy is made when he is depicted by the agitator as both a plutocrat-banker and a parasite who will end up on the relief rolls:

> But it is reliably reported that comparatively few of the Jewish refugees are agriculturists. By far the greater number of them are city dwellers, and small independent merchants—ranging from peddlers to store keepers and bankers. These newcomers, therefore, would not seek colonies in the rural areas but hope to concentrate in our already crowded cities; and since many of them are already penniless, would go on the relief rolls almost upon their arrival.[50]

The agitator endows refugees with characteristics that make them seem distasteful creatures, untouchables whom one avoids as if it were a social commandment to shun them. His picture of the refugee thus becomes a miniature version of the Nazis' notion of the subrace, and his evidence for such an unflattering portrait ranges from the refugee's alleged spiritual corruption to his most superficial mannerisms of behavior.

Ultimately, the refugee is identified with the ancient figure of the outcast, a man cursed by the gods, an exile who does not deserve a better fate. As such he raises a variety of ambivalent feelings among those who are subject to the agitator's appeal. The refugee seems an ideal model for irreconcilability: he has no home, he is accepted neither where he came from nor where he comes to. The refugee and the outcast become symbols of vague unconscious urges, of the repressed contents of the psyche, which, mankind has learned in the course of its history, must be censured and condemned as the price for social and cultural survival. The outcast serves to exorcise the fears as well as the temptations of self-righteous individuals. The hatred for the refugee seems thus a rejection of one's inner potential of freedom.

We may further develop this hypothesis by examining the implications of the fact that the refugee is called a "beggar."[51] One reacts ambivalently to the beggar: his humiliation is gratifying on a subconscious level, while at the same time it produces a feeling of conscious guilt. Once this ambivalence is lifted by the agitator's assurance that contempt for the beggar is not only a respectable but a necessary reaction, he can become a legitimate object of fury and spite. His suffering becomes a valid punishment for the fact that he has suffered at all.

The refugee's homelessness becomes the psychological equivalent of the audience's repressed instincts. Such an equation prepares for a release of banned instincts against banned people; a psychological bridge is constructed between the need of a resentment against repression and the resentment against a people without a country. He who has no home does not deserve one.

Notes

1. CF, June, 1942, p. 2.
2. Phelps, Los Angeles, August 13, 1941, radio.
3. Smith, *Americans! "Stop, Look, Listen,"* radio address, p. 1.
4. AID, Sept. 25, 1945, p. 2.
5. AID, May 5, 1941, p. 4.
6. Smith. *"Labor on the Cross,"* radio address, p. 1.
7. Smith, Detroit, Mar. 22, 1943, meeting.
8. Sanctuary. *The New Deal is Marxian Sabotage,* p. 1.
9. SJ, April 13, 1942.
10. X, Feb. 27, 1948, p. 4.
11. CF, Mar., 1947, p. 913.
12. Mote, *Testimony before the Committee on Military Affairs,* p. 8.
13. Phelps, *An American's History of Hollywood,* p. 5.

14. RC, Oct. 6, 1941, p. 3.
15. SJ, Jan. 19, 1942, p. 5.
16. Smith, Detroit, Mar. 19, 1943, meeting.
17. SJ, Sept. 8, 1941, p. 11.
18. Smith, *The Hoop of Steel,* 1942, p. 22.
19. Coughlin, Speech on Feb. 5, 1939, reprinted in *Why Leave Our Own,* p. 73.
20. Coughlin, Speech on Feb. 19, 1939, reprinted in *Why Leave Our Own,* p. 93.
21. SJ, June 10, 1940, p. 6.
22. AP, Aug., 1944, p. 1.
23. SJ, Feb. 20, 1939, p. 20.
24. SDEF, May, 1940, p. 5.
25. SJ, Dec. 22, 1941, p. 4.
26. DEF, Jan., 1939, p. 6.
27. Phelps, Los Angeles, March 30, 1941, radio.
28. LIB, Apr. 7, 1938, p. 8.
29. White, New York, July 18, 1940, street corner.
30. CF, Dec., 1944, p. 486.
31. Phelps, Los Angeles, July 20, 1941, radio.
32. CF, Aug., 1942, p. 9.
33. Mote, *Testimony,* etc., p. 3.
34. CF, June, 1942, p. 9.
35. CF. Aug., 1942, p. 15.
36. Phelps, Los Angeles, Oct. 20, 1940, radio.
37. Mote, *Testimony Before the Committee on Military Affairs,* pp. 2 & 3.
38. RC, Mar. 10, 1941, p. 6.
39. LIB, Nov. 28, 1940, p. 12.
40. Phelps, Los Angeles, July 27, 1940, radio.
41. Phelps, Los Angeles, July 30, 1941, radio.
42. Phelps, Los Angeles, July 28, 1941, radio.
43. Phelps, Los Angeles, August 4, 1941, radio.
44. Phelps, Los Angeles, Aug. 14, 1940, radio.
45. SJ, Nov. 24, 1941, p. 14.
46. McWilliams, New York, July 13, 1940, street corner.
47. LIB, Sept. 28, 1939, p. 10.
48. X, April 28, 1945, p. 2.
49. CF. Oct., 1944, pp. 455–456.
50. SJ, Nov., 28, 1938, p. 8.
51. Phelps, Los Angeles, July 28, 1941, radio.

5

The Helpless Enemy

The agitator faces a problem: As he frightens his followers with the specter of a ruthless enemy, must he not reassure them that the enemy can actually be defeated?

Most social movements recognize that at the time of their formation they are weaker than their enemy, a situation that is presumably to be changed by the movement's becoming stronger than its opponents. But in agitation there is no need to weaken the enemy, only to unmask his inherent weakness. His strength is based not on actual power or might, but on tricks and deception.

The agitator so constructs his enemy themes that the political attributes of the enemy lead directly and unobtrusively into psychological attributes. In the latter he continues the process of dehumanization already begun in the political portrait, and then twists this dehumanization into helplessness. A low animal, a parasite, a bug is inhuman and therefore undeserving of sympathy; it is helpless and therefore easy to destroy. By portraying the enemy as a criminal, a degenerate, a low animal, a bug, the agitator stirs deep layers of hatred and frustration in his listeners; their itch to violence becomes unbearable, and their hatred of this unspeakable enemy overflows. The agitator steps into the muddy pool of the malaise in order to channelize it into a stream of hate.

Theme 10: Creatures of the Underworld

Criminals

The agitator speaks of his opponents as "down-right villains"[1] or as "hoodlums."[2] The president is "supported mainly by gangsters and racketeers"[3] and is "the kind of stooge the Overseas Gang required to work their program of spoliation through the Congress."[4] Referring to plans for unification of Allied efforts during the war, the agitator finds that "it smells like that page in history which gives account of the attempt on the part of Benedict Arnold to put our troops under the command of a foreign power."[5] He is constantly discovering "widespread suspicion" created by "traitors of both alien and domestic breed" and learns that even Republican leaders are perhaps "only traitors in disguise."[6]

But the enemy is more than a mere traitor, or villain, or hoodlum; he is a murderer. Without naming names, the agitator makes it clear that he holds the enemy responsible for a good many unexplained deaths:

> Christ warned all posterity that the Jews were then and to be "Satan's Chosen People" and that compromise with them spells destruction. Because Christ's warnings have not been heeded by those calling themselves Christians, wars alone, created by "Satan's Chosen People," just the past 25 years, have liquidated over 50,000,000 Christians! To bring this close to home, another recent opponent of NUDEAL, Colorado's *Sen. Alva Adams*, died of a sudden attack, making 19 dead Congressmen so far this year—3 times the death rate of England in 1940 their year of worst blitzkriegs![7]

Such remarks are not isolated: the agitator exploits the conspiracy device to suggest to his audience that accidents and natural events are diabolic plots of the enemy. He sees a sinister significance in the fact that Senator Lundeen was "killed in an airplane accident . . . on his way home to address a rally of people who were protesting any premature entrance into the war";[8] he suggests that this and other deaths reveal the enemy's determination to achieve his ends by any means whatsoever—"if you hew to the line and let the chips fall where they may, anything can happen."[9]

It is noteworthy that in playing up such stories the agitator makes no reference to law-enforcement agencies. The enemy is not only identified with the criminal underworld but is shown as operating with impunity; murder remains unpunished, even uninvestigated. The agitator's harping on the enemy's terrorism might suggest to the audience that political murder is a natural expedient. The enemy gets away with murder, but this works both ways: the potential victim of today can become the executioner of tomorrow.

And so murder and persecution are in the air, ubiquitous, unrelenting, ever-threatening. The enemy is dragged down from the remote realm of power politics, revolutionary theory, and stock exchange manipulations to the vulgar level of the underworld. But these very denunciations of the agitator imply that his audience, until today the victim of this criminal horde, will tomorrow participate in a collective hunt of revenge. The enemy is offered as legitimate quarry. Because the enemy commits such criminal deeds with impunity, can the agitator's followers feel any squeamishness about the methods to be used in retaliation? There is nothing left but for the followers to take the law into their own hands, and the agitator himself will:

> treat personally with John L. Lewis, Robert M. LaFollette, and Samuel Dickstein, as three treasonable and surreptitious disrupters . . . to arrest them as soon as possible with Silvershirt backing, and after presenting due evidence of their traitorous activities to a Silvershirt jury, to confine them upon conviction in a Federal penitentiary for the remainder of the lives.[10]

Degenerates

The enemy is a ruthless criminal and constitutionally inferior. Because he is abnormal, he must be isolated and removed. He is foreign not only because he belongs to another nation or race but also because he is organically incapable of behaving according to norm: "We want neither your physical nor your mental diseases which cause your peoples to engage, incessantly, in mass murder and devilish destruction."[11]

In the description of the enemy, perversion and hysteria are closely connected with destructiveness.

> Why are Winchell's reactions pathological? Why does he rant and rave and become hysterical? Why is he fanatically determined to destroy the reputations of others? . . . [He] is an ego-maniac. . . . He is abnormally sex-conscious . . . a confirmed neurotic . . . and definitely psychopathic.[12]

The enemy, those "Socialists, Communists or psychopathic radicals," is "howling about Fascism in America."[13] "In all his career, Adolph Hitler did not approach the insolence of this minority in the number and grossness of their lies, in the perverse and stubborn nature of their wickedness."[14]

That such epithets of degeneracy are vague does not at all impair their usefulness. For one thing, they arouse distrust of everything the enemy says or does, but more important, they suggest the conclusion that the insane enemy must be isolated. Nor can there be any pity for the insane once their sickness has been designated as socially poisonous.

Here again the agitator's appeal is based on an ambivalent approach to the alleged characteristics of the enemy; the very piling up of the enemy's horrible characteristics implies to his followers the possibility that, in such a situation of extreme social dangers, they too will be able to be released from their inhibitions. By diagnosing the enemy in terms of a syndrome of hysteria, perversion, and insatiable hatred, the agitator stigmatizes the enemy with the disease he is encouraging among his followers.

Low Animals

A criminal or psychopath, however dangerous, may still retain human features, and law and custom provide procedures for handling them. But the agitator breaks this last tenuous link between the enemy and humankind by transforming him into a low animal. Likening the enemy to a vicious animal is more than a metaphor of abuse because the agitator's use of this metaphor is so persistent, so overwhelming, that in effect it usurps the place of its object in the perception of the audience. Like a poet whose inspiration is controlled by his ultimate purpose, the agitator confines himself in his imagery; his animals are of the "unrespectable" kind, rodents, reptiles, insects, and germs. He speaks of "criminal alien rats, and other forms of rodents,"[15] of the "Bolshevik rat's nest."[16] He states expressly that whatever other form the enemies may take is a disguise; in reality they are "poisonous, subversive vipers, regardless of the name they take on."[17] He calls for energetic, ruthless action against the enemy on the ground that "we dare not play with the poisonous venom of a reptile."[18] But it is when evoking insects or bacteria that he is most eloquent:

> Like a cloud of grasshoppers, like vermin in the closet, like white ants in the cellar, like termites in the furniture, a million propagandists have moved in upon us.[19]

He develops a metaphor in great detail:

> These alien enemies of America are like the parasitic insect which lays his egg inside the cocoon of a butterfly, devours the larva and, when the cocoon opens, instead of a butterfly we find a pest, a parasite.[20]

In these foregoing examples the human connotations of terms like *propagandists* or *alien enemies* are literally buried under the mass of insects.

A favorite animal of the agitator's is the termite. In ridiculing one of his pet targets, former Foreign Commissar Litvinov, the agitator refers to him as "The Termite Lit-Val-Hin-Max-Graf-Buch-Har-Stein."[21] The "enemies of America" are seen as "working like termites right here in

America on the pillars of our social, economic, religious, and political life."[22] These "termites have overrun the subway, the theatres, Coney Island, the Lower East Side, Flatbush, the Bronx, Newark."[23]

The microorganism seems to combine all the vicious enemy qualities in the highest degree. It is ubiquitous, close, deadly, insidious; it invites the idea of extermination; and most important, it is invisible to the naked eye. The agitator expert is required to detect its presence: "The propaganda of the alienisms is seeping through the bloodstreams of our national life like a deadly germ."[24] The danger of contamination is too great to leave anyone time to discuss this diagnosis:

> It only takes one venereal germ to destroy the body of a clean young man. It only requires one communist, well placed, to destroy a home, a mill, a factory, a school, or a section of the government.[25]

The terrifying implications of a threat of epidemic are so vivid that the mere accumulation of appropriate terms may suffice to produce the desired associations:

> Disease: Since B#243 quoted THE JEWISH PRESS 9-27-40 that *Polish Jews are typhus carriers,* predicting that such brought into Germany would spread that disease and help destroy Hitler. . . .
>
> The Jewish NY TIMES 11-20-39 quoted special cable from Berlin that Warsaw's ghetto was put under armed guards segregation due to "*Jews* were making profits from the need of the Polish population; furthermore, they were *dangerous carriers* of sickness and pestilence." This is borne out by Board of Health WPA project in 1934–35 in New York City to determine the relation between rats and *typhus fever cases.* . . .
>
> Since hundreds of thousands of such "refugee" Jews have flooded our large cities during NUDEAL (aided and abetted thereby regardless of immigration laws), and since THE JEWISH PRESS boasts that such Jews taken into Germany will cause typhus epidemics, what a danger exists in our midst![26]

Because the enemy is a terrifyingly dangerous insect or germ, he must be exterminated ruthlessly: "What the average Gentile means to say is: 'It's going to take violence to rid the nation of the Locust Swarm, and the sooner we get it over with, the happier for the nation.'"[27] Indeed, people "are tired of the millions of alien Jews flocking like locusts to our country de-housing and de-jobbing native Americans."[28]

Lest this agitational emphasis on low animals seem a mere fantastic aberration, it should be pointed out that European agitation

indulged—and with all too evident effectiveness—in similar characterizations of its enemy. According to an eyewitness account, peasants
recruited from the native population of Nazi-occupied countries to
help in mass murders were given an intensive training course that
lasted only a few hours, and that consisted in the study of pictures
representing Jews as repulsive small beasts. (Cf. Ludwig Hirszfeld,
Historja Jednego Zycia [Warsaw, 1947], ch. 18.) Similarly, in posters
that were widely used by the Nazis to disseminate anti-Semitism
Jews are pictorially distorted to such an extent that the spectator
must actually make an effort of the imagination to rediscover the
human form in what appears to be some strange sort of bug. (Cf.
Jacques Polonski, *La Presse, la propagande et l'opinion publique sous
l'occupation* [Paris, 1946], p. 108.)

How is this extraordinary content of agitation to be accounted for?

The agitator dehumanizes the enemy on several levels: the enemy
seems to the agitator to be a foreigner who comes from suspect
geographical regions; he is a criminal who inhabits reprehensible
moral regions; and he is a degenerate who derives from disgusting
biological regions. To these evocations of the enemy image, the audience responds by experiencing a threat to its livelihood from the
invading strangers; a threat to its emotional balance by the specter of
the ubiquitous criminal whose crime it finds simultaneously repulsive
and seductive; and a threat to its human status from the feared and
filthy subhuman creature.

Various degrees of aversion to small animals are well known in
psychiatric and everyday observations. Clinical experience indicates
that there is a certain connection between extreme detestation of small
animals and feelings of unconscious ambivalence toward childhood
sexual development. Psychoanalysts have tried to show this ambivalence projected through parasitophobia in two ways: (1) the victim
of parasitophobia longs for that phase in infancy in which the child,
like a parasite, clings to and desires the mother, while (2) through his
rejection of the parasite he expresses his subsequent revulsion from
this attachment by means of the sadism into which his longing receded
after being subjected to serious genital shocks and disappointments. In
the parasitophobia the longing is still present but has been repressed
by sadism; the longing continues its subterranean existence while the
sadism is manifestly dominant.

The agitator's tirades against vermin provide a rationalization for the
release of sadistic impulses against the dirty enemies. The gesture with

which a person violently eradicates vermin and the mixture of repulsion and pleasure he may draw from this act, can serve as a vicarious rehearsal for the lust to annihilate more substantial enemies.

The frustrated person (and we must always bear in mind that agitation is aimed at the frustrated) cannot tolerate the lack of frustration that he sees or imagines he sees in other people. Hence he yearns for ceaseless acts of destruction against the vermin as foreigners and against the foreigners as vermin. What agitation tries ultimately to achieve here is to distort and corrupt the very process of the audience's vision and audition. The audience must be conditioned to see the enemy as an animal and to hear the enemy making animal sounds.

There is another aspect of response that the agitator's stress on low animals finds in his audience. Swarms of insects, vermin, and rats seem to be a particularly appropriate vehicle for projection by the masses of their unconscious realization that they are nothing, in many instances, but a mere mass. In violently eradicating the hated vermin, the sado-masochistic person tries symbolically to separate himself from the crowd and confirm his individuality.

Theme 11: Call to the Hunt

The agitator has shown that the wolf in sheep's clothing is actually a sheep in wolf's clothing. But an enemy overtly designated as helpless would cease to be an urgent menace and would not be a satisfactory object for the projection of resentments and fears. The agitator therefore simultaneously dangles both notions before his audience: his enemy is both strong and weak. He reconciles the apparent contradiction by indirectly suggesting that the enemy disguises his weakness by daring to be dangerous: weakness and strength blend in arrogance.

Weakness is inherent in the notion of the enemy as a stranger, an outlaw, a psychopath, and a low animal. None of these images suggests genuine danger. As for the enemy conceived as a germ or scourge, he can be dangerous only if moral taboos or humane considerations hamper efficient antisepsis.

Lacking any solid social support, despised and hated by the people, the enemy has never been able to seize and hold power, has never dared emerge undisguised into daylight. In fact, the enemy is aware of his weakness. He hides like a rat "in alley ways and other dark holes";[29] he lurks "in the shadows of anonymity"[30] and even cultivates "a passion for anonymity."[31] He hatches his plots while traveling "in a special train with the shades drawn."[32]

When he dares come into the open somewhat, the enemy's weapon is manipulation of public opinion. He controls the media of mass communication and operates "among the so-called intellectuals, professional people, school teachers, preachers, student groups."[33] As a trickster, a shady character, an impostor without real strength, the enemy is thus the antithesis of the hard-working, puritanical, and self-restrained entrepreneur who adheres to social convention and rules of moderation and has nothing to hide from the public. But the enemy, nowhere nearly as solid a character, has nothing but his wits at his disposal; he is a dealer in words, in mere ideas, in articles, in speeches. Shut his mouth by force, and he collapses.

The agitator buttresses his suggestion that the enemy is fundamentally weak by linking the various kinds of enemies together in such a way that those who are merely targets of contempt take the edge off, so to speak, those who might symbolize danger. This amalgam of enemies is effected by a verbal device: cumulative enumerations of various enemies. The agitator speaks of "aliens, Communists, crackpots, refugees, renegades, Socialists, termites and traitors."[34] All the doctrines he attacks hardly differ in substance: "Bolshevism . . . regardless of whether it is called New Dealism, Communism, Liberalism, Rooseveltism, Social Democracy or Judaism."[35]

No group has any genuine independent existence, and all are pretty much alike. The very fact that the agitator can speak in one breath of "this radicalism, this racketeering, this sabotage . . . Nazi spies, communist agents"[36] or of "these dictators, these czars, these fascists, these Nazis, these communists, these gangs"[37] may suggest that there is no need to be cautious in attacking any of them. In these enumerations the underlying motive becomes apparent when refugees are linked with crackpots, termites, and traitors. Such combinations deserve not only moral indignation but also contempt. Such an enemy is morally and mentally debased, an "unspeakable gang of alien scalawags. Communist fellow travelers, revolutionary Jews, third generation frustrates, mongrel misfits, and hypocritical humbugs."[38]

The agitator seems occasionally to express surprise at finding such characters together: "an amazing conglomeration of cunning Communists, befuddled fellow-travelers, Utopian dreamers, and revolutionary visionaries, in most every key post of consequence."[39]

By this amalgamation of the various stereotypes of the enemy, the nature of the audience's hostile emotion is transformed. The agitator supplants individual prejudice by mass prejudice. Individual prejudice is an attitude charged with emotional valuations and embodying idiosyncracies. Stubborn, even irrational clinging to idiosyncrasies or prejudices is popularly interpreted as a kind of individualism. But when the agitator amalgamates the various hostile stereotypes of the enemy, the individualistic kind of prejudice gives way to a cold, abstract, standardized fury that is closer to the paranoiac's destructive rage than to the passion of hatred. The enemy is hated with an emotional intensity that can be aroused only by a human being, and treated with a cold pitilessness that can be mobilized only against an inanimate object: "The Jewish Menace has now reached a stage that it can only be dealt with INTERNATIONALLY in the same way that Cancer, Malaria and Leprosy are dealt with and quite calmly at that and without any bloodshed."[40]

While the international financiers, the House of Morgan, Stalin, the Jewish refugees, the Communist, and the fellow traveler are equated and are the objects of the same fury, its immediate target is in this case the weakest group, the Jews. We need not assume that the agitator's followers are completely deceived by the demagogy that attributes dangerous traits to the helpless victim. They may be dimly aware that the object of their fury is really innocent of the charge used as a pretext for attacking it, but precisely because a weak target is singled out, they may remember their own deep-rooted fears of meeting the same fate as the victim-enemy.[41] The enemy's weaknesses come to symbolize the audience's own futile and abortive protest against oppression. In offering members of the audience a quarry to be hunted, the agitator provides them with an effective method of relief: they are to vent their resentment on some helpless victim. Once the various hostile impulses against different enemies have been amalgamated by the agitator, reduced as it were to a uniform gaseous state, they exert equal pressure on all points and tend to break through at the weakest point. Where that is everyone knows.

The act of the frustrated little man who impotently vents his fury on his child or wife is reproduced on a social scale. The individual perpetrator of such an act may realize its irrationality and may feel consciously guilty, but on the social level the concentration of fury on stereotypes of weakness acquires a new connotation. By identifying the victim of persecution with the dangerous persecutor, the agitator sanctions and rationalizes an act of cowardice and impotence and makes it appear as an act of courage and wisdom. At the same time he relieves his followers from one of their basic fears: the fear of being pushed to the bottom of the social ladder. They are offered a group that deserves a fate worse than their own, a group of underprivileged people that they, the manipulated, can manipulate and humiliate with impunity. This transformation of the enemy from a dangerous persecutor into the persecuted quarry is the essence of the enemy theme in agitation.

But it is not a replacement of the persecutor by the quarry; in the image of the enemy the two coexist. Hostility against the quarry can be effectively aroused only when the audience half believes it to be dangerous; the hunt is always conceived as an act of self-defense. In this way the followers are reminded that although they are an elite today, they are in constant danger, and can retain their privileged status only by faithfully following the leader in the constant hunt of the enemy. Not even extermination of the enemy removes the danger he represents; he has to be killed again and again, killed only to be revived once more so that he may fulfill his function indefinitely.

Lumping-Together Device

It is this image of an organically weak and unassimilable enemy that emerges as the result of the lumping together of the various enemy types. In the very process that blurs the distinctions between all the enemy groups, the Jew alone becomes more sharply delineated. From the outset he is present in all the versions of the enemy as their invisible essence, and when the agitator enumerates his various "vicious foes," it is always the Jew who stands out as the most conspicuous, tangible, and accessible target. Consider, for example, the following list:

> the Judaeo-Maxists, Anglophiles, International bankers, radio commentators, Hollywood, Anti-Defamation League, Anti-Nazi League, Friends of Democracy, Rhodes scholars, *PM, Daily Worker, Chicago Sun, The New Masses, The Nation* and *The New Republic.*[42]

Aside from the fact that communism, liberalism, and anti-Nazism are elsewhere represented as Jewish activities, the only group that emerges as clearly identified here is "the Judaeo-Marxists," the Jews. The implication apparently is that an Anglophile, communist, or liberal is recognized through his being a Jew or being associated with Jews; and that to *be* a Jew is equivalent to belonging to a group or organization that the agitator considers pernicious.

Likewise in the list "HIDDEN HAND agencies—Communist Party, CIO, AFL, Federal Council of Churches, Jews, et al.,"[43] the apparently non-Jewish terms only help to throw a more glaring light on the Jews. A member of any of the enumerated organizations is not recognizable as such and may leave it any time, but a Jew must always remain a Jew whether he wishes to or not.

> As Lindbergh said in Des Moines this week, sooner or later the American people are going to be looking for a few flocks of scapegoats. And it's not going to be the Irish, the Spaniards, the Egyptians, or the Hottentots who'll be called to that accounting.[44]

Indeed, the very idea that any group other than the Jews could be a scapegoat is almost comical. The agitator knows very well that he need not be more explicit. But he does not rely on merely existing anti-Jewish stereotypes; he also helps to refurbish them and develop new ones. Reduction of the formidable persecutor to a helpless creature is supplemented by a converse process, to be discussed in the following chapter, in which this helpless creature is endowed with the qualities he must have if he is to serve the agitator's political and psychological purposes.

In singling out the Jews, the agitator need not necessarily resort to explicit "lumping together." He speaks as though he knew that the tendency to single out the Jew as the source of all their troubles is latent in his listeners, and that the very mention of a Jewish name suffices to push all other "enemies" into the background. The procedure is illustrated in a speech made by an agitator who begins by depicting himself as the target of persecution by the powers that be and the communists.[45] It seems that as a result of an insulting remark he made about President Roosevelt,

> orders came down from Washington—I was nineteen years old at that time—orders came down from Washington calling for my arrest. I was imprisoned and indicted by a Federal Grand Jury on charges of threatening the life of the President.

This incident was followed by various tribulations, involving communist activities in the army and the "New-Deal-dominated War Department." His opposition to communism, he went on, made him appear suspect, and he was not allowed to go to the front:

> I immediately volunteered for the D-Day invasion of Europe saying that I wanted to do anything and everything that any other soldier

had to do in this war to demonstrate that I was a true American and a loyal soldier—and a loyal soldier saying that I had volunteered for overseas service; that I loved America and I was a Christian and if I was guilty of anything wrong. I told them to call me up before an investigating board and examine my record and my life.

So I was turned over to one Major Goldstein [laughter] in the psycho-neuropathic ward of the station hospital for observation [laughter].

During the speaker's recital of the sufferings inflicted upon him as a result of insulting remarks, the audience kept quiet as though impressed by this tale of persecuted innocence. Mention of a Jewish name produced laughter—a relief of tension.

The discovery of the Jew among the conspirators has subconsciously been expected all the time; the preceding list of enemies is revealed as a joke, and the Jew is its point. This point is enhanced by the association of the Jew with mental disease, for the suggestion is that not the persecuted hero but the Jew is the real psychopath.

The relief expressed by the laughter is also caused by the realization that there is a simple method of "cleaning up" this "whole bad, smelly mess of persecution."[46] All that is needed is to crush those psychopathic Jews. Behind these horrors there is a man whose name has been made so comical that pronouncing it dispels all fears. The humiliated followers thus become the humiliators, and act out their sense of superiority over their enemy.

The laughter seems to foreshadow the pleasure of the anticipated hunt. The suggestion is that the followers are laughing only because they are generous—they should hit, and hit hard, instead of laughing. Like the cat, they play with the mouse.

Pattern of Obsession

The persistence with which the agitator builds his fantasy image of the enemy stems from a paranoiac conception of his relationship to the world. In any event, the agitator is the least restrained of all figures in public political life. Without inhibition or even the suggestion that he is in any way exaggerating, he can assert that "I read a pamphlet not long ago that said that 67 per cent of the House of Representatives were Jewish. I read a pamphlet that said it and it guaranteed the truth of it, put out by a publisher here in New York. And the Senate is somewhat the same, only a little less, about 59 per cent."[47] Or he can ask with regard to the wartime evacuation of London: "Did you read about the wholesale evacuation of London, ostensibly to get women and children away from the terrible Nazi bombers—that haven't arrived at this writing? *Are Jewish refugees in the evacuated homes now, we wonder?*"[48] And when the agitator is asked by the Library of Congress for copies of his publications, he is again on his guard; he suspects that it is one of the "tricks ... used to trap Christian Americans. . . ."[49] To complete our citations of the paranoiac character of agitational material. we find the agitator discoursing on "why Mussolini turned against the Jews": "One factor compelling immediate action was the question of hygiene. Syphilis in a virulent form is highly prevalent among the natives of Abyssinia. Mussolini resolved to combat both miscegenation and disease. Much to his surprise, he encountered considerable opposition in Italy. He discovered that it came primarily from Jewish sources."[50]

Such paranoiac delusions as are found in the above statements are in reality the projections of hatred. The persecutor always represents some of the features of the person who suffers from the paranoiac delusion. As Freud puts it, the man who thinks "I hate him" twists the thought into a defensive projection: "He hates me." (Cf. Sigmund Freud, *Psychoanalytic Notes upon an Autobiographical Account of a Case of Paranoia,* in *Collected Papers,* vol. 3.) By indulging in this projection, the paranoiac relieves himself of part of his fear of self-destruction. The agitator, by directing his audience's fears onto the image of the enemy, similarly relieves it of some of its fears. But just as the paranoiac finds only temporary relief by fixating the blame on a particular target, so the most the agitator can offer to his audience is a palliative for, rather than a cure of, its fears.

And so he, together with his followers, continues to search. It is this search, rather than any actual object of the search, that seems to characterize the relationship between agitator and audience. Behind one enemy there always lurks another. Suffering from a kind of eternal restlessness, the agitator never seems able to find a terminal and perfect image of the enemy; each version leads to another, each destruction of the enemy's disguise to the renewed discovery that he has still another disguise. It is like a striptease without end.

Agitator and audience seem, however, to find a temporary resting place in their hunt for target of their accumulated resentment. Here at last the "real" enemy seems to have been found: the Jew, who confirms the fantastic fusion of ruthlessness and helplessness.

Notes

1. Smith, Detroit, Mar. 22, 1943, meeting.
2. SJ, Oct. 9, 1939, p. 4.
3. Maloney, New York, July 25, 1940, street corner.
4. Pelley, *What You Should Know About The Pelley Publications*, p. 2.
5. CF, Nov., 1944, p. 466.
6. AP, Sept., 1944, pp. 3 & 4.
7. AID, Dec. 3, 1941, p. 2.
8. Smith, Detroit, Mar. 19, 1943, meeting.
9. Smith, Detroit, Mar. 19, 1943, meeting.
10. LIB, Mar. 28, 1938.
11. Phelps, *An Appeal to Americans*, p. 10.
12. Kamp, *With Lotions of Love . . .* pp. 47–48.
13. DEF, Mar., 1937, Lewis Valentine Ulrey in, p. 19.
14. AP, June, 1945, p. 3.
15. Phelps, Los Angeles, Aug. 27, 1940, radio.
16. RC, Dec. 8, 1941, p. 4.
17. X, Feb. 24, 1945, p. 2.
18. Smith, "Mice or Men," radio address, p. 3.
19. Smith, *"The Next President of the United States"* p. 2.
20. Smith, *"Dictatorship Contes With War,"* radio address, p. 1.
21. Sanctuary, *Litvinoff, Foreign Commissar of the U.S.S.R.*, p. 3.
22. Phelps, Los Angeles, Aug. 6, 1941, radio.
23. AP, Aug., 1944, p. 16.
24. CF, Aug., 1942, p. 13.
25. Smith, *"Americans! Stop, Look, Listen,"* ibid, p. 2.
26. AID, Dec. 30, 1940, p. 1.
27. LIB, Mar. 28, 1938.
28. X, Feb. 13, 1948, p. 2.
29. Phelps, Los Angeles, Sept. 8, 1940, radio.
30. Smith, *"Mice or Men,"* radio address, p. 3.
31. Kamp, *Famine in America*, p. 49.
32. AP, Feb., 1944, p. 6.
33. Smith, *"Mice or Men,"* ibid, p. 1.
34. AP, June, 1945, p. 6.
35. LIB, Mar. 28, 1940, p. 11.
36. Smith, *"Labor on the Cross,"* radio address, p. 4.
37. Smith, Detroit, Mar. 19, 1943, meeting.
38. AP, Sept., 1944, p. 10.
39. Kamp, *How To Win The War*, p. 3.
40. *Women's Voice*, Letter by H. H. Beamish in, Mar. 27, 1947, p. 13.
41. The French historian Mathiez quotes the following excerpt from an official police report written after the execution of twelve persons at the beginning of the Terror: "I must tell you that such executions have the greatest political effects, but the most considerable of them is the appeasement of popular resentment. The wife who lost her husband, the father who lost his son, the merchant who has no trade, the worker who pays everything so dearly that

his wages amount to almost nothing, perhaps resign themselves to their own sufferings only when they see people more unfortunate than themselves and when they think these people are their enemies." A. Mathiez, *La revolution française, Paris* (1928).

42. AP, Oct., 1945, p. 15.
43. AID, May 22, 1939, p. 2.
44. RC, Sept. 22, 1941, p. 2.
45. Lawrence Asman at a Smith meeting, Cleveland, Apr. 4, 1946.
46. Smith, Cleveland, Apr. 4, 1946, meeting.
47. White, New York, July 18, 1940, street corner.
48. LIB, Oct. 7, 1939, p. 5.
49. AID, June 23, 1942, p. 4.
50. SJ, Mar. 27, 1939, p. 11.

6

The Enemy as Jew

The American agitator denounces communists, plutocrats, and refugees without qualification, but he insists on distinguishing between "international" and "American," atheistic and religious, "good" and "bad" Jews. To believe him, his feelings toward the Jews are quite friendly, and he is attacking only so-called organized Jewry. The functional characteristics of the enemy, which he sometimes explains as consequences of racial characteristics, he at other times sees as the cause of racial characteristics. Communist or plutocrat lead to the Jew, but the Jew seemingly leads back to the communist or plutocrat.

The American agitator's failure to develop an explicit and complete anti-Semitic program may be due to the political immaturity of American agitation or to the opprobrium attached in this country to public expressions of anti-Semitism. Whatever the reason, indirect approaches to anti-Semitism actually help the agitator; he can pose as an objective student who is not obsessed by hatred and who should therefore not be denounced as a fanatic. Anti-Semitism, he says, is "one of the mysteries of the centuries"[1] and he merely wonders "if the entire matter of preservation of the Jewish community as a separate and peculiar community should not be given study?"[2]

He can build up a certain suspense: his listeners know that anti-Semitic themes will come but they are not always sure how the agitator will put them across. The agitator can also imply that his reserve in discussing such matters is due to the power of the forces opposing him, but because he always manages to put across his anti-Semitic bias, he suggests that he has succeeded in defying the power of the opposition.

In this chapter no attempt is made to develop a theory of anti-Semitism. We are here concerned only with the stereotypes of the Jew as they appear in agitational material and the way in which the agitator develops and transforms those stereotypes into a logically self-contradictory but psychologically consistent image of the Jew, who appears both as weak and strong, victim of persecution and persecutor, endowed with unchangeable racial characteristics and irrepressible individualism.

Theme 12: The Victim

The Jew is Persecuted

The theme of the persecuted Jew appears in many variations: sometimes he is pictured as a tool or victim of providence; sometimes the severity or existence of persecution is denied; and sometimes the agitator even implies that the Jews stage pogroms against themselves. Whatever the variation, however, the agitator succeeds in keeping his audience constantly aware of the so-called Jewish problem. It matters little whether he denies being an anti-Semite or pretends to explain or even deplore it; in each case he manages to suggest that anti-Semitism is a fundamental and relevant category in the discussion of public issues.

The agitator characterizes persecution of Jews as a kind of natural phenomenon:

> They were thrown out of every country that got a hold of them . . . Mussolini came in and they were thrown out . . . Mr. Hitler came along and he threw them out. . . they were thrown out of Poland . . . they were thrown out of Norway . . . France had to throw them out. France is throwing them out.[3]

The agitator is apparently aware of the public revulsion against the Nazi acts of violence. To counteract the possible effects of it, he absolves fascist leaders from all responsibility:

> We cannot let ourselves be hoaxed into believing that these refugees have fled from the wrath of Franco in Spain, or from the wrath of Hitler when they left Moravia, or Slovakia, or now from Poland. No! *They fled from the wrath of the treacherously outraged peoples of those nations,* as they may one day flee as well from the wrath of a finally aroused populace in America.[4]

Before the spectacle of Jewish misery, the agitator eschews any display of emotion and instead urges his audience to study the question "objectively." He seems to refute the notion that he appeals primarily to passions, and presents the audience with a systematic survey of Jewish history preceded by the following remarks:

> Recurring persecutions and expulsion of the Jews have marked the history of every age and country since the fall of Jerusalem. . . .

> As background for current reading about the Jews—particularly the war mongering of their international financialists and political policymakers [we present the following survey].[5]

Although the explanation is here purely secular, and the fall of Jerusalem is associated with the intrigues of international bankers, the overall purpose of this "background for current reading" is to impress upon the reader the permanent and inevitable character of Jewish persecutions. The personality and motives of the persecutor recede into the background; the Nazi attack on the Jews is a problem that concerns only the Jews, who, because they are destined to suffer, cannot be defended by any earthly power. By summoning them to seek refuge only in spirituality, the agitator drives home the idea of their absolute defenselessness, and he underscores the precariousness of this refuge by comparing it to a bomb shelter:

> If there was ever an occasion for Jewry to abandon its materialism, now is the acceptable day. Until there is a deep spiritual reawakening in the hearts of Jewish leaders, there will be perpetuated the story of Egypt in America and every other nation—a story which will chronicle the worst sufferings of God's once chosen people. Perchance the rich can flee—for a time. But the poor, innocent, misled little Jew will remain, as he always does, to bear the plagues of persecution. . . . Have the Jews forgotten that the more they organize materially against their opponents, the more assaults will increase and the closer they are to persecution? There is no security for Jews except in the bomb shelter of spirituality.[6]

The Jew is not Persecuted

One of the major devices by which the agitator develops his theme of the Jew as victim is often to deny the very existence of persecution. "The persecutions of which the Jews in Germany complained were in reality no persecutions at all,"[7] for even if there were one or two difficulties in Germany, nonetheless "synagogues are open on Saturday the same as usual and rabbis receive their pay without molestation."[8]

Toward such matters the agitator is eager to be as unimpassioned and cautious as possible. One must not be too hasty in accepting news reports: "No one in this country knows the exact truth about German treatment of the Jews except that its severity has been greatly exaggerated."[9] For the fact is that though "the wails of the rabbis about the persecuted Polish Jews clutter up the press. . . we can dry our sympathetic tears; the sob stories are not true!"[10] The agitator is not taken in by mere newspaper reports; he reasons dispassionately: "At present there are three and a half million Jews in Poland and they would not be there if there had been any 'persecution.'"[11]

What does the agitator achieve psychologically by thus flouting the historical evidence of persecution of Jews? For one thing, because the Jewish complaints are branded as exaggerated, the Jews are established as professional complainers who take advantage of the gentiles' kindheartedness. At the same time, the persecutions are reduced to something quite ordinary, normal, and legal, routine activities of a modern state. Here the agitator implies that the term *persecution* does not really apply to the Jews, for the Jews are not quite normal human beings anyway. One does not speak of a termite's or a parasite's rights when it is exterminated. Such creatures cannot be said to be persecuted; they are simply destroyed.

True, the Jews groan and lament, but they are still alive: "On all sides we hear of the 'terrible German pogroms,' *but we have yet to hear of a single Jew killed in one under the Hitler regime*."[12] In fact, hints the agitator, it is not unlikely that Jewish complaints are merely a stratagem to conceal aggressions against Christians: "All this hue and cry about Hitler's persecution was smokescreen to hide the disappearance— mostly to USA is my guess—of millions of Jews in Europe."[13]

And so what appears to others as an attack on a defenseless group becomes a struggle between the forces of order and a cunning enemy whose demand for rights is merely a pretext for securing unfair advantages. Only the suckers can pity Jews, only those who allow their pity to make them the victims of the Jews. One must suppress one's altruistic impulse in relation to them as one suppresses it when witnessing the arrest of a criminal. The impunity with which actual persecution of the Jews is denied seems to imply that whoever joins the hunt of the Jews need not fear punishment or moral disapproval, for, says the agitator, the persecuted are really the persecutors.

Anti-Semitism Disavowed

The agitator's repudiations of anti-Semitism, or even direct assertions of pro-Semitic feelings—"I am a friend of the Jews"[14]—are variations of the rhetorical figure of apophasis (mention of something while denying intention to mention it). The form, sometimes the mere tone, of such statements belies their presumed content. The audience always knows, for the agitator manages to insert an anti-Semitic insinuation in the very midst of his disclaimer. For example: "*Liberation* has never deliberately dealt in rancors. It has picked no quarrel with the Jew as individual but strictly what his race represents in the mass."[15] Whether the individual is blamed for the group or the group for the individual, the effect is the same.

The existence of anti-Jewish animosity is justified by innuendo: the Jews are behind both capitalism and communism. The same ambiguity is developed in the guise of careful definitions:

> Neither Father Coughlin nor *Social Justice* is anti-Semitic. . . in the sense that it is opposed to any individual Jew, to any religious Jew, to any group of Jews.

> We are opposed, however, to having atheistic Jews *impose their code of life upon our political structure, our social structure, our economic structure and our national structure.*[16]

Such formulations actually define the anti-Semitic tactics: the Jew must always be attacked on some pretext; the fact that the Jew is persecuted must be exploited politically. If despite all the agitator's sincere efforts to the contrary anti-Semitism still flourishes, it is not his fault. He even promises to defend the Jews, and takes this opportunity to outline a program of action for the anti-Semitic extremists:

> Will I ever assail Jewry in general? Ridiculous!

> If and when the day should come when the anti-Semite radicals will grow strong enough as a result of the depression and Communist aggression to rise against the Jews, I will be in the front ranks of the Cohens, the Franklins, the Issermans, the Wises, the Bambergs and the other sons of Israel fighting in their defense.[17]

Although these denials afford the agitator an additional opportunity to keep the so-called Jewish problem alive in the minds of his audience, they are especially helpful in the dissociation of anti-Jewish action from anti-Jewish sentiment. Even those who do not harbor any anti-Semitic feelings must be mobilized for the hunt, or at least neutralized. It is as though the agitator were aware of the fundamental difference between the kind of "bona fide" suburban anti-Semitism, which is not usually associated with a conscious political purpose, and totalitarian anti-Semitism, in which the Jew is primarily an object of political manipulation. An anti-Semite of the traditional type may recognize that at least some Jews are good citizens, although he would not care to meet them socially. What the agitator aims at is to impress upon his audience the need to persecute all Jews, the "good" and the "bad," a distinction he does not take very seriously in any case. And by developing the idea of collective responsibility of the Jews, he provides the rationalization for this attitude.

All Are Guilty

The agitator professes to be so opposed to anti-Semitism that he often gives the Jews advice on how to combat it. "Why don't the Jews who want peace and quiet repudiate such character assassins as Walter Winchell?"[18] Or he addresses himself directly to Jewish religious leaders: "The evil doers in their own midst must be cried out against by the rabbis."[19]

By suggesting that the "bad" Jews are able to engage in their destructive activities because they enjoy the passive support of the "good" ones, he smuggles in the notion of collective responsibility.

> I say to the good Jews of America, be not indulgent with the irreligious, atheistic Jews and Gentiles. . . be not lenient with your high financiers, and politicians who assisted at the birth of the only political social and economic system in all civilization that adopted atheism as its religion, internationalism as its patriotism and slavery as its liberty.[20]

The agitator does not run any risk of being misunderstood in his timeworn distinction between the good and bad Jews. Jewish solidarity and Jewish collective responsibility are treated as so self-evident that the very idea that some "good" Jews might escape the wrath of the aroused gentiles appears as ridiculous. As though to make this clear, the agitator playfully refers to a fictitious central Jewish organization that could correct any Jewish transgressors:

> FOR THEIR OWN PROTECTION I sincerely wish that the General Jewish Council would take some of their incorrigible children to the woodshed. A few lightning flashes properly aimed and a few thunder claps efficaciously yelled would do much to rectify the barometer of class hatred. . . .[21]

The agitator's seemingly casual reference to racial tensions as "class hatred" serves to intimate that all Jews belong to the same social group, the well-to-do.

Anti-Semitism Explained

The trouble with the Jews is that they do not listen to the agitator's advice; otherwise, he suggests, all might be well. For some inexplicable reason, they reject his sincere offers of friendship: "Why do these short-sighted Jews continue to goad us? Why don't they cultivate our friendship instead of inspiring our animosity?"[22] The agitator drives to an extreme the idea, still held by many Jews themselves, that Jewish behavior or character accounts for the hostility against them. He denounces the narrow-minded ethnocentrism of the Jews:

> If you want to arouse an anti-Jewish sentiment in America that will sweep like influenza across the fields of our nation, break down these immigration barriers. . . . Be temperate and satisfy the needs of your people instead of the racketeers within your own midst who are raising money with which to build up straw men and knock them down again.[23]

The agitator is particularly indignant at the Jewish effort to combat anti-Semitism. Such an idea is denounced as outright madness: "National Committee to Combat Anti-Semitism . . . this crazy organization should be folded up by the Jews themselves."[24] Anti-Semitism is nothing but a reaction to the Jewish persecution of anti-Semites: "These merciless programs of abuse which certain Jews and their satellites work upon people who are not in full agreement with them create terrible reactions."[25]

From the idea that the Jews promote anti-Semitism by their stupidity there is only one step to the idea that they promote it deliberately: "Kahn is one of those Jews who is devoting his life to the promoting of anti-Semitism. God save the race from such Jews."[26] Opposition to anti-Semitism is depicted as a method for escaping all criticism and for attacking innocent gentiles:

> "Anti-Semitism" is a defense mechanism. Its origin is very ancient. It is a label used by Jewish scoundrels to protect themselves against *just* as well as *unjust* criticism. No other race claims any such general immunity from criticism. The label frightens many persons with weak spines.[27]

No wonder that the agitator in exasperation accepts the label: "Inspired press constantly calls me anti-British, as well as pro-Nazi, and anti-Semitic. If following Christ's footsteps makes me 'anti-Semitic'—so be it."[28]

The persistent denial of anti-Semitism thus becomes a proud admission of it, with the suggestion that such admission is an act of courage.

Unseriousness

Obviously, the agitator has the time of his life in discussing anti-Semitism. One moment he may strike a pose as someone too frightened for words: "We cannot be specific in describing the race responsible for the hatred campaign because we Americans would lose our necks if we would dare to speak up."[29]

Or he gives a clownish display of bewilderment:

> As my followers know, I am opposed to racism in all its varied forms, but for some reason, which I cannot figure out, there is a certain clique of Jews in every community who stop at nothing short of murder itself to prevent our people from assembling. I must continue to believe, until I am convinced otherwise, that these people are financed . . . by Josef Stalin.[30]

Or he imitates the techniques of the money-back-guarantee advertisement:

> *Lie Number 12:* Gerald Smith is anti-Semitic. He answers this by saying that if any person can find a written or public utterance he has ever made against any race or any creed, he will retire from public life.[31]

He may also throw in an ambiguous reference to how efficiently he would deal with the question if he were in power: "If we will put Christ first in America and the problems of America first in our hearts, these unhappy conditions involving racial groups will be ironed out in a hurry."[32]

Or he directly combines a protestation of tolerance with a transparent threat: "I am not religiously intolerant. I don't care if the Jew stays in the synagogue all day long. Then I would know where he was."[33]

It is noteworthy that the last utterance was answered from the audience with the remark "They go in there to count their dough." In discussing the Jews the agitator knows that he can get away with anything. It does not matter whether he calls himself a friend of the Jews with reservations or an adversary without reservations. It does not matter what the Jews feel about it. The fact that Jewish helplessness can become an occasion for jokes shows how he can succeed in suppressing human feelings in the audience and in promising more substantial pleasures when the real hunting season opens. The Jew is the victim, and victims are there to be victimized. The Jew *should* be persecuted because he *is* persecuted—this is the core of the agitational theme of the Jew as victim.

It is now possible to trace the dynamics of the enemy themes. In portraying the enemy as ruthless, the agitator prepares the ground for neutralizing whatever predispositions for sympathy for the underdog his audience of underdogs may feel. If the enemy is ruthless, then there is no reason to feel sympathy for his simultaneous—if contradictory—helplessness. In this way the Jew as victim becomes legitimate prey.

Moreover, the agitator can play upon the ambivalent feelings toward the weak who even as they are objects of sympathy, are also the objects of suspicion and hatred. It is dangerous to become identified with the weak; one avoids the persecuted victim almost as a matter of course. From such distrust of the weak to joining a hunt against them is a step that implies the complete repression of altruistic motives. Such repression is not innately rooted in human character but is determined by specific social conditions, one such condition being the mob appeal that rallies citizens to hunt down a criminal. But if a more convenient quarry can be substituted for the criminal, the innocent will be persecuted as if he were a criminal, and the fact of his misfortune and weakness will be seen as proof of his guilt.

Theme 13: The Other

The theme that says the Jew should be a victim because he is a victim is developed into the notion that he would not and could not be singled out for persecution if he were like everyone else. The Jew must have done something to deserve the general hostility directed against him, and he has done this because he is by nature unassimilable.

The Jew is caught in a trap. When viewed as the Other, he is primarily accused of refusing to adjust himself, but if he shows the slightest sign of trying to be like the gentiles, he is told that he cannot change and is accused of malicious motives in wanting to change.

> Native Americans have no lasting patience with a people that stresses its *differences*, when it dares to do so, and retreats to an imaginary haven of its *likenesses*, after its differences have become a source of acute and general annoyance.[34]

The agitator uses a number of devices to suggest that it is the Jews' otherness that is the cause of their persecution.

The Jew as Anti-Christ

The most ancient explanation of anti-Jewish feeling is that the Jews rejected Christ. This explanation implies that the Jew has not been singled out by his enemies but has rather singled himself out. As a result the status of the Jew is fixed for the entire Christian era:

> Take history and go back. I could take you back 400 years ago, and the same little minority group were thrown out of Spain. Why? Because they deliberately refused to live like any other man in the country.[35]

Striving to exploit religious sentiment, the agitator consistently refers to the Jews as the "deadly enemies of Christianity itself"[36] and "the hidden anti-Christ power,"[37] and as indulging in a "ghastly assault on the Christian religion."[38] But this kind of conscious religious "argumentation" offers, especially in modern times, rather limited possibilities for the agitator, if only because—theoretically at least—the Jews can escape hostility by conversion.

The agitator therefore strives to strike deeper psychological chords in his audience by perverting the universalistic nature of Christianity into an endogamic religion that is equated with "Americanism." More important, he uses traditional religious language to stir certain ambivalent attitudes that arise from the Christian recognition that Jesus was a Jew. Images of blood and violence occur abundantly in his denunciations of Jews as anti-Christians. The Jews are absolutely ruthless, they "expect to show no mercy to Christians."[39] In fact, their persecution of Christ has never ceased. "Though He had many friends, there was no one to speak out in His defense: 'For fear of the Jews no one spoke out openly of Him.' It has always been so. It will always be thus."[40]

By vividly depicting this allegedly eternal hostility, the agitator is able to present his audience with sadistic images:

> Why is there in this world such deadly animosity for the name of Christ? . . . Pilate ordered that he be scourged, whipped—but even the show of blood upon his back did not satisfy the sadistic mob of Hell. They could be satisfied with nothing but crucifixion, death on the cross.
>
> So, down through the centuries, the Satanic sons and heirs of Beelzebub have continued to cry. "Crucify! Crucify!," whenever the name of Christ is mentioned.[41]

Thus the ambivalent image of the Jew persisting from childhood religious training is transformed by the agitator into an image of an unchangeable group that consistently opposes every aspect of the Western tradition. While pretending to preach Christian ideals, the agitator becomes the advocate of a radical anti-Christianity that denies the possibility of redemption to unbelievers.

For genuine believers, the condition of the unconverted can be the cause not only of disapproval but also of pity. But the agitator's "theological" explanation of the Jew's stubborn refusal to be converted cannot lead to pity; it leads, on the contrary, to the suspicion that the Jew's refusal to see the light of truth is based not on ignorance but on some secret superior knowledge. While the Christians chase the mirage of eternal salvation, the Jews grab all the material goods. The Jews do not have to worry about the restrictions imposed by Christian ethics—and as the pious Christian prays, they empty his pockets. The Jews thus enjoy all the fruit forbidden to the Christians.

As a result, the agitator's repeated charge that the Jew is a "businessman first, last and always,"[42] and that "the only God whom he worships is the calf of gold"[43] has implications contradicting the agitator's occasional excursions into theology. The agitator is here simply appealing to a strictly secular feeling: envy of unfair advantages. The Jews are so ruthless and money-mad that they exploit even their status as a persecuted minority to gain extra privileges:

> They [the Jews] are unwilling to share the common fate of their fellowmen but they are demanding *special* consideration as a "minority," a "stateless" class, a "homeless" race, a "helpless" people, a "persecuted" religion.[44]

The Jew makes a racket even out of his role of anti-Christ.

Clannishness

The Jews refuse to conform—in making this traditional accusation the agitator speaks out as a serious educator who wants each fellow to mingle with the crowd. He is disturbed by snobbishness and pretension of superiority:

> Let the Jews remember that too many Americans are conscious of some of the tenets of Judaism. Jews are so ultra-clannish that they frown upon a Jewish girl's marrying a Gentile boy because the Goyim is not good enough, either morally or intellectually, for the girl.[45]

Trying to make capital of the age-old fact of Jewish seclusion as though it were simply a manifestation of Jewish character, the agitator intimates that the Jew must be kept apart from the community, and then accuses the Jew of seclusiveness.

The charge of clannishness also helps suggest that Jews are primarily concerned with their own needs and indifferent to the welfare of the country in which they live:

> No one should expect from an American Jew the same devotion to American traditions, or to the stability of American society or even to the perpetuity of our constitutional government, as from other racial and national elements of the population.[46]

Ferment

The Jew refuses to change himself, but at the same time he constantly changes his environment. The epitome of restlessness for its own sake, he is never satisfied with his place in society.

The Jews, suggests the agitator, are troublemakers, if only becuase they try to improve their status. But the Jews are blamed for this very rebellion against the situation that produces their insecurity: their restlessness is attributed to an irrepressible will to power. The homelessness of the Jews is their own doing: "They have no country, never had one and never intend to have one. . . ."[47] In the countries where they find temporary rest, they plot to achieve dominance:

> Jews so far forget their kindly and just treatment in this Christian land as to take the lead in every subversive movement for its overthrow; when they carry on continual agitation against our economic system and our form of government in their open forums and conclaves of their rabbis.[48]

When the Jews act as troublemakers they have come out of their seclusion. Hence, the agitator's denunciation of their subversion is an implicit call to drive them back to the ghetto. But the image of the Jew as the irrepressible agent of change seems to have a still deeper psychological impact on an audience that is itself restless and insecure for in a turbulent world where others, including the agitator, are compelled to grope hesitantly and often blindly and to fall back upon such vague notions as imminent doom or conspiracy, the Jews seem to feel at home. Using their "age old tactics," [49] they have somehow managed, suggests the agitator, to preserve their identity over the ages, evil though it is; their troublemaking enterprises, whether directed toward financial control of the world or revolutions against the world or both, always show that the Jews have a clear goal. In a world of shattered and atom-ized personalities, the image of such an enemy as it is unconsciously conjured by the agitator seems both attractive and dangerous to his audience. By attributing these secretly desirable traits to the Jews, the agitator stirs his audience's envy, and to feel envy of the helpless, hunted foe is to increase the desire to use violence against him.

Spotting the Jew

The image of the Jew as Anti-Christ and its secular derivations of the Jew as clannish and the Jew as social ferment are the more conceptual-ized symptoms of Jewish otherness. But the Jew can also be detected by other, more primitive characteristics that are sometimes so elusive as to defy description. While the conceptualized traits reflect the Jews' unwillingness to conform, these other traits reflect the Jews' inability to conform because of their idiosyncrasies. The former may sometimes be concealed, but the latter show through every disguise, and are the best way to identify a Jew. The agitator plays the part of a bloodhound always hot on the scent of the Jew who cannot hide his true identiy.

Among these alleged distinctive traits, there is first of all the Jew's undefinable foreignness. The word epitomizing this trait of foreignness is *oriental* or *Asiatic*. The agitator speaks deprecatingly of "orientals who are American citizens,"[50] of oriental concepts of government, of oriental mobs that overrun the White House, of oriental aliens that invade our nation and rifle the cash register, etc., etc. Associations of the forbidden, immoral, and luscious seem to play a role in the use of the term *oriental.*

The attribute of foreignness is supplemented by a wealth of more specific references to Jewish history. The agitator can dispense with using the word *Jew* when he speaks of Pharisees, money changers, the goldmongers clan, the usurpers of Christian liberties. He can content himself with mentioning "those flagless citizens,"[51] or indulge in a kind of "guess who" test: "Every classification of decent citizens in this country—except perhaps one—has openly condemned Communism."[52] He can name the Jew without naming him: "If Churchill says it is O.K., then it is all right from Hyde Park all the way down to the East Side of New York, from which district some big names have come."[53]

He can also, just as in the case of anti-Semitism, take advantage of the official prohibition and resort to the rhetorical figure of apophasis: "There were certain over the radio unnamable naturalized persons living in America."[54]

Sometimes several attributes are merged, as in the following quotation in which the traits of anti-Christianity, anti-Americanism, control of propaganda apparatus, psychopathic behavior, and sinister business machinations all point to the Jew:

> I do not subscribe to the proposition that if we have prosperity we must have war. That is Satan's gospel. Peace is the gospel of Christ. The radio and the press are filled with the propaganda of war. Should we Americans engender an artificial hatred towards any nation to satisfy the merchandisers of murder and the owners of debt?[55]

Public censorship of broadcasts only partly accounts for the agitator's habit of designating the Jews by indirection; the device serves purposes other than mere circumvention of the law. It is a game, a rehearsal of the anticipated hunt and a verbal reproduction of the age-old hunt of the persecuted. But this game in addition to its entertainment value serves also to teach the audience to discover spontaneously what the agitator wants it to discover. The attention of the audience is concentrated on the Jews more effectively when they are not mentioned explicitly. Look into the rat holes, the agitator seems to say, I don't have to tell you whom you will find there.

At the same time the agitator seems to match the enemy's tactics by entering into a conspiracy with his followers in which he speaks to them in the anti-Semitic in-group language: he summons his followers not to reveal the esoteric knowledge he has imparted to them, thus strengthening the bonds between him and them.

The prohibition against uttering the enemy's name is an archaic heritage. By not naming the Jew, the agitator suggests that he is so powerful that the mere act of calling him "the Jew" might mean danger. But simultaneously he suggests another implication. The Jew is so despicable and wretched that even the mere mention of his name is repulsive. When the Jew is not mentioned in the same way decent people are, his character as outcast is stressed, and he seems to the audience a weak and helpless figure. In this way, again, the agitator develops the device mentioned in the previous chapter: the Jew's strength, a cause for hating him, is shown as merely a façade of his essential weakness, a reason for persecuting him.

Yet the Jew remains ubiquitous. Foreign while yet familiar, he can be encountered everywhere, hiding under every mask and always spotted by the agitator. The Jew is unable to cover up his tracks.

Jewish Names

The climax in the process of spotting the Jew occurs when Jews, still without being called Jews, are referred to by Jewish-sounding names. Now at last the quarry has been trapped and is ready for the kill. The audience reacts with laughter; in the agitator's apocalyptic oratory, such moments of triumphant detection seem to provide one of the few bits of relief: "Sidney Hillman, or more correctly Schmuel Gilman"[56] or, "Karfunkelstein, alias Leon Blum"[57] or "Meyer Genoch Moisevitch Wallach, sometimes known as Maxim Litvinov, or Max-movitch, who had at various times adopted the other revolutionary aliases of Gustave Graf, Finkelstein, Buchmann, and Harrison was a Jew."[58]

The agitator suggests that he for one cannot be cheated: he always discovers the essence behind the appearance. It is not true, he seems to say, that a name is just a name; if we look at it more closely, if we find its origin and pronounce it correctly, its true meaning is revealed. The Jewish name is a label that makes clearly visible the nature of its bearer; it is a stigma, it pins the Jew down, and he can no longer escape.

The strong emotional reaction that the mention of Jewish names always seems to produce suggests that they are not perceived as ordinary names, i.e. conventions, but that they are felt to be an integral part of Jewish personality. The fact that Jews can be recognized merely by their names seems to bear this out; and the fact that the Jews have preserved their names despite all historical vicissitudes (in the course of which they lost every other conventional sign of national identity) makes their names an important symbol of their historical continuity. But the Jewish name is also a symbol of the continuity of the persecution to which the Jews have been exposed. By bringing out this latter aspect, by forcing the Jew who actually or allegedly uses an alias to show his real name, the agitator twists the badge of pride into a badge of disgrace.

The agitator's frequent recourse to cumulations of Jewish names suggests that the device reverses the symbolic significance of such names in still another way. The repetition of Jewish family names creates the impression that they are all more or less the same, consequently that their bearers are all the same, and can be dealt with simultaneously and equally. Instead of denoting an individual, the Jewish name is made to indicate a species, a race. The name becomes a stereotype of nonindividuality: if you know one Jew you know them all.

The Jewish name is transformed into a term of abuse, and in hurling it at the enemy the agitator engages in name-calling in the literal sense of the term. As a mocking epithet, its sound is not only foreign but ridiculous. It strikes the audience as a joke: "Walter Lipshitz Winchell—I'm not joking—that's his name."[59]

The agitator sometimes engages in painstaking heraldic research:

> It is known, however, that Winchell's father used the name of Jacob Laino, and that Winchell assumed the name of "Lawrence" in his youth. "Our real name," he once wrote with a show of impatience, is "Schmaltz." *Our guess would be that Winchell's real name (if it ever comes out) is, or should be Vevele Weinschul, which is a good, honest, respectable name.*[60]

The family name, envied token of tradition and heritage for non-Jews, becomes a symbol of degradation for the Jews. What the gentiles are proud to display, the Jews seem eager to hide. Their history is made into their curse and disgrace. By evoking a past when the Jews were persecuted (or, as in the above quotation, reminding the audience that the Jew who enjoys American freedom was once a subject of an anti-Semitic country), the agitator verbally reenacts the injustice previously done to the Jews.

Mimicking

We come here to what is perhaps one of the most crucial anti-Semitic stimuli: mimicking (Cf. Max Horkheimer and Theodor W. Adorno, *Dialektik der Aufklärung* [Amsterdam: Querido, 1947], pp. 212ff.), which is not limited to the pronunciation of Jewish names. Striking examples are to be found in the agitator's way of describing Jewish complaints. He suggests that the Jews do not speak like human beings but make weird sounds; whenever they express emotions, they are loud, conspicuous, unbearable, and comical. The agitator refers to "the wailing yelps and weird wails of subversive Jews and Communist gangs"[61] or imitates sounds supposedly made by Jews among themselves: "America's Jewish Kommissars Screech, Squabble and Scrap."[62] When the Jews want to protest against Hitler, these "alien-minded super-collectivists" indulge in "loud sneers and jeers and hymns of hate";[63] on other occasions, they yell, howl, whine,[64] and so on.

What the Jews are here implicitly blamed for is that they seem to challenge both the discipline of civilization, which prescribes restraint, and the suppression of the urge to display one's own emotion. They appear free to act out their passions and desires, their demands and fears, their sympathies and above all their antipathies. Once again, the

Jews refuse to conform, this time on a deeper emotional level. They are portrayed as despicable and dangerous, for they insist on the right to be individuals. The agitator discredits such expressions of individualistic rebellion.

This condemnation of Jewish expressiveness is accompanied by its caricaturing imitation. The followers are forbidden to indulge in such expressiveness for themselves, but they are permitted to imitate manifestations of it in their alleged enemies.

The fact that the audience enjoys such caricatures and imitations of allegedly weird Jewish behavior shows that this Jewish foreignness is not as external to them as it might seem. They feel it in their own flesh, it is latent in them; the Jew is not the abstract "other," he is the other who dwells in themselves. Into him they can conveniently project everything within themselves to which they deny recognition, everything they must repress. But this projection can be effected only on condition that they hate the Jews and are permitted to realize the repressed impulse in the form of a caricature of the enemy. They find an outlet for their repressed aspirations only by simultaneously condemning them.

Theme 14: The Menace

According to the agitator, Jewish influence is behind every threat to society and every frustration of his followers' hopes. From the idea that the Jews are persecuted to the idea that they are persecutors, the transition is not too difficult; it has been made often enough in the past to become a kind of stereotype. But this stereotype is not merely the product of anti-Jewish agitation; it would seem that the history of the Jews and interpretations of this history have contributed to the creation of an idea of the Jew in which persecuted and persecutor are inextricably blended.

The fate of the Jew has always been an object of theological speculation; his survival has struck many thinkers as a mystery that could not be explained by natural causes. A well-known religious philosopher who was by no means hostile to the Jews refers to them as a "pre-eminently historical people (Nicolas Berdyaev, *The Meaning of History* [New York, 1936], pp. 86ff.) who

> according to the materialistic and positivist criterion ought long ago to have perished.... The survival of the Jews, their resistance to destruction, their endurance under absolutely peculiar conditions and the fateful role played by them in history; all these point to the particular and mysterious foundations of their destiny.... The Jewish destiny

is characterized by a particular dramatic intensity which makes the purely Aryan spirit seem dull by comparison. . . . The Jewish spirit constitutes a distinct racial type. . . . It is still animated by the aspirations towards the future, by the stubborn and persistent demand that the future, should bring with it an all-resolving truth and justice on earth, in the name of which the Jewish people is prepared to declare war on all historical traditions, sacraments, and associations.

The above passage is based on an explicit rejection of a "materialist" or "naturalist" approach to history, but even on the level of the "ideal" or the "transcendent" the image of the Jews as persecuted leads almost irresistibly to the idea that they are essentially different from and opposed to the world as it is.

In the agitator's language the idea of the sacred mission of the Jew acquires a negative sign. The theologian's "mysterious foundations" are transformed into a deliberate Jewish conspiracy; the "particular dramatic intensity" of "the Jewish spirit" into Jewish ruthlessness and cunning; and the "war on all historical traditions, sacraments, and associations" into vicious aggression against the gentile world. Awe and admiration can be sublimated forms of fear and envy; and when the agitator reduces the emotions inspired by the "idealist" theological interpretation to those of his own level, he transforms the awe and admiration into fear, envy, and hatred. The sheer fact that the Jews have managed to survive through so much suffering seems to him and his followers evidence that they must have certain secret and menacing powers. Because they are and have been persecuted they can be plausibly charged with having the vindictive and cunning mentality of slaves; because they have survived all persecutions, they can be plausibly assumed to command extraordinary resources, and to be endowed with an extraordinary vitality. They alone seem to be self-sufficient, and able to preserve their individuality in a world that suppresses individuality.

Vindictiveness

During the prewar and war years one of the persistent themes of agitation in the United States was that the Jews had instigated a crusade against Hitler to revenge themselves for his persecutions:

Day after day, and far into all these pregnant nights, we hear the ceaseless, senseless din of propaganda, all of which is for the purpose of making us war-minded enough to go to war to save World Jewry's financial, political, economic and social fortunes.

Ever since the Armistice of November, 1918, Jewry's International High Command has been making plans for the next World War—which is now-beginning in Europe.[65]

To drive home his point more effectively, the agitator may characterize Jewish machinations as a well-established and understandable reaction, only then to accuse the Jews of cowardice and selfishness:

We would not condemn the Jews so much for their culpability in declaring and prolonging this war if they would manifest sufficient intestinal fortitude to say that the war now being waged is to protect their vast international business interest.[66]

However, the audience is not allowed for one moment to think that Jewish hostility to Hitler is justified. The Jews are vindictive by nature: "It is a matter of record that Jews over the world, particularly the United States, long ago 'declared war' on Germany," created "a distorted impression of events in Central Europe." and generated "antagonisms and retaliations, until finally the flame ignited."[67] They

bristle with hate because their pride has been hurt by Adolf Hitler. They have a persecution complex and they want America to go to war . . . even if it costs the lives of ten million Americans, as long as they can have their revenge.[68]

Jewish lust for revenge is depicted as unrestrained, as directly pathological. As the war approached its climax, the agitator's line was that "Jewish leadership insists on annihilating and enslaving all people of German blood, regardless of their innocence or their guilt," and he prophesied that "they [the Jews] will likely bring down on their heads a reaction even worse than that through which they have just passed."[69]

The notion that Hitler's treatment of the Jews was a "reaction" to their vindictiveness follows a sentence in which the Jewish interest in this war is described as "understandable." The agitator speaks as though there were no distinction between the idea that the Jews are vindictive because they were wronged and the idea that he is wronged because they are vindictive. He seems to have no difficulty in blaming the persecuted for the worst actions of the persecutors. Alluding to a report that the Gestapo forced some Jews into its service, he concludes:

In view of savagery displayed in Russia, by Jewish OGPU, wherein torture carried to unmentionable extremes helped liquidate during

> past 25 years some 50,000,000 persons; and in view of *Rabbi Alstat's* admissions, can it be that the gruesome liquidations now attributed to the Gestapo were carried out by some kind of beasts?[70]

No matter how lurid the colors with which alleged Jewish power is painted, the agitator always suggests that this power is ultimately imaginary. The idea that the Jews are helpless is perhaps nowhere stressed more strongly than when the agitator refers to their power. The unserious and sometimes directly grotesque connotations in such references do not seem to weaken the basic implication that there is an identity between the persecutor and persecuted. Like sadist and masochist, the two are not distinguished in the unconscious.

Persecution of the Jews even comes to be conceived as a prerequisite of Jewish power. The idea is presented with a touch of irony.

> Space is too limited to comment on why Jews hired gangsters to stage pogroms against other Jews. But it IS necessary that Jews be persecuted. If they were not, their whole international system would collapse. That is why it was necessary that Hitler be made to kill so many before the United States would destroy Germany. By Jewish reports. Hitler killed every Jew in Germany about six times. It is hard to believe that a Jew could be killed that many times, have all his property confiscated, and then show up at a refugee camp with a fur coat and suitcases full of money, clamoring about his sacred right to come to the United States.[71]

The identity of the persecutor and the persecuted is explicitly stated by an English street orator who, referring to the refugees of the *Exodus 1947*, complained that "now Britain was a fifth-rate nation, dictated to by four thousand Jews afloat in British ships." (Quoted by Woodrow Wyatt, *New Statesman and Nation*, August 30, 1947.) It is difficult to believe that even a profascist audience fails to perceive such a charge as a joke—but it is a startling joke, a proof of the agitator's impudence or prowess and his determination to resort to any means to attain his end. It is proof that against the Jew everything goes; just because he is helpless he can be hit below the belt. But the charge also sets associational trains in motion: the refugees, after all, *are* a stubborn and troublesome lot, and if they do not dictate to the British Empire, they certainly tried to, and they do force the government to waste a great deal of time on them. The idea of their power is a good joke, but it is not "dismissed" as other jokes are—quite the contrary.

Cunning

The Jews do not satisfy their lust for revenge openly. They always act behind the scenes, and it is they who are "the power behind *all* dictators."[72] The agitational texts suggest that the most important Jewish instrument of domination is, next to money, the manipulation of public opinion.

The agitator exploits certain actual occupational facts. The relatively high percentage of Jewish participation in the motion picture and radio industries and in the press is used in two ways. First, the Jews are depicted as the absolute masters of the media of mass communication. "We recognize the tremendous influence which the sons of Jewry wield in the press, the cinema and on the radio, the three chief sources which control public opinion."[73] In fact, all "movies . . . are run by Jews";[74] the Jews "control the press . . . control the motion picture industry a hundred per cent,"[75] and "press and radio in the United States is definitely under Semitic domination."[76]

Second, this alleged position of the Jews is depicted as a consequence of their innate intellectuality. This may be stated in the form of a compliment:

> My fellow citizens, I am not ignorant of Jewish history. I know its glories. I am acquainted with its glorious sons. I am aware of the keen intellectuality which has characterized its progress in commerce, in finance and particularly in the field of communication.[77]

Resentment against the Jews as wielders of intellectual power is fed by the obscure realization that such power is basically precarious; the agitator has a way of suggesting that success spells danger for the Jews: "In the fields of publicity, finance, commerce, communications, amusement and industry, the Jews have risen to perilous heights."[78]

The Jews seem to have succeeded in using standardized products of mass culture for the pursuit of their own exploitive ends: "The Jew combines owning and controlling the movies and radio have a cheap trick in their method of Hollywood clowns using radio programs to advertise and glorify each other."[79]

The followers' own ambivalent attitude toward mass culture, the feeling that in the last analysis they are somehow betrayed by what they read and hear and see, is exploited for agitational purposes. While manipulating the others—so the agitator tells his audience—the Jews protect their own interests. Mass culture is a product of intellectuality, and intellectuality is above all seen as a means of exploitation.

The Jews are conceived as living by their wits and avoiding physical work. They achieve their goals by means of intellectual machinations, stock exchange manipulations, or revolutionary propaganda, but they never seem to toil in the sweat of their brows. This is a trait common to the banker and communist, and is one of the elements of the paradoxical image of the communist banker.

Significantly enough, the agitator rarely accuses the Jews of violent crimes. The Jews are depicted as crooks, conspirators, warmongers, revolutionists, but they never seem to do things with their hands. Compared to them, a common murderer or burglar is a laborer with tools and skills who must engage in physical work to achieve his ends. The Jews are not even such hard-working criminals. Work without hardship is identified with exploitation, and to the followers the vision of a people who enjoy life without paying for it is intolerable. Hence the accusation that the Jews aim at compelling the gentiles to perform all the "dirty" work:

> I speak of the International Organized Jewry who seeks a One World government, mongrelizing of the races (of all except their own) a world police force, world court, (again Jew-dominated) and a one world government with once free and independent Christian Americans as the slaves to till the soil, sweat in the industries, fight the wars and be the slaves.[80]

These old motives of resentment may be intensified by an obscure suspicion that the intellectual no longer fulfills his traditional function of serving the spiritual needs of the community. He is identified with the best-selling author, the movie script writer, and the successful newspaperman. He seems to make a good living by producing a content that serves merely to divert those engaged in less gratifying tasks.

Domination by intellect is experienced as usurpation because it is not backed by actual physical power and ultimately it depends on the consent of the dominated or on deception. Consistently depicted as oversophisticated, practicing debauch, enjoying forbidden things, tempting the suckers by futile entertainment, and pursuing destructive aims, the modern intellectual, as the agitator sees him, is a secular variation of the devil. But the agitator is not in the least against the principle of manipulating people by means of the entertainment industry; he merely objects to the fact that it cannot be used for his own "righteous" purposes: "The moving picture business today is largely in the hands of Satan and his emissaries. . . . Satan has things pretty much his own way in a sphere that ought to be a powerful factor for righteousness."[81]

Self-Sufficiency

Our list of traits that the agitator ascribes to the Jews includes several that supposedly define the Jews' character: for instance their freedom from the shackles of Christian morality, their readiness to help each other, their irrepressible dynamism, their expressiveness, their cunning. All these traits are denounced as despicable and hateful, yet they also lend themselves to another interpretation, for they can be viewed as desirable assets in the individual's struggle for existence. On some occasions the agitator almost explicitly indicates that he conceives the Jews as people who somehow manage to get more out of life than the gentiles:

> I am not an anti-Jew. The Jew has his place but he has it no more than you or I. He has a place where we will put him in time, and when he gets there he won't be able to spend much money, not more than we have now.[82]

But the strain of envy present in such an accusation is not confined to the stereotyped notion that the Jews possess inexhaustible financial resources. The other traits referred to above also seem worldly assets that have been appropriated by the Jews, while the non-Jews have lost or are losing them.

The very multiplicity of Jewish attributes is significant. The Jew appears as a colorful figure: he is interesting, he attracts attention, he does not have to stress his originality, he is allegedly recognized by innumerable obvious signs, by his language, manners, ideas. The very fact that he is a Jew distinguishes him from the anonymous crowd. It is true that his characteristics are contradictory. He is persecuted and privileged, strong and weak, rich and poor, religious and atheistic, clannish and promiscuous, modern and archaic. But the Jew somehow synthesizes all contradictions; despite his multiplicity he remains one, easily and clearly identifiable. A remarkably integrated personality, he gives free expression to individualistic impulses that others must repress; at the same time he has a highly developed rational faculty, and has not lost the sense of collective solidarity.

The Jew's capacity for enjoying life creates the illusion that in an era when the individual is under tremendous pressure, the Jew, by defying the trends of the day, remains an individual and profits from it. To an audience obsessed by feelings of insecurity, the agitator suggests that the Jews are a people who have succeeded in weaving a continuous historical texture of their own since the beginnings of time and who know at any given moment how to cut this material to meet any new situation. He often refers to Jews by epithets or images taken from the Bible or from their ancient and medieval history; even their most modern techniques of propaganda are nothing but a repetition of age-old devices: "technique and its [propaganda] terminology from the Sanhedrin and from the Sanhedrin's progeny."[83]

The Jew, the agitator intimates, is at home in every country, he is not fettered by linguistic, geographic, ethnographic frontiers. He is ubiquitous—everywhere on the earth and everywhere in history. He has solved the problem of belonging, and although he is an individual, he is never isolated. And he shapes his own fate; while the other peoples are never held responsible for their misery, the Jew is responsible for both his own and the other nations' fate.

His fate as an individual is also the fate of his people. The Jews always help one another, sacrifice themselves for one another, and as we have been told, even stage pogroms against themselves when this can serve their purposes. Although unique individuals, they act like a swarm of insects and invade other countries like epidemics.

The image of the Jew who escapes the heavy demands of self-discipline, whose morals are easy, who does secret and forbidden things, and who enjoys life without paying for it is all the more provoking because the Jew seems able to do all this even while his power is so precarious. For Jewish power, the agitator implies, has no solid foundations in reality; it is based solely on manipulations and machinations. It cannot withstand the exercise of brute force, and brute force is something that the Jews never have at their disposal. The very survival of the Jews can thus be felt as a challenge, for it seems to refute the idea that ultimately everything in life is based on physical power, and that those deprived of it must submit to those who wield it. The Jews symbolize the utopia of harmony that has come to be regarded as a deception. This almost automatically suggests that they can enjoy happiness only by deceiving others.

At a time when bare survival comes increasingly to be felt as the sole value, and conformism as the sole method of assuring one's survival, Jewish survival seems an intolerable challenge. If the world has borne with the Jews for centuries, it cannot bear with them any longer. They must be liquidated because they are doomed; there is no place for the individual in the world today. In the last analysis, elimination of the

Jew does not seem to be motivated by expectation of material gain but by the fact that in modern life individual happiness seems to become so exceptional that the presence of a group that seemingly continues to pursue it is felt as an affront and a menace.

It would be erroneous to represent the Jew as the ultimate enemy of the agitator. Although the agitator's invectives converge on the Jew, his attack is aimed at all forces in society that he finds reprehensible. The Jew becomes the symbol on which he centers the projections of his own important rage against the restraints of civilization.

Such sentiments are not unique to American agitation:

> I also want to talk to you, quite frankly, on a very grave matter . . . I mean the clearing out of the Jews, the extermination of the Jewish race. It's one of those things it is easy to talk about—"The Jewish race is being exterminated," says one Party member, "that's quite clear, it's in our program—elimination of the Jews, and we're doing it, exterminating them." And then they come, 80 million worthy Germans and each one has his decent Jew. Not one of all those who talk this way has witnessed it, not one of them has been through it. Most of you must know what it means when 100 corpses are lying side by side, or 500 or 1,000. To have stuck it out and at the same time—apart from exceptions caused by human weakness—to have remained decent fellows, that is what has made us hard. This is a page of glory in our history which has never been written and is never to be written, for we know how difficult we should have made it for ourselves, if—with bombing raids, the burdens and the deprivations of war—we still had Jews today in every town as secret saboteurs, agitators and troublemongers. We should now probably have reached the 1916–17 stage when the Jews were still in the German national body.
>
> We have taken from them what wealth they had. I have issued a strict order, which SS Obergruppenführer Pohl has carried out, that this wealth should as a matter of course be handed over to the Reich without reserve. We have taken none of it for ourselves. Individual men who have lapsed will be punished in accordance with an order issued at the beginning which gave this warning: Whoever takes so much as a mark of it is a dead man. A number of S.S. men—there are not very many of them—have fallen short, and they will die without mercy. We had the moral right, we had the duty to our people, to destroy this people which wanted to destroy us. But we have not the right to enrich ourselves with so much as a fur, a watch, a mark, or a cigarette or anything else. Because we have exterminated a bacterium we do not want, in the end, to be infected by the bacterium and die of it. I will not see so much as a small area of sepsis appear here or gain a hold. Wherever it may form, we will cauterize it. Altogether,

however, we can say that we have fulfilled this most difficult duty for the love of our people. And our spirit, our soul, our character has not suffered injury from it. [Speech of the Reichführer-SS Heinrich Himmler at the meeting of S.S. major-generals at Posen, October 4, 1943, quoted in *Nazi Conspiracy and Aggression* (Washington, 1946), p. 558.]

The use of the stereotypes of Jewish greed and sabotage, and the metaphor of the bacteria cannot obscure the fact that something more than wealth and hygiene is involved. Although the speaker uses terms such as *spirit, soul,* and *love of our people,* the essential point he wants to impress upon his listeners is this: under no circumstances must they succumb to human impulses. The dehumanization and killing of the Jew cannot be carried out effectively unless the killer too is dehumanized, unless he extirpates in himself every claim to human existence as an individual.

Notes

1. CF, Apr., 1945, p. 556.
2. CF, Oct., 1945, Upton Close letter in, p. 653.
3. McWilliams, New York, July 18, 1940, street corner.
4. LIB, Sept., 28, 1939, p. 10.
5. SJ, Nov. 17, 1941, p. 18.
6. SJ, Apr. 20, 1942, pp. 7 & 8.
7. LIB, June 3, 1933, Mrs. Anna B. Sloane in, p. 10.
8. DEF, Sept., 1937, p. 5.
9. AP, Feb., 1945, p. 8.
10. LIB, Apr. 21, 1940, p. 12.
11. SJ, Mar. 13, 1939, p. 11.
12. LIB, Nov. 7, 1938, p. 9.
13. AID, June 10, 1945, p. 2.
14. Smith, Cleveland, May 11, 1943, meeting.
15. LIB, Nov. 28, 1940, p. 2.
16. SJ, July 7, 1941, p. 4.
17. SJ, June 5, 1939, p. 2.
18. CF, Sept., 1945, p. 635.
19. Smith, St. Louis, Mar. 25, 1944. meeting.
20. Coughlin, Detroit, Nov. 20, 1938, radio.
21. SJ, June 5, 1939, p. 2.
22. CF, Oct., 1944, p. 452.
23. Smith, Detroit, Mar. 19, 1943, meeting.
24. CF, Mar., 1945, p. 540.
25. CF, Dec., 1943.
26. CF, Feb., 1945, p. 519.
27. AP, July, 1944, p. 1.
28. AID, May 6, 1942, p. 1.

29. Phelps, Los Angeles, October 20, 1940, radio.
30. CF, July, 1945, p. 604.
31. CF, July, 1942, p. 3.
32. CF, June, 1943, p. 215.
33. McWilliams, New York, July 25, 1940, street corner.
34. AP, Nov., 1944, p. 3.
35. McWilliams, New York, July 18, 1940, street corner.
36. Phelps, Los Angeles, Aug. 20, 1940, radio.
37. DEF, Feb., 1940, p. 4.
38. AP, Nov., 1944, p. 12.
39. PW, June 10, 1936.
40. SJ, Mar, 30. 1942, p. 16.
41. CF, May, 1942, p. 3.
42. SJ, Sept. 29, 1941, p. 19.
43. Coughlin, Speech on Jan. 22, 1939, reprinted in *Why Leave Our Own*, p. 45.
44. AP, Feb., 1945, p. 10.
45. SJ, Sept. 29, 1941, p. 19.
46. DEF, Nov., 1939, p. 22.
47. McWilliams, New York, July 18, 1940, street corner.
48. DEF, July, 1939, Lewis Valentine Ulrey in, p. 22.
49. AID, Jan. 27, 1941, p. 2.
50. SJ, Sept. 15, 1941, p. 5.
51. Coughlin, Speech on Feb. 5, 1939, reprinted in *Why Leave Our Own*, p. 73.
52. SJ, Dec. 4, 1939, p. 6.
53. Phelps, Los Angeles, Oct. 13, 1940, radio.
54. Phelps, Los Angeles, Dec. 26, 1940, radio.
55. Coughlin, Speech on Jan. 22, 1939, reprinted in *Why Leave Our Own*, p. 45.
56. Kamp, *Vote CIO . . . and Get a Soviet America*, p. 14.
57. Coughlin, Speech on Feb. 5, 1939, reprinted in *Why Leave Our Own*, p. 67.
58. Sanctuary, *Litvinoff, Foreign Commissar of U.S. S. R.*, p. 4.
59. Smith, St. Louis, Mar. 25, 1944, meeting.
60. Kamp, *With Lotions of Love . . .* p. 28.
61. X, Feb. 17, 1945, p. 3.
62. LIB, Feb. 28, 1938, p. 6.
63. Kamp, *Native Nazi Purge Plot*, p. 5.
64. Cf. CF, May, 1942; RTL, Oct., 1941.
65. LIB, Oct. 28, 1939, p. 6.
66. AID, Dec. 9, 1940.
67. DEF, Apr., 1940, p. 5.
68. Phelps, Los Angeles, Oct. 20, 1940, radio.
69. CF, May, 1945, p. 565.
70. AID, Apr. 30, 1945, p. 1.
71. *The Individualist*, Mar. 31, 1947, p. 4.
72. AID, Dec. 9, 1941, p. 2.
73. Coughlin, Speech on Jan. 29, 1939, reprinted in *Why Leave Our Own*, p. 48.
74. Mote, Cleveland, July 1, 1942, meeting.
75. Maloney, New York, July 25, 1940, street corner.

76. DEF, June, 1941, p. 16.
77. SJ, Nov. 28, 1938, p. 10.
78. SJ, Sept. 29, 1941, p. 19.
79. X, Mar. 3, 1945, p. 2.
80. X, June 6, 1947, p. 2.
81. DEF, Feb., 1941, p. 17.
82. White, New York, July 18, 1940, street corner.
83. AP, Sept., 1944, p. 3.

7

A Home for the Homeless

As a would-be leader of a popular movement, the agitator cannot content himself with articulations of malaise and denunciations of the enemy; he must offer some kind of statements about his goals and the means by which he proposes to reach them.

The "positive" statements of any advocate of social change may be discussed under four heads:

1. Descriptions of the values and ideals that are to replace the rejected values and ideals.
2. Formulations of goals that contain some assurance that the factors leading to present frustrations will be eliminated, and that a situation will be created in which frustrated needs will be fully gratified.
3. Descriptions of the methods of realizing these goals: a practical program of action.
4. References to the character of the movement's adherent as contrasted with the character of the enemy. The adherent is not merely one who is exempt from the enemy's vices; he also has positive virtues. (A prohibitionist, for instance, is not merely a teetotaler but also a man who, precisely because he does not succumb to the vice of drink, is an upright citizen, faithful husband, and a thrifty, far-sighted, self-controlled individual.)

This last group of statements will be discussed in the next chapter. In this one we shall take up the first three, dealing respectively with the agitator's values, goals, and methods of achieving them. Of all agitational themes, those that might be described as programmatic are the least well developed.

Platforms and Programs

As soon as we examine the platforms and programs of the agitator, we find that there is a considerable dearth of materials. When formulating a specific objective, he almost cynically aims to go one better than the government, his most dangerous competitor. For instance, he proposes a "Serviceman's Reconstruction Plan," which provides that "each member of the United States Armed Forces, upon his honorable discharge, be paid $7,800."[1]

When the agitator does issue a "Statement of Principles" it is as vague as the following document of the "Committee of 1,000,000, a patriotic and dynamic crusade which began with nine constituents and now has more than 3,000,000":[2]

> The foundation principles of this committee, which have been unchanged since its beginning in 1937, are as follows:
> 1. To rebuild the spirit of America.
> 2. To wipe out to the last vestige Communism, Nazism, and Fascism in all forms. (In view of the attempt now being made to join us in a political union with foreign countries, we express our bitter objection to all such schemes to compromise the sovereignty of America, such as "Union Now With Britain." "Federal Union, Inc." etc.)
> 3. To redefine the American national character.
> 4. To instill a new spirit in American youth, dedicated intellectually and physically to the maintenance of American institutions.
> 5. To issue a call to farmers and laborers to resist what is now known to be an international plot to make them part of a world revolution.
> 6. To rededicate the citizenry of America to the family altar and to the spirit of the Church.
> 7. To secure the maintenance of a well-defined standard of American living.

Some of the points in such platforms are restatements of the stereotyped images of the enemy (the communists must be wiped out); others are examples of shadowboxing; and still others are merely glittering generalities. It would be easy enough to go through such platforms and show their internal inconsistencies as well as the contradictions between what they proclaim and what the agitator says on other occasions, but such exercises would have slight value.

Reaction Patterns

The agitator seems to steer clear of the area of material needs on which liberal and democratic movements concentrate; his main concern is a sphere of frustration that is usually ignored in traditional politics. The programs that concentrate on material needs seem to overlook that area of moral uncertainties and emotional frustrations that are the immediate manifestations of malaise. It may therefore be conjectured that his followers find the agitator's statements attractive not because he occasionally promises to "maintain the American standards of living" or to provide a job for everyone but because he intimates that he will give them the emotional satisfactions that are denied them in the contemporary social and economic setup. He offers attitudes, not bread.

Actually, he fails to touch upon the roots of emotional frustration in our society. He does not present his followers with a prospect of joy or happiness but, rather, encourages a verbal discharge of emotion. Significantly, the whole meaning of the agitator's movement is represented as a reaction: "I assure you, we are aroused and your challenge is hereby met by a mightier challenge."[3] The followers are invited to hit back at those who direct history against them. Rather than a movement expressing universal aims, the agitator's movement proposes itself as a kind of protection agency that will ward off the enemy.

All the while, the audience is expected to act not because of desires or motives of its own but only out of exasperation, when it has been goaded beyond endurance by the enemy's depravity. "When enough Gentiles have been booted out of jobs, the Gentiles are reactively bound to arise and boot out Jews."[4]

Theme 15: Either-Or

The Agitator's Values

Agitation differs from both the reform and revolutionary types of social movements in that it attacks values not in open, explicit terms but surreptitiously, under the guise of a defense of existing ideals. In that way the agitator can both reject current values and avoid the task of formulating a new set of values. Nowhere does he explicitly indicate, even in the most rudimentary fashion, any adherence to universal standards or criteria that could take the place of discarded ideals and form the nucleus of a new moral, philosophical, religious, and political outlook.

It would be false, however, to imagine that his work of disintegration results in a complete vacuum. To destroy loyalties to universal beliefs, the agitator always insists that all ideals and ideas cannot be taken at face value but that they are rather mere camouflage for the enemy's will to survive. This will to survive now becomes the agitator's implicit frame of reference. As a result, his picture of the world and of the problem of man's conduct in that world are tremendously simplified. Instead of a variety of more or less complex situations that are judged in terms of a set of differentiated ideas, the agitator proposes to view the world as split between two irreconcilable camps. There is no possibility of working out a solution acceptable to all, or even a solution in which everyone will find a satisfying place. The adversary can never be won to the agitator's cause, even if and when the desired condition for which the agitator works is achieved; the only way to deal with the enemy is to exterminate him. The agitator assimilates opposing human groups to hostile biological species, and ultimately, in his view, the march of history relapses into the processes of nature.

In such a world people are neither guided nor inhibited by moral standards. All ethical problems are reduced to the single problem of choosing between the stronger and weaker camp, that is, of discovering which camp will ensure one's survival. The enemy, by his very nature, is unable to choose, but those who have the privilege of choice must adhere to the most powerful camp if they are to avoid destruction. Here, then, is a world in which values may in fact interfere with the crucial choice even if they do not already serve as tricky means of insuring the enemy's victory. It is an Either-Or world—survive, by no matter what means, or perish, with no matter what good intentions. Either-or—for or against—this fundamental dichotomy is basic to the agitator's world outlook.

In the Either-Or world constructed by the agitator, the essence of human life is violent conflict, a conflict that is unavoidable and present on all levels of human existence.

> The great masses of humanity are divided by a deep and wide chasm. On the one side of this chasm are the real producers of wealth—the underpaid farmers producing the food and fiber for all and the underpaid laborer processing the food, the fiber, the homes and all the material things of a civilization.
>
> On the other side of a deep wide chasm is a little group of wealthy men. Every capitalistic system under the sun is perfectly satisfied with things as they are within the state and yet not satisfied that their economic domination is enough.[5]

This economic dichotomy is transposed to the sphere of international politics. "It is a war between the 'Haves' and the 'Have-nots.' . . . In plainer language: because Jewish international bankers own or control the gold of the world, *it is their war.*[6] According to the agitator the same division will continue after the war: "The Jewish Agency is the *united front of Jewry* (a kind of Jewish League of Nations impenetrable to Gentiles) against the non-Jewish world, regardless of any internal dissension in their own midst."[7]

In the field of domestic politics the motif of self-preservation is invoked directly:

> As far as I am concerned, we have been reduced to that one simple elementary problem of self-preservation. . . . Head-choppers in Washington might become so ambitious as to create an unhealable disunity by their extreme practices.[8]

More often the appeal to self-preservation is clothed in ideological garb, as in the following:

> We are coming to the crossroads where we must decide whether we are going to preserve law and order and decency or whether we are going to be sold down the river to the Red traitors who are undermining America.[9]

or

> The Talmudic philosophy of Europe-Asia-Africa and Nudeal is directly opposite that of Christian.[10]

The conflict, whether conceived in biological or dressed in ideological terms, is pictured as all-embracing and omnipresent; no situation or issue is outside its fatal orbit. The profoundest causalities in history— "Every serious student of world affairs today knows that the mighty conflict of the centuries is under way and must move on to its final, inevitable and devastating climax"[11]—as well as such trivial matters as the shape of the traffic lights in New York City are alike experienced as consequences of the same Manichean struggle. To cope with such a situation requires the most drastic measures: "'*We do not want the Franco way for America,*' is the common theme of these editorial critiques. To be sure we don't; *neither did Spain!* But the alternative is Islam, or, in our day, Red godless Communism."[12]

The dilemma is absolute:

> God pity you blind business men who think that there is any cure for a situation thus poisoned. Unless you stand up and fight you

will wake up some night and face the knife of a revolutionist at your throat just as they did in Russia, Spain, Mexico, and elsewhere.[13]

Those who choose wrongly will suffer the consequences:

> The "bloodless revolution" phase is about over. Time will soon be, when you and others like you, will have to decide what leadership you will follow. The wrong choice means terror, rape, murder, starvation and destruction—besides which what occurred in Europe and Asia will be tame.[14]

The Either-Or dilemma seems to cut deeper than even the most fundamental political or social conflicts; it seems to be a universal characteristic of existence, a kind of predestination of human, subhuman, and superhuman conflicts. The agitator presents his vision of this Either-Or world not as the logical outcome of his deprecation of values but as a given and unquestionable existential insight. Actually the Either-Or situation is an unavoidable corollary of a world without universal values, without the hope of a final redemption that is an integral part of Western religious and philosophical thought. The agitator offers no vision of a better world, no hope that men will ever be able to live as brothers. All that is possible, he implies, is to survive in a dog's world, to band together as an elite in order to take from others what we want for ourselves. Moral values yield to a sober estimation of the problem of self-survival:

> May I say this to you, ladies and gentlemen: There are five hundred million people starving in the world today. There are five hundred million people that are paupers of the war. We face the same problem you have to face when you go down a poverty-stricken street; you have got your little payday check and you make $60 a week; you have got the boy in school, you want to be generous, you want to be a Christian, you want to do all you can, but just the moment you stop and dissipate all you have upon these people of the street, you have deserted your own, you have violated nature and you have struck suicide to your own household.[15]

Inherent in this whole attitude is the agitator's tendency to shift the emphasis of discussion from a defense of ethical values to biological self-defense. This shift involves a far-reaching change in the structure of human belief. In a liberal society the concept of loyalty involves capacity for judgment, feeling, and exercise of will; ideally speaking, a man's choice of belief is determined by his rational insight. In the agitator's world, the ideational components of belief are largely eliminated, and one's acceptance or rejection of a creed is summoned, so to speak, to function independently. All the agitator's listeners are supposed to raise their hands when the agitator asks them to accept an attitude, and to shake their fists in fury when the agitator bids them to reject it. This simple acquiescence is the result of the Either-Or choice.

Theme 16: Endogamic Community

The Agitator's Goal

In his role as a social therapist, the agitator is a strong believer in the exogenic theory of disease: every pathological symptom is traced to a foreign agent. But if the agitator's ideas about pathology are definite, his concept of what is normal is remarkably vague. All he can offer is a rededication to the established institutional and ideological framework of the American republic as it has persisted since the founding fathers. "I challenge Americans to reconsecrate themselves . . . to America,"[16] he exclaims. If anything has gone wrong, it can be only because we Americans have bothered with concerns that are not American or have strayed from American ways.

Offhand, it might seem that just as on other occasions the agitator tries to don the mantle of populism, he is here trying to identify himself with the conservative tradition. Unlike his European counterparts he is always eager to tie up his cause with respectable ideas and names; in his speeches he frequently mentions Washington, the Founding Fathers, Lincoln, and congressmen known for their conservative views.

Another conservative implication of the agitator's nationalism is his insistence that every social issue involves a conflict between the ingroup and the out-group; he consistently refrains from analyzing social problems in terms of internal conflicts. Unemployment, for example, he sees as due to an influx of undesirable aliens; likewise, the problem of food distribution has nothing to do with variations of purchasing power within the nation, but is caused by the insatiable appetites of other countries. In the name of "Americanism" the agitator expressly denies class and social differences; "Americanism is like pure water which tastes just as good to a ditch digger in Chicago as to a Supreme Court judge in Washington,"[17]

The image of "pure water" is perhaps not accidental; except for purity the agitator seems to have great difficulty in assigning any specific content to his nationalism. In the agitator's eyes, nationalism means first of all negation of its opposite, internationalism.

He sometimes justifies this negation by debunking the liberalistic doctrines of world peace, by exposing the power politics that goes on behind the scenes of international bodies, and by sneering at the "advocates of world peace" who "don't agree among themselves."[18] But his main argument is: "We can't solve internal problems, so how can we claim to solve international problems?"[19] On the other hand, the only internal problem he stresses is the presence of foreign reds and Jews.

Even when he tries to anticipate the charge that he is always negative, and proposes a positive goal, the best he can do is to restate his essential negativism:

> If Christians are determined to establish a Christian front, let not their motives be misinterpreted. Certainly it is not an anti-Semitic front. It is a front for Christ and for His principles. It is a militant front which is not content to let the enemies of Christ, be they Gentile or Jew, dis-establish Christ in our government, our commerce, our industry, our factories, our fields or our institutions of education. Our militancy, however, may not be negative; may not be anti-Semitic. It must be positive and for Christ.[20]

At the point where the agitator gets to his fundamental notions about Americanism, he parts company from the conservative by interpreting the imperative of patriotism as a call for endogamic seclusion. All of the arguments or pseudoarguments by which he tries to buttress his extreme nationalism are overshadowed by an absolute, almost instinctive rejection of everything foreign. For the agitator, the act of joining an international body not only is equivalent to the surrender of national sovereignty but also involves the distasteful prospect of having to mingle with other people in a gathering "made up of a few Orientals and a few Russians and a few Europeans . . . and a few South Americans"[21]—a prospect he does not find pleasing.

The ancient distrust and fear of the stranger seems to be at the base of the agitator's nationalism, for when he does try occasionally to give political concreteness to his nationalism, all he can produce is a few threadbare phrases: free enterprise, individualism, protective tariffs, and simple flagwaving. "The spirit of the founding fathers is still in our midst."[22] Or: "Let American individualism function—let free enterprise produce."[23]

Can a present-day audience, no matter how low its intellectual level, be satisfied with such an arid collection of clichés? Can it be satisfied with the distinctly unpleasurable note of denial that reverberates beneath the agitator's nationalism? For instead of material and moral security the agitator offers his listeners nothing but a refurbishment of slogans that have clearly not sufficed for protection from the foreign evils against which he warns them. Only when taken against the background of the world the agitator conjures, the Either-Or world hopelessly divided into incompatible camps, does the affirmation of endogamic exclusiveness seem to hold primitive attractions that might compensate for its apparent aridity as the goal of a movement.

To disappointed and disoriented listeners, the affirmation of exclusiveness may mean the assurance that their identity will be preserved. Their sense of alienation may thereby be somewhat relieved, and replaced by a sense of belonging to something, no matter how vague. As the opponent of "the scourge of internationalism,"[24] the agitator plays the role of the head of a family who is worried about the hardships his children suffer far from home and summons them to come back. He is less concerned with complex international political problems than with such humble questions as money, material comfort, health:

> I swear to my God that not a single dime of any money I may ever get my hands on will ever be sent to Europe's afflicted as long as one single American citizen remains destitute, jobless, paralyzed and suffering from neglect.[25]

In these humble concerns food occupies a prominent place. Before giving to others, Americans must be sure that they eat their fill and eat what they want:

> We assume that treaties and agreements and understandings shall be reached with other nations, but we want no League of Nations, we want no world court and no world congress . . . any more than we want our neighbor, three houses down the street, telling us whether we're going to have coffee or milk for breakfast.[26]

As late as March 1947, the agitator, in the name of food, denounces the Truman doctrine:

> Giving our food and supplies to foreign nations or even selling them to them in credit which we will never get paid for, keeps prices high because of "shortages" and that is exactly what the New Deal International money changers have been and are imposing upon us.[27]

His solicitude goes as far as the pettiest detail. Like a stingy house-wife who frowns upon her children's extravagant habit of inviting guests for dinner, and who wants at least to save the best morsels for her own family, he advises his listeners: "I believe absolutely, when you have got one shipload of oleomargarine and one of butter, send the oleomargarine . . . and keep the butter at home!"[28]

If the agitator refrains from outlining a detailed program for abundant living, he is at least vocal in assuring his listeners that whatever is available will fall into the right hands, for—and here we find another possible element of gratification in his arid appeals to preserve what exists—his listeners are promised to play a privileged role in the nation as he conceives it. Just as with material goods, so the spiritual benefits of Americanism are to be enjoyed only by an endogamic elite of Christian Americans.

The basic implication of the agitator's "defense" of American principles is that the human rights he proclaims should be transformed into a privilege. Even this doubtful privilege is nowhere defined clearly, except in contexts where its meaning comes down to the right to persecute minorities. The agitator speaks in grandiose terms of "the final judge-and-jury of what's what in America . . . the American people." But when this final judge-and-jury that "has yet to render its decision" finally does it, the only result "will be a decline of the Jewish population in both Washington and Hollywood. No, we do not mean a pogrom! We refer to migrations."[29]

The privilege here offered to the endogamic elite includes the essential promise to implement their rights as Americans by a vague permission (made more thrilling because it is accompanied by an apparent denial—"No, we do not mean a pogrom") to participate in the coercive functions of society. The promise of beneficent dependence in a nation that will be like a family is supplemented by the promise to the obedient followers that they will enjoy power over their prodigal and wicked brothers.

Theme 17: Housecleaning

The Agitator's Methods

Even more vague than the agitator's statement of his goals is his definition of the means by which he tends to achieve power. By virtue of his almost total silence on this matter, the agitator implicitly suggests that in this respect at least his movement is like a traditional political movement that intends to use orderly and democratic methods to change the government. At the same time, the agitator seems to promise his audience a more active role in the liberation. "This meeting," he reminds his audience, "is not a lecture course, it is not an open forum. . . . We are making history here today."[30] For though he has no wish other than to take power by the most peaceful and orderly means, the enemy may force him to use force; if so, "we will fight you in Franco's way."[31] Similar threats of a general uprising are to be found in his vague references to "Thirty Thousand 'Minute Men'" who are reported to be training at Lexington and Concord[32] and in his prophecies that the enemies' "days are numbered."[33] In a bolder mood, he declares that "there will be no stopping the blood running in our city streets"[34] and that "the country's due for civil war, anyway."[35]

Yet it must be emphasized that the agitator's calls to direct action are at least as vague as his definitions of his goal. It would be erroneous to believe that his programmatic silence is merely a cover for preparations for an armed uprising. In fact, the agitator takes care to make clear that his proposed uprising is not really a revolution. Throughout his remarks there runs a strong current of respect for institutionalized force. It is not accidental that the agitator who attacks the executive, legislative, and even judiciary branches of the government with indiscriminate virulence, will invariably identify himself with the forces of law and order, especially the police, and occasionally discover quite imaginative arguments to persuade them to take his side: "The Police of USA well know that the first to be liquidated in the event of a 'takeover' by the Synagogue of Satan (Organized Jewry-Intl. Finance) thru 'revolutionary' tactics, are the Police men."[36]

The agitator becomes quite lyrical when he speaks of armed forces. In 1943, while the nation was engaged in an unprecedented war effort, he demanded, as though no one else had thought of it before him,

> a line of fortifications built on land and water and in the air around the United States, that can be pierced by no alien force. It will be made up of cruisers, destroyers, gunboats, mosquito fleets, anti-aircraft guns, and airplanes, both bombers and fighters, troop transports, merchant vessels and a perfectly trained army, navy and marine force.[37]

The spontaneous rebelliousness the agitator wants to set in motion is to remain unstructured and unorganized; it is to be confined to an immediate emotional reaction. To describe this reaction, the agitator falls back upon familiar clichés: there is going to be trouble, "hell is going to pop."[38] But seldom does he suggest anything more specific or far-reaching than a march on Washington.

Even as a demagogue he never goes so far as to call upon the masses to take power into their own hands and establish their own governmental authority. Such a proposal would contradict his whole approach to his followers. As he describes it, the influence of the masses on the government must always be, at most, an indirect one; their aroused fury is to be kept in a kind of indefinite suspension, a perpetual and never fulfilled threat against the legislators and officials who might act against their wishes. The agitator never lets himself be carried away by his revolutionary élan; he knows when to stop and transform it into its opposite. This is one point at which he seems always to have himself most completely under control. Even when he does offer his followers a picture of a successful upheaval, it hardly involves any fundamental change in government:

> With a determined *MARCH* on *WASHINGTON* you could expect the guilty cowards in both House & Senate to run away, leaving the patriots, who could then go thru with the impeachment proceedings. That patriotic remnant of the Congress then could enact a law declaring who would serve as Pres., V-P, etc., until next election. That is the law![39]

The agitator takes it for granted that after the purge the people will withdraw to their homes and leave the government in the hands of the "patriotic remnant." In his eyes the masses remain essentially passive. The agitator's quarrel with the government is not at all basic, it merely involves a desire to see it manned by satisfactory personnel: "Place the Nation's affairs—every department—every agency—every job—in the hands of capable, experienced, honest experts whose loyalty to American principles of government has never been questioned."[40]

In fact, it seems that one of the objections that the agitator has to the government is that it does not govern: "The chaotic results of the bad government which has been inflicted upon us . . . point to the conclusion that some reorganization is necessary for a system of government which fails to govern."[41]

Behind the apparent contradictions between the agitator's call for rebellion and his desire merely to effect changes in the personnel of the government, is his reliance on the old European device of a *putsch*, in which there is a realignment of ruling circles without the intervention of the masses of people. It may therefore be asked why this proposal should be found attractive by the agitator's listeners. If the agitator were desirous of offering an opportunity for social action to an audience that suffers from a sense of nonparticipation in public life, the results of his *putsch* would necessarily be extremely disappointing: a brief, sensational flareup after which nothing of consequence would have been changed. The movement, on the face of it, has no goals nor does it seem to offer an appreciable field of action for its followers; it seems merely a movement for the sake of movement, a futile excitement for nothing at all.

We may find a clue to a possible answer to our question if we examine the content of the practical steps that the agitator advocates to end existing abuses, and the imagery he employs in such contexts. These steps consist almost uniformly of metaphors of discarding, throwing out, eliminating, as preparatory to extermination. "All refugees . . . should be returned to the lands from which they came";[42] "All aliens and former aliens should be deported."[43] The United States will "throw the Reds out"[44] and "kick out" the Jews.[45] Sometimes the orderliness and police character of the procedure is indicated by references to the need for "so called Refugees" to "be cataloged"[46] or for compiling lists of names[47] of the undesirables to be deported. The accompanying imagery is consistently drawn from the realm of hygiene. The word purge occurs directly: "We must purge America of every un-American organization and activity which might menace our national defense in the hour of a great crisis,"[48] and in innumerable variations. Thus the agitator talks about "cleansing America."[49] He advocates a "cleansing bath . . . of violence,"[50] a purge "of every 'ism.'"[51] the "political sterilization of the Jewish internationalists."[52] and "an internal fumigation to rid ourselves of European germs before we succumb to their diseases."[53]

The agitator's output is full of references to the present condition of the country as an ill-kept house. He complains that the enemies "have littered our fair land."[54] that "ideological and intellectual disease germs"[55] and contaminating the United States, and that it is "time to clean house."[56] He denounces "this whole smelly mess" with which this nation has become afflicted[57] and speaks of the necessity of "yanking this country from its devil of a mess!"[58]

Like the Low Animal metaphor this hygienic metaphor occurs too consistently and too profusely to be dismissed as accidental. It seems on the contrary to perform significant functions in the agitator's speeches and writings, one of which may be to make respectable his proposed political operation by presenting it in the guise of a harmless and familiar housecleaning. By comparing his rebellion with an act of elementary hygiene, he suggests that essentially everything is all right and that all we need is some more "order" or "orderliness."

The idea of a "housecleaning" seems to have a reassuring effect on both listeners and potential backers: nothing too extreme is contemplated. At the same time it serves as a substitute for genuine political activity. The great decisions are made by the heads of the family, while the rest of the family (that is, the audience) can busy itself with keeping the place clean, picking up the "mess," and protecting the house from foreign burglars. Consequently, the gruesome or bloody consequences of the agitator's purge become a mere unavoidable by-product of the community's renewed health and well-being. The agitator uses as his emblem the oversized American housewife with a fly swatter in one hand and a broom in the other: an image of the harmless and aggressive follower, of harmlessness transformed into aggression. For all his ruminations about apocalypse, for all his warnings about threatening catastrophe and for all his insistence on the Either-Or nature of the impending showdown, the agitator can summon no more glorious picture of his great act of liberation than this simultaneously ridiculous and threatening picture of a housewife doing her chores.

These remarks on the political content of the "housecleaning" theme may be supplemented by others based on psychoanalytical theory. According to this theory, education for cleanliness is one of the most difficult experiences a small child ever encounters. The child offers tremendous resistance to it, and even after he has been habituated to follow the social codes of cleanliness, the traumatic experience of cleanliness training exerts far-reaching consequences on both the conscious and unconscious layers of his personality. One of the major devices used to coerce children into cleanliness habits is threats that they will become sick and be punished for their sickness if they violate the rigid hygienic codes. As a result, they find the more obvious manifestations of uncleanliness repellent. The theory that there are significant and dynamic connections between the reorganized anal drives (as psychoanalysis describes the socially formed attitudes toward cleanliness) and such character traits as order, exactness, and pedantry is well known. So also is the notion that suppressed infantile instincts reassert themselves in later life through neurotic symptoms—among other ways, as delectations in the forbidden sphere of dirt.

The agitator is a virtuoso in manipulating such susceptibilities. In stigmatizing the enemies as people who live in the midst of the most offensive rubbish and refuse, he permits his audience to toy with verbal equivalents of the outlawed infantile pleasures. By insulting the enemy—that is, by attributing to the enemy familiarity with dirt and filth—it is possible to come into contact with forbidden materials and to perform forbidden acts. The same person who would be consciously ashamed to display even the slightest inclinations towards such infantilism grasps this occasion to indict the enemy for his own lust—and thereby finds an involuted method for expressing that lust. But simultaneously the projection of repressed desires onto the enemy reminds the audience that there is something shameful and disgusting about such desires. Projection makes possible simultaneous enjoyment and rejection.

Stereotypes utilizing the symbols of dirt, filth, and odor are used to impress the audience with the fact that all speeches and literature put out by the enemy should be discarded at once. Because the agitator counts upon the willingness of people to listen and to read, he must make the reaction of refusing to hear the views of his competitors quasi-automatic. This automatism cannot be achieved merely by discrediting the competitor's wares as fraudulent. It requires an immediate negative emotional reaction, which is obtained by the warning that the enemy's material should not be touched because it is filthy.

Perhaps the deepest layer of personality that can be psychologically organized or manipulated is the complex human reaction toward odors. When people smell a bad odor, they quite often do not turn away from it; instead they eagerly breathe the polluted air, pretending to identify it while complaining of its repulsiveness. One does not have to be a psychoanalyst to suspect that in such instances the bad smell is unconsciously enjoyed in a way somewhat similar to that in which scandal stories are enjoyed. We probably here touch upon phenomena quite successfully repressed in the collective unconscious of mankind, a last faint reminder of animal prehistory, of the way animals walk face downward while using their nose as a means of orienting themselves. The idiosyncratic violence with which various disgusting odors are rejected, and on which the agitator speculates, points to a repressed and forgotten origin. What the agitator does here, as in so many other instances, is to encourage these atavistic predispositions. The dark and forbidden things the listener enjoys with such insistent indignation are the very same things he would like to indulge in. Whether the agitator is conscious of his manipulation of these susceptibilities or is subject to them himself, is a moot point; what is important is that he does manipulate them in a sustained and patterned way.

It is no accident that metaphors of stench and slime are prominently represented among the agitator's hygienic metaphors. He speaks of the "cesspools of Europe,"[59] he likens capitalism to "a stinking corpse,"[60] and he refers to enemy propaganda as "malodorous." He does not hesitate to compare himself to a sniffling dog: "Well, I didn't have to sniffle him very long to find out he had the Willkie smell all over him."[61] But this evil smell is combated by a pleasant smell: "I resolved in 1940 when I got nipped by that financial smell that came down from Wall Street and rolled on to the flats of Indiana to get the smell of horse and cow—I vowed never again would I fall for such a trick."[62]

The audience, it is interesting to note, applauded the reference to the good smell, while laughing at the reference to the bad one.

In the agitator's view of the world, the atmosphere is permeated with foulness. When the audience reacts to his portrait of this world in terms of its socially conditioned response and prejudices, the image of the dirty and evil-smelling enemy solicits reactions that range from moral indignation to outright fury against those who create such an atmosphere. The prevalence of moral and material rubbish demands the most thorough sanitary measure. Such legitimate catharsis purifies the enjoyment that accompanies the delight of fantasies about forbidden dirt.

Those of his followers who expected to move into a new home are given only the same old shack—thoroughly housecleaned.

Notes

1. McWilliams, *The Serviceman's Reconstruction Plan*, p. 1.
2. CF, June 1942, p. 2.
3. Coughlin, Newark, N.J., July 30, 1939, radio.
4. LIB, Jan. 14, 1939, p. 9.
5. SJ, Jan. 1, 1940, p. 7.
6. SJ, Aug. 11, 1941, p. 3.
7. AID, June 9, 1942, p. 4.
8. CF, Oct.–Nov., 1942, p. 10.

9. CF, Feb., 1946, p. 714.
10. AID, May 14, 1941, p. 1.
11. LIB, Apr. 7, 1940, p. 1.
12. SJ, Feb. 12, 1940, p. 2.
13. Smith, *"Mice or Men,"* radio address, p. 3.
14. AID, July 10, 1939, p. 4.
15. Smith, Detroit, March 19, 1943, meeting.
16. Smith, *"Mice or Men,"* radio address, p. 4.
17. CF, Sept., 1942, p. 12.
18. Smith, Detroit, Mar. 22, 1943, meeting.
19. Smith, *ibid.*
20. Coughlin, speech on Feb. 19, 1939, reprinted in *Why Leave Our Own,* pp. 98–99.
21. CF, Oct.–Nov., 1942, p. 8.
22. Coughlin, Speech on Mar. 26, 1939, reprinted in *Why Leave Our Own,* p. 161.
23. Kamp, *Famine in America,* p. 50.
24. DEF, Aug., 1939, p. 4.
25. Phelps, Los Angeles, Sept. 8, 1940, radio.
26. CF, Oct.–Nov., 1942, p. 8.
27. X, Mar. 22, 1947, p. 2.
28. Smith, Detroit, Mar. 19, 1943, meeting.
29. LIB, Mar. 14, 1940, p. 5.
30. Smith, Detroit, Feb. 7, 1943, meeting.
31. Coughlin, Newark, N.J., July 30, 1939, radio.
32. SJ, Dec. 25, 1939.
33. Maloney, New York,, July 25, 1940, street corner.
34. AID, July 24, 1939, p. 1.
35. LIB, Mar. 28, 1938.
36. AID, June 15, 1942, p. 3.
37. Smith, Detroit, Mar. 22, 1943, meeting.
38. Smith, New York, Oct. 20, 1936, meeting.
39. AID, Oct. 7, 1941, p. 1.
40. Kamp, *Famine in America,* p. 50.
41. SJ, Apr. 4, 1938, p. 10.
42. Smith, *The Plan,* p. 4.
43. Phelps, Los Angeles, Oct. 2, 1940, radio.
44. SJ, Nov. 27, 1939, p. 6.
45. Maloney, New York, Aug. 3, 1940, street corner.
46. X, April 28, 1945, p. 2.
47. Cf. PW, Sept. 23, 1936, p. 2.
48. Smith, *Enemies Within Our Gates.*
49. McWilliams, New York, July 29, 1940, street corner.
50. LIB, Dec. 30, 1933, p. 12.
51. DEF, Sept., 1939, p. 6.
52. LIB, July 28, 1940, p. 6.
53. Phelps, Los Angeles, July 28, 1941, radio.
54. SJ, Feb. 20, 1939, p. 20.
55. Smith, *Enemies Within Our Gates.*

56. Kamp, *How To Win The War*, p. 2.
57. CF, July, 1942, p. 13.
58. LIB, Feb. 14, 1938, p. 5.
59. Phelps, Los Angeles, July 28, 1941, radio.
60. SJ, June 7, 1937, p. 2.
61. Smith, Detroit, Oct. 21, 1942, meeting.
62. Smith, *ibid.*

8

The Follower

In the movements of all traditional advocates of social change one can find incipient versions of their hopes for the future. The movement embodies the advocate's goal in embryo, the new world within the shell of the old. The harmonious and friendly relations that flourish or are supposed to flourish among the adherents anticipate the society they are trying to build.

Agitation is distinguised by a remarkable lack of such positive symbols. Nazi propaganda tried to conceal the essentially negative and reactive nature of the "Aryan" by developing the notions of the biological race and the hemmed-in nation. But these notions, obviously irrelevant to American life, are of little help to the American agitator when he attempts to portray his adherent. Yet, as the advocate of the endogamic community, he can hardly define his followers in terms of a social class. The American agitator falls back on the clichés of professional patriotism, Fourth of July Americanism.

The invention of the Aryan race and the agitator's glorification of the Simple American are symptomatic of similar efforts to strengthen social coercion. Both the *Volksgemeinschaft* of the Nazis and the community of pure Americans proposed by the agitator are actually pseudo-*Gemeinschaften,* or pseudocommunities. Such notions are deceptive solutions of the problem created by the disintegration of individualism. The agitator seems aware of this disintegration, but he conceives it as caused by an external force rather than as inherent in the structure of contemporary society: "There are forces at work which . . . would destroy the individuality of Americans and make of them automatons."[1]

The agitator bars the way toward understanding those forces. His normative image of the follower, built simply as a reactive response to the image of the enemy, is as ambivalent as that of the enemy: deceptive strength and real impotence. In the face of the formidable threat represented by the enemy, the adherents are made to believe that they can survive only by huddling together in an exclusive community and by obeying the orders of the leader. But if the enemy must be exterminated, the adherent can just be saved from extermination. In the last analysis, both are equally contemptible: the enemy as the projected target of the adherent's fury, and the adherent because he can do nothing but resort to such projections.

Theme 18: Simple Americans

Striving to recruit the largest possible number of people to his banner, the agitator tries to transcend traditional political or social divisions and to appeal directly to

> the great common body of the American people, who are deacons of churches, trustees of churches, who go to High Mass on Sunday morning, who build the fires and keep the doors of the synagogues, who grub the stumps and husk the corn and chop the cane, and do the work.[2]

The majority of Americans, he intimates, support his cause. His estimates vary: "these seventy-five to one hundred million real, plain, simple American folks,"[3] or "75% of the American people."[4] In more expansive moments he is certain [that] more than eighty percent of the American people are getting sick and tired of being misled by foreign fraud."[5] "Everybody who is against war and communism is called an anti-semite. 85% of America followed Nye, Smith and Coughlin."[6] And finally reaching a rhapsodic climax, he proclaims that "mine is not the cry of just one American citizen. It is the plea and the prayer of millions of Americans."[7]

The most obvious purpose of such assertions is to instill in the listeners the feeling that, just as they cannot be wrong when they buy a nationally advertised product, so they cannot be wrong when they represent a general political trend. In addition to this reassuring function, these claims to mass following help to emphasize the basic weakness of the helplessly outnumbered enemy.

Friends and allies are equipped with seemingly unmistakable identification marks. The agitator makes his followers feel that they are something special. They must be convinced that they belong to an elite even if the elite presumes to include the vast majority of the people.

As soon as the agitator tries to define this elite, he apparently encounters insuperable obstacles. The poverty of the characteristics attributed to the follower is in striking contrast with the richness of characteristics assigned to the enemy. When the agitator tries to characterize this elite socially, he only borrows various stereotypes. When he predicts that "some day Gentile Americans are going to wake up to what is being done to the 'forgotten man' "[8] or denounces any offenses against "the common man" and his "welfare."[9] he is borrowing from the arsenal of progressive clichés. When he refers to his adherents as "we old-fashioned Americans"[10] or as "individualists who still believe in Constitutional government and the American way of life,"[11] he is using the language of conservatism. And when he speaks of the "poor stockholders . . . the forgotten men."[12] he is using the middle-of-the-road stereotype designed to impress prospective middle-class adherents.

The inadequacy of such symbols is obvious: they are not sufficiently distinctive to become the exclusive property of the agitator. Still trying to construct a portrait of his followers, the agitator resorts to nationalism described as the exclusive property of Christians, the "Christian Nationalists."[13]

The Christian is defined in negative terms: he is the non-Jew, who can remain a Christian only by never mingling with Jews. The mark of purity, by which the adherent can remain faithful, is a refusal to mix with the contaminating Jews. A Christian who associates with Jews is contemptuously referred to as "Shabes-goy";[14] such people are condemned as "those Gentiles to whom Christ referred as being 'two-fold more the child of hell' than the Jewish leaders of that Synagogue of Satan."[15]

To complement his notion of the Christian follower as one who is not a Jew. the agitator tries to adapt the Nazi notion of a pure Nordic race. The results are pathetically poor; all he can produce is a vague biological intimation in "Americans of the original species."[16] In the characterization "real Americans"[17] the abstract adjective *real* barely conceals the negative meaning of *non-nonreal.* What the agitator implies is that his adherents are all those who do not fall under any of the categories of the enemy. His elite or in-group is essentially negative; it depends for definition on those in the out-group. It is what the "other" is not, a pure residue. The very leveling of class differentiations and cultural distinctions involved in this image makes impossible any kind of specific or positive identification of his followers.

The agitator makes no genuine appeal to solidarity. Even when he addresses himself to the vast majority of "American Americans,"[18] he suggests that what unites them is the common danger they face in the Jew. By making their precarious situation their major sign of identification, he retains his manipulative power over them. Under the guise of granting his followers identity, the agitator denies it to them. He says in effect: If you belong to the common people you need not ask for something else because it is quite enough to be considered one of the common people rather than an enemy of the people. Anything else might expose you. Both he and his audience feel that the cement of our social structure is not love, solidarity, or friendship but the drive to survive, and in his appeal to his followers, as well as in his portrait of their characters, there is no room for solidarity. There is only fear.

Grassroots Anti-Intellectuals

That the agitator refers to his followers as common folk, a kind of "proletarian elite," might seem offhand to suggest that he seeks to disavow the antidemocratic implications of his discriminatory statements by the use of a well-tested device. But this is also a device that by its very nature often tends to transform democratic psychological patterns into totalitarian ones. Closely related to the common resentment against anyone who dares be different and hence implicitly directed against minority groups, it establishes conformism as a moral principle, a good in itself.

Seizing on the "simple folk" theme as a pretext for fostering an aggressively anti-intellectual attitude, the agitator describes his American Americans as a people of sound instincts and, he is happy to say, little sophistication. He suggests that, on one level, the conflict between his followers and the enemy is nothing but a clash between simple minds and wise guys, level-headed realists, and crazy sophisticates. He delights his followers by proclaiming his own lack of intellectuality:

> I do not understand political science, as an authority from an academic viewpoint. I am not familiar with the artistic masterpieces of Europe, but I do say this tonight: I understand the hearts of the American people.[19]

Implying that intellectual pursuits are inherently depraved, he refers contemptuously to "the parlors of the sophisticated, the intellectuals, the so-called academic minds."[20] Heavy is the responsibility of the "Scribes and Pharisees of the Twentieth Century . . . [who] provide a nation with its dominant propaganda including seasonal fashions in politics, religious attitudes, sub-standard ethics and half-caste morals."[21]

Here the agitator is, first of all, playing on the resentment of uneducated people against the educated, a resentment he often transforms into sneering anti-intellectualism. But in addition to this attitude, which the agitator can expect to find ready-made in his audience and merely inflates, he exploits another and at the moment perhaps more significant attitude: the modern disappointment with rationality. All the symbols of liberalistic enlightenment are the targets of his attack. Psychology, especially psychoanalysis, is singled out for vehement and sarcastic denunciation, for among other crimes, "by uncovering secrets of rich men and women," it wields " 'control' over the subject."[22]

Offering typical patient "resistance" to psychoanalysis, the agitator scorns any suggestion that his audience of simple Americans might be frustrated. "'Frustration'? No wonder Freud is worshipped in certain quarters. Did he not invent a label that enables any suspect to take the offensive against his accusers?"[23] No, not frustration but sound, healthy instincts and common sense characterize his followers. They are not taken in by

> that old city-slick, tweedle-dee, tweedle-dum stuff. . . . We will come out with a crusading, militant America First Party and we are going to take this government out of the hands of these city-slickers and give it back to the people that still believe two plus two is four. God is in his Heaven, and the Bible is the Word.[24]

Theory, discussion, interchange of opinion—all this is futile, an impediment to the struggle for self-preservation. The situation is too urgent to permit the luxury of thought. Having discovered that "actions are more realistic than hypocritical catchwords,"[25] the agitator tells his followers that there is no point in wasting time in talk. As the result of anti-intellectualism, the speech-maker denounces speeches: his group "is not 'another organization.' We hold no banquets. We waste small time in speech making. *The Silver Legion* comes to Christian citizens who want ACTION."[26]

The agitator's doctrine of aggressive intolerance is represented as the "natural reactions of plain people to [having heard] the truth."[27] He hardly bothers to veil his function of releasing the emotions of those simple Americans who are his followers:

> Our people frequently do not express themselves because there are only a few of us who speak with abandon in times like this, but in the hearts of our people are pent-up emotions which go unexpressed because they fear their vocabularies are insufficient.[28]

The agitator, in praising the simple folk, praises only their humble and folky ways, in which the latent savagery and brutality that is both repressed and generated by modern culture, still manifests itself. He offers them little else.

Attracted by the promise of a new spiritual home, the audience actually gets the tautological assurance that Americans are Americans, and Christians Christians. The simple American is a member of an elite by virue of birth but in the last analysis, he can be defined only in negatives: he is a Christian because he is not a Jew; he is an American because he is not a foreigner; he is a simple fellow because he is not an intellectual. The only positive means the agitator has of identifying the Simple American is as a follower. The adherent who turned to the agitator in the vague hope of finding identity and status ends as more than ever an anonymous member of a characterless mass, a lonely cipher in an army of regimented ciphers.

Theme 19: Watchdogs of Order

Hypnotic Alertness

For all their strength, the Simple Americans are apathetic and lethargic, they are like a "slow, muscular, sleeping giant."[29] This fact fills the agitator with a kind of despair; he argues, implores, cajoles, shouts himself hoarse to arouse them to awareness of their danger: "O God! When will the American people awaken and snap out of their lethargy? When will they arouse themselves to the dangers which confront them internally as well as externally?"[30] He summons them to alertness: "Wake up, Americans! It is later than you think! ACT BEFORE IT IS TOO LATE!"[31]

Offhand, this call to alertness may seem like that of all other proponents of social change who also excoriate apathy and indifference. But the agitator's warnings and admonitions seem hardly to have any genuine relationship to a situation. Even the most trivial of occasions elicits the call to alertness: that "character assassins have smeared our two greatest heroes—Lindbergh and Rickenbacker—should be enough to wake up America."[32]

Significantly, the agitator never tries to justify his call to alertness by subsequent explanation, even of the most rudimentary kind. Although it is possible to detect signs of similarity between the agitator's call and religious revivalism, their actual functions are quite different. In a sermon the call to awareness is addressed to the soul of the individual, with the aim of strengthening his conscience or superego; likewise, the reformer as a rule endeavors to inculcate a stronger social sense among his adherents by lifting their concerns from the private to the general level. But the agitator, under the guise of pursuing a similar purpose, actually invites his listeners not to change themselves

126

spiritually or socially but simply to place all blame, all sin, on the external enemy. He asks them not to become more conscious of the causes of their difficulties but simply to give vent to their feelings: "I challenge all true Americans today to come out from your place of hiding, express yourselves, give vent to your opinions, stand squarely upon your feet. . . . America awake!"[33]

In such direct appeals to the people to cease being "very patient and good-natured,"[34] in such warnings that "long enough we have been apathetic,"[35] and in such direct statements as "That's the way I like my people to be, angry,"[36] the agitator defines the alertness of his Simple Americans as something that is the opposite of alertness. They are invited, not to organize rational responses but to act out their impulses. The agitator plays on his audience's predisposition to seek escape from rigid psychological controls. People want unconsciously to "give in," to cease being individuals in the traditional sense of self-sustaining and self-controlled units. The ability to control oneself reflects a more basic ability to compete with others and thereby determine one's economic and spiritual fate. But today the social pressures to which each individual is subjected are so overwhelming that he must yield to them both economically and psychologically. He must act according to the pattern of conformist social behavior rather than according to the needs of his individual personality. The social and cultural pressures to which he is subjected become the determining factors in molding his personality. As a result, the very diminution of his "ego" decreases his ability and his willingness to exercise self-control. Hysteria, an extreme expression of this lack of self-control and a psychological trait that is rapidly spreading through all of society, is the audience reaction on which the agitator banks when he calls for displays of anger and emotion. When the agitator so insistently demands such outbreaks, he lifts an already tottering taboo from the conscience of his audience and suggests to its members that an abandonment of self-control has by now become the socially correct mode of behavior.

Because he was the one who released the instinctual urges of his listeners, the agitator is in an especially favorable position to control and manipulate them. The alerted Simple Folk rush hysterically in obedience to the agitator's call. Where do they go? Responding constantly, they are kept in a perpetual state of mobilization and are not given an opportunity to collect their thoughts. What takes place is not an awakening but rather a kind of hypnotic trance that is perpetuated by constant admonitions to alertness.

Just as the enemy never rests—"certain Jewish organizations are working day and night to open America's borders to five million Jewish refugees"[37]—so the Simple Americans are asked to be on guard constantly and indefatigably. The audience is driven to submit to the agitator's incessant harangues until it is ready to accept everything he says in order to gain a moment's rest. Once aroused, the simple folk "are known to be *pure hell!*"[38] but the very way in which they have been aroused merely perpetuates their inferior status.

"Let's Go"

In designating his followers as Simple Americans, the agitator no doubt seeks to give them a sense of superiority and strength, yet, as we have seen, the image of the adherent that he constructs is singularly lacking in positive gratification. Themes like the "Endogamic Community" and "Housecleaning" suggest some sort of spiritual gratification, but even these indulgences and gratifications prove to be essentially negative. At no point does the agitator promise any substantial improvement in his adherent's status. Perhaps, then, we might infer that the agitator is appealing to the notion that the poor man should be content with his lot on the dubious grounds that he is somehow morally superior to both the rich and those who rebel against the rich. Such an inference is only partly correct.

When the agitator appeals nostalgically to the "good old times," he can at most be vaguely sentimental—hardly an attitude by means of which to solidify his followers in his movement or to present them with a satisfactory image of themselves. It is difficult to believe that "dreams of little white houses with blue roofs, built near singing streams, with sheep and cattle grazing in quiet pasture land"[39] or the maudlin account of a party where "the women baked yummy cakes, sold refreshments, etc. We all sang and had a jolly, sociable and inspiring time besides. . . . Rich people are noticeable by their absence in this cause"[40] represent the sole positive stimulus available to the agitator. For somewhere, somehow the agitator must give his followers the feeling that his calls to alertness have some reality basis and that by heeding his appeals they will get something worthwhile.

One possible clue may be found in the extreme aridity of the agitator's statements. Although he does not explicitly advocate a dangerous and frugal life, as the Fascists did to some extent, his dubious and often directly negative attitude toward material benefits and pleasures suggests that what he does dangle before his followers' eyes is the prospect of participating in a Spartan elite—an elite without special happiness or privileges but with greater access to the centers of social power. The American American is always seen as surrounded by dangerous and cunning enemies, and all that he can do is to use social power as a means of self-preservation. The agitator intimates to his audience that the thing that matters is not so much possession of goods as social control; once you are "in," you are likely to get a share of what can be had. Such a promise of a share in actual social control may serve as a very powerful antidote to the pervasive and frustrating sense of exclusion from which his audience suffers. The agitator, unlike all traditional advocates of social change, does not promise a good society, he does not tell his followers that there will be delicious fruits to be had once power is attained. All he tells them is that power in itself is worthwhile.

Not the traditional "gravy" promised by politicans, but power construed as the right directly to exercise violence is what the agitator offers his followers. And here again the agitator is perhaps less unrealistic than might appear offhand. By permitting his followers to indulge in acts of violence against the enemy group, the agitator offers them the prospect of serving as semiprivileged agents of a social domination actually exercised by others. But the followers nonetheless do share in the reality of power, for power ultimately is grounded on force, and they are to be the dispensers of brute force. True, the followers are to get only the dregs of power, the dirty part of the game—but this they will get. And hence their feeling that "it's the right of Christian Americans to be the master in the United States of America,"[41] has some psychological justification. Though they have only the prospect of becoming watchdogs of order in the service of other, more powerful groups, the watchdogs do exert a kind of subsidiary power over the helpless enemy.

This promise of sadistic gratification is relayed through linguistic stimuli. Intimating that the act of venting pent-up emotions on a scrapegoat is, if not quite desirable, something natural and hence unavoidable, the agitator says that "good Americans are boiling inside and some of them, unfortunately, are looking about for something, perhaps a group on which to focus their attention, on which to lay the blame for conditions."[42]

He clearly indicates the direction in which they are supposed to look: "Liquidate the millions of burocrats . . . kick out the top heavy

Jew majority, many foreign born that NOW dictate and direct our domestic and foreign policies."[43]

The outbreak of violence is justified by the agitator in legal terms by being implicitly compared to a police action: "The rank and file of sober, sincere, and peaceable citizens [should] pull them [New-Dealers] out of power and lock them up, pronto, as their crimes may be proven."[44]

As justification for such calls to violence, the agitator paints vivid pictures of the enemy's brutality, for though the group is seen as inhuman, its members are allowed one all too human characteristic: enjoyment of cruelty. They "would actually and physically crucify Father Coughlin . . . there is in their hearts a sadistic thirst for blood."[45] They have an apparently unquenchable thirst for blood; they would like "to drink the blood of every German"[46] and "with their own foul tongues, they would lap up the blood of their own critics."[47]

Blood and Death

Perhaps the most effective though indirect method by which the agitator encourages violence is his consistent use of images that condition the audience to accept violence as "natural" and respectable. In his world murder and death are invariable parts of the landscape. His threats are couched in the language of brutal action, of explosions of anger that sweep everything aside. He predicts that the enemy's activity will "dynamite a Boulder Dam of public reaction which will create a domestic crisis unequaled in the history of our people."[48] The people ought to march on Washington "with monkey wrenches and lead pipe"[49] once his ideas have begun to "ignite in the public mind."[50] He complains that he is

> smeared in the press, boycotted, liquidated, described as a menace, fired from his job, relieved of his command, viewed with suspicion, editorialized against, hounded with gossip, preyed on by character assassins, ripped from gut to nose, he must be socially disemboweled, economically wrecked, burned out with the sulphur of editorial excoriation, banished if possible, exiled wherever practical, scorned, branded as psychopathic, isolated as one of the lunatic fringe.[51]

This torrent of words exemplifies a basic function of modern agitation: rehearsal. The verbal fury of the agitator is only a rehearsal of real fury.

Can his followers then have any qualms about the retaliatory methods they use against the enemy? For against such a background of enemy ruthlessness, in an atmosphere that reeks of cruelty and murder, the sadistic urges of both agitator and follower are unloosed. Perhaps unconsciously and perhaps not, the agitator slips in an anticipatory description of his followers' cruelty: "We pushed you out of Coney Island, Rockaway, Long Beach and we will push you outta here—out into the ocean."[52] He loves to imagine how fearful and cowardly the enemy is: "Winchell is perhaps best known for his physical cowardice . . . afraid to pass an undertaking parlor by himself . . . terrified at the smell of embalming fluid."[53]

Indulging in verbal equivalents of the violence he evokes, the agitator wishes he "could write messages that would burn the trousers off the brazen intolerants who have the unmitigated gall to criticize us."[54] Or he gloats at the thought that "many Americans of the original species would like to see the Hon. Hans von Kaltenborn broadcast with his bare feet on a hot brick."[55] And he promises that "there'll be some fat, greasy scalps hanging on the wall."[56]

In the guise of a warning that the destruction of the enemy will not be fun, he promises fun, and while urging restraint he spurs his followers to violence: "Hanging hordes of Jews in apple orchards, or even watching the cracking of their Communist front with satisfaction, has nothing to do with yanking this country from its devil of a MESS!"[57] Or in the guise of a little joke, he continues to urge violence: "Next time, let's plow under the international bankers instead of the pigs and cotton."[58]

A favorite symbol of sadism, the delighted description of whipping, also occurs in agitation:

> Christ, we recall, took the cord of his garment and physically lashed the money changers out of the portico of the sacred Temple in Jerusalem. Was Christ precipitate? Are we to be more "Christian" than Christ? . . . Let's go![59]

> Reaching macabre depths of perversity and sadism, he adds: "So you might well start adjusting your thinking to the inhuman orgasm that's ahead, before America singes her Locust-Swarm savagely."[60]

The Elder Brother

By encouraging such sadistic fantasies the agitator does not, like most political leaders, appear in the role of the restraining or moralizing father but rather as the elder brother who leads the small-fry gang in its juvenile escapades. Yet it would be erroneous to infer that he preaches free and wild joy in aggression, for with every gesture that urges his audience to indulge in violence, he reminds his followers, no matter how indirectly, that their aggression involves the forbidden, that they are still weak and can free themselves from the enemy's tyranny only by submitting unconditionally to his leadership. In the anticipated hunt, the followers can expect no spoils: they must be satisfied with the hunt itself.

Though they are destined to be the watchdogs of order tomorrow, today they are still weak: "Do not think for a moment that it will be easy—or fun."[61] The blending of strength and weakness that characterizes the agitator's image of the enemy also holds for his followers. Like the enemy conspirators, the followers must shun the light of day, for they are always in danger of attack by the enemy. Here, as in so many other instances, the image of the adherent is merely an inversion of the image of the enemy. The agitator confesses to this weakness:

> A man said to me, "Come to Houston and talk to my friends." I went over there and there were about one hundred of them, and when I got over there I was supposed to have a meeting at a public place, but they said, "We are going to have it out in one of the houses because we are afraid of the reprisals of the New Deal if we held it in a place where our names are known."[62]

So the agitator, for all his claims to the support of the overwhelming majority of the people, has no recourse but to turn to conspiracies. He urges his followers to form "platoons of 25 persons that are pliable. They can be suddenly thrown into action in their respective districts in the work of teaching the principles of social justice to others."[63]

The agitator's gift to his audience—his permission to indulge in violence—is a Trojan horse. Even the promised violence is hard to deliver, even that one last shred that might give some measure of positive personality to the image of the adherent turns out to be illusory. All that remains is the immediate condition of constantly renewed excitement and terror; the followers are allowed no rest, they must constantly ward off enemy attacks that never occur, they are called to the most heroic and self-sacrificing acts of violence that never take place. In the end the follower again becomes an "innocent bystander" who is the most deeply involved accomplice.

The adherent is nothing but an inverted reflection of the enemy. He remains a frustrated underdog, and all the agitator does is to mobilize his aggressive impulses against the enemy. The underdog becomes watchdog and bloodhound, while yet remaining essentially an underdog, for the most he can do is to react to external threats. The image of the adherent thus serves indirectly to condition the audience to authoritarian discipline.

Notes

1. SJ, Mar. 4, 1940, p. 19
2. Smith, New York, Oct. 20, 1936, meeting.
3. Smith, New York, Oct. 20, 1936, meeting.
4. CF, June, 1942, p. 14.
5. Phelps, Los Angeles, Aug. 14, 1941, radio.
6. Smith, Cleveland, May 11, 1943, meeting.
7. Phelps, Los Angeles, Aug. 18, 1940, radio.
8. AID, July 24, 1939, p. 1.
9. AP, Feb., 1944, p. 9.
10. Smith, *Stop Treason,* radio address, p. 3.
11. Kamp, *With Lotions of Love* . . . p. 4.
12. Phelps, Los Angeles, Aug. 3, 1941, radio.
13. CF, Feb., 1946, p. 714.
14. BR, Feb. 26, 1945, p. 4.
15. AID, June 2, 1942, p. 3.
16. AP, Feb., 1945, p. 3.
17. Smith, *Mice or Men,* radio address, p. 1.
18. Kamp, *Vote CIO . . . and Get a Soviet America,* p. 6.
19. Smith, New York, Oct. 20, 1936, meeting.
20. Smith, St. Louis, Mar. 25, 1944, meeting.
21. AP, Aug., 1944, p. 1.
22. AID, May 5, 1941, p. 2.
23. AP, Feb., 1944, p. 13.
24. Smith, Detroit, Mar. 19, 1943, meeting.
25. Coughlin, Speech on Mar. 26, 1939, reprinted in *Why Leave Our Own,* p. 161.
26. LIB, Oct. 14, 1933, p. 11.
27. CF, Jan., 1948.
28. Smith, Detroit, Mar. 22, 1943, meeting.
29. Smith, *The Next President of the U.S.,* radio address, p. 4.
30. Phelps, *An Appeal to Americans,* p. 22.
31. Sanctuary, *New Deal is Marxian Sabotage,* p. 2.
32. CF, Feb., 1943, p. 152.
33. Smith, *Which Way, America?* radio address, p. 1.
34. Smith, *Labor on the Cross,* radio address, p. 1.
35. Coughlin, Newark, N.J., July 30, 1939, radio.
36. Smith in an interview with the New York Post, quoted in E. A. Piller, *Time Bomb,* New York, 1945, p. 124.
37. CF, Mar., 1945, p. 530.
38. LIB, Dec. 30, 1933, p. 12.
39. Phelps, Los Angeles, July 30, 1941, radio.
40. PRB, Oct. 8, 1942, p. 4.

41. McWilliams, New York, Aug. 3, 1940, street corner.
42. Phelps, Los Angeles, Aug. 14, 1941, radio.
43. X, Nov. 21, 1947, p. 2.
44. RC, Apr. 21, 1941, p. 16.
45. CF, May, 1942, p. 4.
46. CF, Nov., 1944, p. 475.
47. AP, Aug., 1944, p. 1.
48. Smith, Detroit, Mar. 22, 1943, meeting.
49. Mote, *Testimony Before Senate Military Committee,* p. 3.
50. AID, Jan. 13, 1941, p. 1.
51. CF, Feb., 1946, p. 710.
52. SJ, Nov. 24, 1941, p. 14.
53. Kamp, *With Lotions of Love* . . . p. 29.
54. Phelps, Los Angeles, Aug. 10, 1941.
55. AP, Feb., 1945, p. 3.
56. Coughlin, quoted in A. B. Magil, *l.c.,* p. 15.
57. LIB, Feb. 14, 1938, p. 5.
58. Smith, Los Angeles, Nov. 3, 1945, meeting.
59. SJ, Dec. 4, 1939, p. 6.
60. LIB, Jan. 14, 1939, p. 9.
61. SJ, Nov. 27, 1939, p. 6.
62. Smith, New York, Oct. 20, 1936, meeting.
63. SJ, June 13, 1938, p. 23.

9

Self-Portrait of the Agitator

The democratic leader usually tries to present himself as both similar to and different from his followers: similar in that he has common interests with them; different in that he has special talents for representing those interests. The agitator tries to maintain the same sort of relationship to his audiences, but instead of emphasizing the identity of his interests with those of his followers, he depicts himself as one of the plain folk, who thinks, lives, and feels like them. In agitation this suggestion of proximity and intimacy takes the place of identification of interests.

The nature of the difference between leader and follower is similarly changed. Although the agitator intimates that he is intellectually and morally superior to his audience, he rests his claim to leadership primarily on the suggestion of his innate predestination. He does resort to such traditional American symbols of leadership as the indefatigable businessman and the rugged frontiersman, but these are overshadowed by the image he constructs of himself as a suffering martyr who, as a reward for his sacrifices, deserves special privileges and unlimited ascendancy over his followers. The agitator is not chosen by his followers but presents himself as their prechosen leader—prechosen by himself on the basis of a mysterious inner call, and prechosen as well by the enemy as a favorite target of persecution. One of the plain folk, he is yet far above them; reassuringly close, he is yet infinitely aloof.

Although spokesmen for liberal and radical causes refrain, for a variety of reasons, from thrusting their own personalities into the foreground of their public appeals, the agitator does not hesitate to advertise himself. He does not depend on a buildup manufactured by subordinates and press agents, but does the job himself. He could hardly trust anyone else to paint his self-image in such glowing colors. As the good fellow who has nothing to hide, whose effusiveness and garrulousness know no limit, he does not seem to be inhibited by considerations of good taste from openly displaying his private life and his opinions about himself.

This directness of self-expression is particularly suitable for one who aspires to be the spokesman for those suffering from social malaise. The agitator seems to realize almost intuitively that objective argumentation and impersonal discourse would only intensify the feelings of despair, isolation, and distrust from which his listeners suffer and from which they long to escape. Such a gleeful display of his personality serves as an ersatz assertion of individuality. Part of the secret of his charisma as a leader is that he presents the image of a self-sufficient personality to his followers. If they are deprived of such a blessing, then at least they can enjoy it at second remove in their leader.

Those who suffer from malaise always want to pour their hearts out, but because of their inhibitions and lack of opportunities they seldom succeed. Conceiving their troubles as individual and inner maladjustments, they want only a chance to be "understood," to clear up the "misunderstandings" that others have about them. On this need the agitator bases his own outpouring of personal troubles. When he talks about himself the agitator vicariously gratifies his followers' wish to tell the world of their troubles. He lends an aura of sanction and validity to the desire of his followers endlessly to complain, and thus his seemingly sincere loquacity strengthens his rapport with them. His trials are theirs, his successes also theirs. Through him they live.

By seemingly taking his listeners into his confidence and talking "man to man" to them, the agitator achieves still another purpose: he dispels any fear they may have that he is talking above their heads or against their institutionalized ways of life. He is the elder brother straightening things out for them, not a subversive who would destroy the basic patterns of their lives. The enemy of all established values, the spokesman of the apocalypse, and the carrier of disaffection creates the atmosphere of a family party in order to spread his doctrine the more effectively. Blending protestations of his weakness with intimations of his strength, he whines and boasts at the same time. Cannot one who is so frank about his humility also afford to be equally frank about his superiority?

The agitator's references to himself thus fall into two groups or themes: one covering his familiarity and the other his aloofness, one in a minor key establishing him as a "great little man," and the other in a major key as a bullet-proof martyr who despite his extraordinary sufferings always emerges victorious over his enemies.

Theme 20: Great Little Man

Unlike those idealists who, sacrificing comfort in behalf of a lofty social goal, "go to the people," the agitator comes from the people; in fact, he is always eager to show that socially he is almost indistinguishable from the great mass of American citizens. "I am an underdog who has suffered through the depression like most of the people."[1] Like millions of other Americans, he is "one of [those] plain old time, stump grubbing, liberty loving, apple cider men and women."[2] Yet he is always careful to make it clear that he is one of the endogamic elite, "an American-born citizen whose parents were American born and whose parents' parents were American born. I think that's far enough back."[3] There is no danger that anyone will discover he had an impure grandmother.

Not only is he one of the people, but his most ardent wish is always to remain one and enjoy the pleasures of private existence. He hates to be in the limelight, for he is "an old-fashioned American" who, he cheerfully admits, does not even know his "way around in the circles of high society at Washington."[4] If it were really up to him and if his conscience didn't tell him otherwise, he'd spend all his time on his favorite hobby: "If we had a *free* press in America I doubt if Gerald Smith would publish *The Cross and the Flag*. I am sure I wouldn't publish AMERICA PREFERRED. In my spare time I'd play golf."[5] Even when he finally does seek office, it is only after a heart-rending conflict and after he has received the permission of his parents: "First, I would have to get the consent of my Christian mother and father, because years ago I had promised them that I would not seek office."[6] And on those rare occasions when he can escape from his duties for a few minutes of relaxation, he proudly tells his listeners about it: "Well, friends, Lulu and I managed to get time out to attend the annual carnival and bazaar of the Huntington Park Chapter of the Indoor Sports Club."[7]

Even at this rather uncomplicated level of identification the agitator is ambiguous. By his very protestations that he is quite the same as the mass of Americans he smuggles in hints of his exceptional status. Public life, he intimates, is a bother, and whoever deserts his private pleasures in its behalf must have some good reason for doing so. By constantly apologizing for his abandonment of private life and his absorption in public life, the agitator suggests that there are special provinces and unusual responsibilities that are limited to the uniquely endowed. If one of the plain people, such as he, gains access to such privileges and burdens, then it must surely be because of his unusual talents. He has embarked on a difficult task for which he is specially qualified, and therefore his followers owe him gratitude, admiration, and obedience.

A Gentle Soul

Although he is, by virtue of his special talents, a man who has risen out of the common people, the agitator remains a kindly, gentle soul—folksy, good-natured, golden-hearted. Far be it from him to hold any malice against any fellow human being, for "if we must hate, let us hate hate."[8] Nor is he "the kind of person who carries hatred or bitterness for any length of time . . . In spite of all I have gone through . . . I have never lost my sense of humor, my ability to laugh, even right into the face of seeming disaster."[9]

Like all other Americans, he is a good and solicitous father to his children, and in a moment of difficulty appeals touchingly to his friends for help: "My son, 9½ years old, is pestering me, wanting a bicycle. Get in touch with me, please, if anyone knows where I could obtain a second-hand bicycle very cheap."[10] But his virtues come out most clearly in his role as model husband. He regales his audience with bits of intimate family dialogue: "I said one day to my sweet wife."[11] And even he, the would-be dictator, does not hesitate to admit that the little, or not so little, wife is the boss at home: "If I don't look out I'll be looking for a boss' lap on which to sit and chew gum. Well, Lulu's the boss and, having gained about 25 pounds during the past six months, she has plenty of lap on which to sit."[12]

As he makes the rounds of his meetings, his faithful wife accompanies him: "A few weeks ago found Mrs. Winrod and me spending Sunday at Sioux City, Iowa, holding meetings in the Billy Sunday Memorial Tabernacle."[13] And when he wishes to express his gratitude to his followers, it is again as the gentle soul, the faithful family man: "The wife and I are very grateful for the prayerful letters, kind words, and sums remitted so far."[14] So sweet and lovable are both his personality and his family life that he offers family pictures for sale: "How many have received 1. Calendar of Mrs. Smith, me and Jerry? 2. A copy of my 'undelivered speech'?"[15]

Troubles Shared

One of the agitator's favorite themes is his economic troubles, about which he speaks to complete strangers with perfect ease:

> I must confide to you without reservation . . . I have spent everything I have; I have surrendered every possession I had in this world in

order to carry on this fight. I will not be able to borrow any more money; I have nothing left to sell.[16]

Another agitator complains that by engaging in political activity he has embarked on "a gamble with the security of my wife and children at stake."[17] And still another offers the audience a detailed financial statement:

> The taxes on my Kenilworth home are unpaid and there are some $1800 in outstanding bills accrued since I stopped depleting my few remaining securities, although I have paid light, phone and groceries . . . his [her husband's] refusal to give us any of the milk check income from my farm, his continuing to spend this income while associating with the woman he brought to sleep in my own bed at my farm, finally made it necessary to take some legal steps to protect the family.[18]

The agitator is just as frank about the condition of his health as about his financial or marital contretemps. We find him making great sacrifices that cause him to commiserate with himself: "I come home and say to Mrs. Smith. 'How does this old heart of mine keep up?' . . . But I know how men like that go—they go all of a sudden."[19] And even when his heart does not bother him, his teeth do: "The last time I saw Charlie Hudson, he still had been unable to afford to get needed dental work done. His wife takes roomers."[20] His afflications threatened to handicap his political work:

> My dentist informed me I must have four teeth removed at once. I don't mind that so much as I do the fact that I may come on the air tomorrow, after the teeth have been extracted, and sound like a dear old gentleman who has been drawing old-age pension for forty years or more.[21]

By multiplying references to his family, his health, and his finances, the agitator tries to create an atmosphere of homey intimacy. This device has immediate, gratifying implications. The personal touch, the similarity between agitator and audience, and the intimate revelations of "human interest" provide emotional compensation for those whose life is cold and dreary, especially for those who must live a routinized and atomized existence.

Equally gratifying to listeners may be the fact that such revelations help satisfy their curiosity, a universal feature of contemporary mass culture. It may be due to the prevalent feeling that one has to have "inside information" that comes "from the horse's mouth" in order to get along in modern society. Perhaps, too, this curiosity is derived from an unconscious infantile desire to glimpse the forbidden life of the grown-ups—a desire closely related to that of revealing and enjoying scandals. When the listener is treated as an insider his libido is gratified, and it matters little to him whether he hears revelations about crimes and orgies supposedly indulged in by the enemy or about the increase in weight of the agitator's wife. He has been allowed to become one of those "in the know."

Public Privacy

When the agitator indulges in his uninhibited displays of domesticity and intimacy, he does so not as a private person but as a public figure. This fact endows his behavior with considerable ambivalence. His lyrical paeans in praise of the pleasures of private existence imply *ipso facto* a degrading of this privacy when he exposes it to public inspection. This gesture has the double meaning of an invasion of the agitator's private life by his public life and of his public life by his private life. In this way the traditional liberal differentiation between the two is made to seem obsolete and in any case untenable. Privacy is no longer possible in this harsh social world, except as a topic of public discussion.

Finally, these revelations of private life serve to enhance the agitator's stature as a public figure, who, it has already been suggested, vicariously symbolizes the repressed individualities of his adherents. He establishes his identity with the audience by telling it of his financial troubles and other kinds of failures, but he also underlines the fact of his success. He has risen from the depths in which the followers still find themselves; in contrast to them, he has managed to integrate his public and private personalities. The proof of this is simple enough: is he not talking to the followers and are they not listening to him? As a symbol of his followers' longings, the agitator centers all attention on himself, and soon his listeners may forget that he is discussing not public issues but his qualifications for leadership.

That the agitator simultaneously stresses his own weakness, that he pictures himself as all too human, does not impair the effectiveness of his attempt at self-exaltation. By the very fact that he admits his weaknesses while stressing his powers, he implies that the followers too can, if to a lesser extent, become strong once they surrender their private existence to the public movement. They need but follow the path of the great little man.

Theme 21: Bullet-Proof Martyr

Aside from his remarkable readiness to share his troubles with his fellow men, what are the qualities that distinguish the great little man from the rest of the plain folk and make him fit to be one of "those . . . who lead"?[22] Here again the agitator is ready to answer the question. Although the agitator calls himself an old-fashioned Christian American, Christian humility is hardly one of his outstanding virtues. For all his insistence that he is one of the common folk, he does not hesitate to declare that he is an exceptionally gifted man who knows and even admires his own talent.

That he has no difficulty in overcoming conventional reticence about such matters is due not merely to his quite human readiness to talk about himself but also to the fact that his prominence is not merely his own doing. As he has emphasized, his natural inclination is not to lead humanity; he would rather play golf. But he cannot help it—forces stronger and more imperious than his own will push him to leadership. Both because of his innate dynamism and because he has been singled out by the enemy, the mantle of leadership, like it or not, falls on his shoulders.

The Inner Call

Suggesting that his activity is prompted by sacred command, the agitator speaks of himself as the "voice of the great unorganized and helpless masses."[23] He is "giving vocal expression to the thoughts that you have been talking about around your family tables."[24] But it also comes from holier regions: "Like John the Baptist." the agitator is "living just for the sweet privilege of being a voice in the wilderness."[25] As such, the agitator does not hesitate to compare himself to Christ: "Put down the Crown of Thorns on me."[26] He sees himself continuing the work of the "Divine Savior."[27]

But for all his suggestions that he has a divine responsibility, the agitator does not pretend to bring any startling new revelation. He does not claim to make his audience aware of a reality that they see only partially; he does not claim to raise the level of their consciousness. All he does is to "say what you all want to say and haven't got the guts to say it."[28] What "others think . . . privately," the agitator says "publicly."[29] And for this purpose he is specially talented: as one agitator says of another, he delivered what was "perhaps the greatest address we have ever had on Christian statesmanship."[30]

Like a new Luther, he bellows defiance of established powers without regard to consequences: "I am going to say some things this afternoon that some people won't like, but I cannot help it, I must speak the truth."[31] Nothing can "halt and undo the innermost convictions of stalwart sons of Aryan blood,"[32] not even the ingratitude of those who spurn him: "Nevertheless, there I will stand demanding social justice for all even though some of the ill-advised whom I am endeavoring to defend will take a pot-shot at me from the rear."[33]

Nor is the agitator's courage purely spiritual:

> If the Gentiles of the nation back up Pelley now in his challenge to the usurpers of American liberties, they are going to get a "break" that they have never dreamed possible till Pelley showed the spunk to defy the nepotists.[34]

The agitator, aware of both his qualifications and his courage, knows that

> when the history of America is written . . . concerning the preservation of the American way of life. I am going to be thankful that in the day when men were cowardly and overcautious and crawled under the bed and allowed themselves to be bulldozed by a bunch of wire-whiskered Communists and atheists and anti-God politicians, that there was one man by the name of Gerald L. K. Smith that had the courage to be an old-fashioned, honest to God, Christian American![35]

And the agitator knows too that his courage extends to somewhat smaller matters as well:

> When I went to the Auditorium, although it was very cold, probably five degrees below zero—twenty degrees the first time, five degrees the second time—the place was packed and every inch of standing room was taken. I had to pass through a picket line, one of those vicious picket lines organized by Reds and enemies of our meeting there.[36]

It is this blending of seriousness and unseriousness, of the sublime crown of thorns and the toothache that characterizes the agitator's approach to composing his self-portrait as well as to the other themes of his speeches and writings. He is both the little man suffering the usual hardships and the prophet of truth: Walter Mitty and Jeremiah rolled up into one.

Such an indiscriminate mixture of trivial and sublime symbols might appear blasphemous or simply disgusting, but the agitator seems to count on a different kind of reaction. Instead of imposing on his listeners the difficult task of following a saint, a task that might after all cause them to feel that they too must assume some of the traits of sainthood, he gratifies them by dragging the lofty notions of sainthood down to a humdrum, *kleinbürgerlich* level. The followers thereby are offered an object of admiration, the image of the desanctified saint, that is closer to their own level of feeling and perception. The agitator imposes no strain on them.

There is still another gratification for the audience in the agitator's narcissistic outbursts of self-praise. A courageous and self-reliant man might be disgusted with the spectacle of someone celebrating himself as the repository of all the manly virtues, but people who are acclimated to self-denial and self-hatred are paradoxically attracted by the selfish narcissist. As a leading psychoanalyst puts it: "This narcissistic behavior which gives the dependent persons no hope for any real love arouses their readiness for identification" (O. Fenichel, *The Psychoanalytical Theory of Neurosis* [New York: Norton, 1945], p. 510). Accordingly, the agitator does not count on the support of people capable of self-criticism or self-reliance; he turns to those who constantly yearn for magical aids to buttress their personalities.

Persecuted Innocence

Like any advocate of social change the agitator appeals to social frustration and suffering, but in his output there is a striking contrast between the vagueness with which he refers to the sufferings of his listeners as a social group and the vividness with which he documents his personal trials. He speaks as though the malaise resulted in tangible hardship in him and him alone. His trials and ordeals are truly extraordinary, almost superhuman, and by comparison the complaints of his followers seem merely to refer to minor nuisances, insignificant reflections of his glorious misfortunes. He is the chosen martyr of a great cause: himself. As they compare their lot to his, the followers cannot but feel that they are almost like safe spectators watching a battle between the forces of evil and their own champion of virtue.

In building up this image of persecuted innocence, the agitator uses religious symbols. He "has come through the most heart-rending Gethsemane, I believe, of any living man in America today,"[37] and he does not hesitate to compare himself to the early Christian martyrs: "Many leaders . . . sneered at Father Coughlin and turned thumbs down on the Christian Fronters. as did the Patrician population of Rome turn their thumbs down on the Christian slave martyrs."[38]

But these religious associations are only decorations for ordeals that are strictly secular; the agitator's sufferings are of this world. Here he runs into a difficulty. In actual fact, he has met with little interference from the public authorities. (Except for those involved in the war-time sedition trial and one agitator convicted as an enemy agent, the American agitators have suffered only from exposures and criticism.) Yet he realizes that as a man with a mission, he must be persecuted. If the past will yield no evidence, perhaps the future will, for who is to deny him the right to premonitions:

> I don't know what is going to happen to me. All I ask you to do is, don't be surprised at anything. If I am thrown in jail, if I am indicted, if I am smeared, if I am hurt physically, no matter what it might be, don't be surprised at anything, because everything in the calendar is now being attempted. . . . I am glad to make that sacrifice.[39]

One reason that the agitator has difficulty in specifying the persecutions to which he is subjected is that his enemies work in secret. They force him to the most surreptitious behavior: "I, an American, must sneak in darkness to the printer to have him print my booklet and to get it out to the people like a bootlegger."[40] He is beset by vague dangers that are difficult to pin down: "One of these newspapermen, according to another newspaperman, is said to have predicted somewhat as follows: 'Two Jews from England were over here to see that Hudson does not get home alive.'"[41]

But when the agitator gets down to bedrock, it becomes clear that what he most resents is public criticism, which he describes as "smearing" and "intimidation." He complains that "Jewish New-Dealers in the Congress . . . started a mighty ball rolling to smear Pelley from the scene."[42] And "because I dare to raise my voice foreigners are intimidating me and trying to get me off the air."[43] Nor does he feel happy that "frequently we have heard it prophesied over the radio by such noble patriots as Walter Winchell and others, that we were about to be incarcerated in concentration camps."[44]

A Slight Case of Murder

However insubstantial the evidence he can summon for his martyrdom, the agitator, it must be admitted, works it for all it is worth. He continually suggests that he has embarked on a dangerous career and that he is actually risking his life. The threat never abates, as we shall see in tracing it during the course of one agitator's statements over a period of twelve years.

As early as October 1936. he realized that his death warrant had been signed. Like his political boss, who was assassinated, "it may cost my life."[45] And not without reason: "Ten threats came to me within twenty-four hours here in New York City."[46]

Three years later these threats of murder were still harassing him: "I continued to receive all sorts of threats against my life."[47]

By 1942 the rather slow-working murderers had a definite objective: to keep him out of the Senate. "I am convinced that there are men in America who would rather commit murder than see me in the United States Senate."[48] Other murderers, or perhaps the same ones, found his literary output more objectionable than the possibility of his becoming a senator: "I have been warned that I will not live to complete this series of articles."[49]

Half a year passes, and the enemy is still intent on murder. "A certain set of ruthless men in this nation have actually called for my assassination."[50] The murderers seem finally to have worked up enough energy or courage to come within striking distance:

> I held a meeting down in Akron, Ohio, one time and my Committee resigned the afternoon of the meeting. . . . I had to walk into that armory alone. . . . I walked from the hotel over to this place which seated about 6,000 people alone, and when I got over there, the place was packed. . . . I walked down the center aisle, walked right up to the microphone and the first thing I said was this, "There are men in this room who would like to see me killed tonight."[51]

Yet even then there is no record of the murderers doing anything. Two more years went by and by the spring of 1945 the still-healthy agitator noted that the threat to his life had become so real that it was even confirmed by police authorities: "Shortly before the end of the meeting I received a message from the police detectives to the effect that they were convinced that there was a definite plot to do me great injury, perhaps kill me."[52] Nothing seems to have come of that danger, but by the summer of the same year the agitator reported that "people who know what is going on are convinced that a plan is on foot to actually get me killed at the earliest possible moment."[53] As of the moment of writing, the agitator remains alive and unharmed, never having once been the victim of assault or assassination. As late as April 29, 1948, he still maintained that he was the object of an attempt on his life, this time by means of "arsenic poisoning."[54]

That he has no genuine factual data to support his charges does not seem to disturb the agitator: he persists in believing that an evil force is out to get him. His recital of fears, smearing, premonitions, anonymous letters—all this adds up to the familiar picture of paranoia. The paranoiac's conviction that he is persecuted cannot be logically refuted because it is itself extralogical. In agitation the leader acts out, as it were, a complete case history of persecution mania before his listeners, whose own inclinations to regard themselves as the target of persecution by mysterious forces is thus sanctioned and encouraged. Nevertheless it is the agitator who remains at the center of the stage; it is on him that all the imaginary enemy blows fall. By symbolically taking upon himself all the burdens of social suffering, he creates unconscious guilt feelings among his followers, which he can later exploit by demanding their absolute devotion as recompense for his self-sacrifice. And because the enemy exacts the heaviest penalty from him, he has the implicit right to claim the highest benefits once the enemy is defeated. Similarly, because the enemy singles him out for persecution, he has the right to engage in terroristic reprisals. All of these consequences follow from the agitator's self-portrait as martyr.

But simultaneously the agitator, for all the dangers to which he is exposed, does manage to survive and continue his work. He is not merely the martyr but also the remarkably efficient leader, and on both counts he deserves special obedience. Because he is both more exposed and better equipped than his followers, his claims to leadership are doubly vindicated.

The Money-Minded Martyr

There are many indications that, at its present stage at least, American agitation is a racket as well as a political movement. To what extent the agitator actually depends on his followers' financial contributions it is difficult to say with any degree of certainty. In any event, he does not account for the use of the money he collects. It seems probable that at least some agitators have been heavily subsidized by anonymous wealthy donors, and it is known that some of the smaller fry make a living by selling their literature.

When the agitator appeals to his followers for money, he strengthens their devotion to the cause by leading them to make financial sacrifices. In agitation such psychological factors are probably of greater importance than in other movements, for it must be remembered that in agitation the follower has no precise idea what his cause is, that the whole background of the agitator's appeal is one of destruction and violence, with a meager minimum of positive stimuli. What remains then is the agitator himself—his inflated personality and his pressing needs. The agitator does not hesitate to act the insistent beggar. He begs meekly: "Oh, I'm just a common American citizen, friends, poor in the world's gifts, depending on the quarters and dollars of friends and radio listeners."[55] But he also begs for himself as the agent of history: "It is a long grind to get the thousands of dollars absolutely necessary as a minimum in this way. But it must be done if the fight is to go on."[56] "Why hold back your financial aid NOW—when revolution itself is being shouted from our public rostrums?"[57]

He begs for aid, but he also warns that those who do not come through now may live to regret it: "If any of you don't agree with the principles of America First and don't care to contribute to our cause, this is the time for you to get up and walk out."[58] Those who do not comply face the dreaded penalty of exclusion: they have to walk out and be alone with themselves.

Magic of Survival

That he has managed to survive under terrible financial handicaps and political persecution arouses the agitator's self-admiration. "How could he emerge unscathed with such colossal forces arrayed to smash him?"[59] His invulnerability is remarkable and is only slightly short of miraculous. His safety is, in fact, adduced as proof that he has gone through dangers, and as he concludes his report of the plot hatched against him by English Jews, he remarks with a note of defiance in his voice: "I arrived safely Sunday night."[60] His life seems to him protected by an anonymous providence: *Pelley is an absolute fatalist . . . he believes that nothing can harm him until he has done the work which he came into life at this particular period to do!*[61] And he always returns to the fight: "I intend to . . . toss off the shackles that have been thrown around me . . . to spread my wings again . . . and to soar to new heights to carry on the battle."[62] His powers of exertion are tremendous: "I speak two hours here and two hours there, and write all night and talk all day to people and write letters and work . . . and everything else, and still I always seem to have the strength to do what lies before me."[63]

Seen from one perspective, all this bragging is rather harmless. A narcissist naturally believes himself invulnerable and omnipotent, and his slightly ridiculous posturings only endear him to his audience. He is reduced to a level that is within their vision. Like the extraordinary exploits of the hero of a movie or a cheap novel, the agitator's adventure ends on an ultimately happy note: the hero is saved. From this harmless relapse into an adolescent atmosphere, the followers, together with the agitator himself, draw a certain simple gratification. They have been in the company of a hero who is not too heroic to be akin to them.

And yet somewhere in the interstices of this harmless braggadocio there lurk the grimmer notes of violence and destruction. The agitator's self-portrait of miraculous survival has a solid reality basis; he really does enjoy a high degree of impunity. He is safe and sound, magically immune, secretly protected, and this despite his verbal violence and scurrilous denunciations of the powers that be or of some of the powers that be. If his enemies do not carry out their threats of murder, it is not because they would not want to but because they do not dare. Their power, the agitator thereby suggests, is rather less impressive than it appears; they have only the façade of power. Real power is on his side.

Behind this defiance of the enemy's threats lurks another suggestion: when the hour strikes and the seemingly strong enemy is revealed in his true weakness, the agitator will take revenge for the torments of fear that have been imposed on him. Perhaps it is not too bold to conjecture that as the agitator continually stresses his own bodily vigor, he is implicitly developing a complementary image to his leading metaphor of the enemy as a Low Animal. His own body is indestructible, but the helpless bodies of the enemy—those parasitical and disease-breeding low animals—are doomed to destruction. Behind the whining complaints and the triumphant self-admiration of this indestructible martyr looms the vision of the eugenic storm troops. The agitator is a good little guy, to be sure; he is a martyr who suffers endlessly; he survives by virtue of superior destinies; but in the long run he makes sure to protect himself.

Tough Guy

The agitator knows that sometimes he must bare his teeth. Often he does it with the air of a youthful gang leader testing his hoodlums:

> I am going to test my people. I am going to see if the fathers that left their bones on the desert had real sons. I am going to find out if the children of the men that rebuilt San Francisco after the earthquake are real men.[64]

Such vague anticipations of the agitator's future role are supplemented with more direct hints about his present strength. He means business, even if he is a great little man. "I am a tough guy. I am tough because I have got the goods on them."[65] The easygoing braggart is also a brutal swashbuckler. "They can threaten me all they want to. I am not a damned bit afraid to walk the streets of New York all by myself. I don't have to. I have the toughest men in New York with me."[66] Nor does he always have to sneak in the dark to his printer: "Huskies of my 'American Group' protect me when I take my printed booklets from the printer's plant."[67]

The bodyguard, however, is used not merely against the enemy. The same bodyguard that protects the leader from the enemy also protects him from any interference from his listeners; their role is to listen, not to participate. When he speaks, you had better listen—or else. In this way the agitator already establishes himself as a constituted authority. The agitator brags about this:

> So as we moved down through the middle of the meeting I said. "Now, we are not going to have any disturbance, we are not going to be heckled and the first man who attempts that, we will throw him out through the nearest window." So one fellow like this boy, way up in the balcony said something and somebody didn't understand what he said and he was almost pitched out of the window.[68]

It is in this atmosphere, in which even the followers are threatened with manhandling if they step out of line, that the agitator tests out a future device: the totalitarian plebiscite. "Do you authorize me to send a telegram to Senator Reynolds . . . put up your hands. . . . All right, that is number one."[69] He feeds them cues: "I bid for the American vote under that flag. Give that a hand."[70] Such presentiments of the plebiscite are in themselves trivial enough, but they serve to emphasize the agitator's role as the sole legitimate voice to which everyone must listen in silence except when told to speak up in unison.

Inside Knowledge

Not only is the agitator physically powerful and something of a terrorist to boot but he also has access to secret and highly important information, the source of which he is most careful not to reveal. He quotes mysterious "sources" that enabled him "to correctly diagnose 3 years ago that the 1940 presidential election would not be bonafide."[71] He asserts that "there has fallen into my hands a copy of these confidential instructions which came out from New York City concerning the underground science."[72] By miraculous but unspecified means he manages to penetrate into the heart of the enemy fortress where his sharp ears hear the confidences that "Zionists in America whispered with secret circles."[73]

On other occasions the agitator can offer only promises of revelations to come: "I shall try to keep you posted concerning the diabolical conspiracy."[74] Or his information is too horrible to disclose: "I personally have had some experiences in the last year that would make your blood run cold, if I could tell you what they were."[75] Or he is bound by professional secrecy:

> Two contacts, best unnamed on account of nature of information divulged, inform: ". . . believes that he has discovered the hdqtrs. of what seems to be Grand Orient Masonry . . . uptown in New York City. A building in the middle of a large block, surrounded by apartment houses; in a sort of courtyard, with a high barbed wire fence around it. No one is ever seen to enter this place, altho access could be had underground from one or more of the surrounding houses. A large telephone cable, sufficient for over 100 lines, goes to the place which is guarded night and day by armed guards."[76]

The agitator uses the language of an adolescent gang leader. He seeks to ingratiate himself with his listeners by promising them some highly important information. Some day the listeners will be "let in." But the agitator uses this technique of innuendo in ways other than the relatively harmless promise to divulge secrets. He withholds information in the very gesture by which he seems to give it out. He reveals not secrets but the existence of secrets; the secrets themselves are another variety of "forbidden fruit." Those affected by the promise to be "let in" are even more affected by the fact that the agitator has access to information inaccessible to them. To listen to innuendo and to rely on deliberately vague statements requires a certain readiness to believe, which the agitator directs toward his own person. So long as he does not reveal the "sources" of his knowledge, the agitator can continue to command the dependence of his followers. Unlike the educator, he never makes himself superfluous by revealing his methods of gaining knowledge. He remains the magical master.

This secret knowledge, like his toughness, is a two-edged weapon. It implies an ever-present threat from which no one is quite safe: "Some day that thing is really going to come out, and when it comes out it is going to smell so high that any man that is connected with them, with that outfit, will be ashamed to say that he ever knew them."[77] Or: "I have written a letter containing some mighty important information which I have placed in the hands of attorneys in this city. . . . The letter will not be printed . . . if we arrive home safely at the end of our campaign."[78]

Behind such statements there is the suggestion that he knows more than he says, and that nothing can ultimately remain hidden from him. If his self-portrait as a tough guy anticipates the storm trooper, then his insistence on his "inside knowledge" anticipates the secret files of the totalitarian police, which are used less against the political enemy, known in any case, than as a means to keep the followers in line. Sternly the agitator indicates this to his followers: get used to the idea now, if you want a share in this racket, you have to obey its rules—and I make the rules.

The Charismatic Leader

The self-portrait of the agitator may seem a little ridiculous. Such an absurd creature—at once one of the plain folk and the sanctified leader; the head of a bedraggled family and a man above all material considerations; a helpless victim of persecution and a dreaded avenger with fists of iron! Yet contemporary history teaches us that this apparently ridiculous braggart cannot be merely laughed away.

In establishing this ambivalent image of himself the agitator achieves an extremely effective psychological result. In him, the martyr ultimately triumphant over his detractors and persecutors, the adherents see all their own frustrations magically metamorphosed into grandiose gratifications. They who are marginal suddenly have a prospect of sharing in the exceptional; their suffering now can appear to them as a glorious trial, their anonymity and servitude as stations on the road to fame and mastery. The agitator finds the promise of all these glories in that humdrum existence of his followers that had driven them to listen sympathetically to his appeals; he shows them how all the accumulated stuff of repression and frustration can be lit up into a magnificent fireworks, how the refuse of daily drudgery can be converted into a high explosive of pervasive destruction.

The self-portrait of the agitator is thus a culmination of all his other themes, which prepare the audience for the spectacle of the great little man acting as leader. Taking advantage of all the weaknesses of the present social order, the agitator intensifies his listeners' sense of bewilderment and helplessness, terrifies them with the specter of innumerable dangerous enemies and reduces their already crumbling individualities to bundles of reactive responses. He drives them into a moral void in which their inner voice of conscience is replaced by an externalized conscience: the agitator himself. He becomes the indispensable guide in a confused world, the center around which the faithful can gather and find safety. He comforts the sufferers of malaise, takes the responsibility of history and becomes the exterior replacement of their disintegrated individuality. They live through him.

Notes

1. Phelps, Los Angeles, Sept. 26, 1940, radio.
2. Smith, New York, Oct. 20, 1936, meeting.
3. Phelps, Los Angeles, Aug. 7, 1941.
4. Smith, *The Hoop of Steel,* p. 23.
5. AP, May, 1945, p. 8.
6. CF, May, 1942, p. 8.
7. Phelps, Los Angeles, July 28, 1941, radio.
8. Coughlin, Speech on Jan. 29, 1939, reprinted in *Why Leave Our Own,* p. 57.
9. Phelps, Los Angeles, July 21, 1941, radio.
10. Phelps, Los Angeles, Sept. 19, 1940, radio.
11. Smith, New York, Oct. 20, 1936, meeting.
12. Phelps, Los Angeles, Aug. 1, 1941.
13. Winrod, *Letter,* Feb. 1943, p. 3.
14. Hudson, letter to subscribers of his Bulletin, July, 1942.
15. Smith, Detroit, Apr. 9, 1942, meeting.
16. Smith, *Why is America Afraid?*
17. Phelps, Los Angeles, Aug. 18, 1940, radio.
18. RTL, Feb. 28, 1942, p. 3.
19. Smith, Detroit, Mar. 19, 1943, meeting.
20. PRB, Apr. 8, 1942, p. 1.
21. Phelps, Los Angeles, Jan. 14, 1941, radio.
22. CF, July, 1945, p. 604.
23. CF, May, 1942, p. 9.
24. Stewart, New York, July 13, 1940, street corner.
25. Smith, Cleveland, May 11, 1943, meeting.
26. Smith, Detroit, Apr. 9, 1942, meeting.
27. DEF, Oct., 1942, p. 11.
28. Smith, St. Louis, Mar. 25, 1944, meeting.
29. SJ, July 7, 1941, p. 4.
30. CF, Aug., 1945, p. 616.
31. Smith, *Why Is America Afraid?*
32. LIB, Sept. 21, 1939, p. 7.
33. SJ, June 5, 1939, p. 2.
34. RC, Oct. 20, 1941, p. 16.
35. Smith, Detroit, Mar. 19, 1943, meeting.
36. Smith, *ibid.*
37. DEF, Nov., 1940, p. 5.
38. SJ, July 7, 1941, p. 4.
39. Smith, Detroit, Mar. 19, 1943, meeting.

40. Phelps, Los Angeles, Nov. 20, 1940, radio.
41. AID, June 23, 1942, p. 4.
42. Pelley, *What You Should Know About The Pelley Publications*, p. 4.
43. Phelps, Los Angeles, Sept. 29, 1940, radio.
44. Smith, Detroit, Mar. 22, 1943, meeting.
45. Smith, New York, Oct. 20, 1936, meeting.
46. Smith, *ibid.*
47. Smith, *"Reds On The Run,"* radio, p. 2.
48. CF, May, 1942, p. 9.
49. CF, Oct.–Nov., 1942, p. 3.
50. CF, Feb., 1943, p. 154.
51. Smith, Detroit, Feb. 7, 1943, meeting.
52. CF, Apr., 1945, p. 557.
53. Smith, *Letter,* "The Battle of Babylon," July, 1945, p. 1.
54. Smth, St. Louis, April 29, 1948, meeting.
55. Phelps, Los Angeles, Sept. 8, 1940, radio.
56. PRB, Aug. 10, 1942, p. 5.
57. SJ, Nov. 27, 1939, p. 19.
58. Smith, St. Louis, Mar. 25, 1944, meeting.
59. Pelley, *What You Should Know About The Pelley Publications*, p. 5.
60. AID, June 23, 1942, p. 4.
61. Pelley, *Official Despatch,* p. 4.
62. Phelps, Los Angeles, Dec. 31, 1940, radio.
63. Smith, Detroit, Mar. 19, 1943, meeting.
64. Smith, New York, Oct. 20, 1936, meeting.
65. Phelps, Los Angeles, Oct. 8, 1940, radio.
66. McWilliams, New York, July 29, 1940, street corner.
67. Phelps, Los Angeles, Nov. 12, 1940, radio.
68. Smith, Detroit, Feb. 7, 1943, meeting.
69. Smith, Detroit, Mar. 19, 1943, meeting.
70. Smith, New York, Oct. 20, 1936, meeting.
71. AID, Jan. 19, 1942, p. 4.
72. Smith, *"Dictatorship Comes with War,"* radio, p. 3.
73. SJ, July 14, 1941, p. 7.
74. Smith, *Letter,* Mar., 1943.
75. CF, Feb., 1943, p. 154.
76. AID, Nov. 26, 1941, p. 2.
77. Smith, New York, Oct. 20, 1936, meeting.
78. Phelps, Los Angeles, Feb. 7, 1941, radio.

10

What the Listener Heard

In Europe, Hitler and Mussolini openly advocated a radical break with contemporary society. They explicitly repudiated capitalism and liberalism, and negated the democratic way of life in favor of a system based on charismatic leadership. To make their ideas attractive they resorted both to a glorified evocation of the preliberalistic past and to a distorted version of contemporary revolutionary ideologies. The very name National Socialist shows how the Hitler movement tried to incorporate elements of ideologies that appealed both to the past and the future.

These preliberalistic and revolutionary elements of the fascist appeal in Europe served to mask the actual meaning of the movement. In practice Nazi totalitarianism was no more feudal than it was socialist. Its break with contemporary society took place only on the cultural and ideological level; the old liberalistic values were ruthlessly pushed aside for the needs of an industrial war machine. Old forms of economic and social coercion were perpetuated and strengthened.

The American agitator, however, has no preliberalistic tradition on which to fall back; he does not find it expedient to pose as a socialist, and he dares not explicitly repudiate established morality and democratic values. He only indirectly and implicitly assumes the mantle of charismatic leadership. He works, by necessity rather than choice, within the framework of liberalism.

Study of our themes shows that this limitation does not prevent him from conveying the principal social tenets of totalitarianism to his audience. The themes point to the disintegration of existing institutions, the perversion and destruction of democracy, the rejection of Western values, the exaltation of the leader, the reduction of the people to regimented robots, and the solution of social problems by terroristic violence. The American agitator shows that manipulation of people with a view to obtaining their conscious or unconscious adherence to his movement need not take the detour of preliberalism or perverted socialism; that the psychological attitudes and social concerns that flow from the crisis of liberal society provide a sufficiently fertile soil for the growth of anti-democratic tendencies. It is as though the American agitator had evolved a method of directly converting the poisons generated by contemporary society into the quack remedies of totalitarianism; he does not need to resort to pseudofeudal or pseudosocialist labels. His themes could be transplanted to another country, much more easily than corresponding Nazi slogans could be transplanted to the United States. The mythical notion of the pure-blooded Nordic Aryan German superman would have to undergo many profound changes before becoming an effective appeal in this country, but the agitator's Simple Americans could be used in other countries as Simple Germans, or Simple French, or Simple Britishers, and so on. One is tempted to say that the American agitation is a standardized and simplified version of the original Nazi or fascist appeals.

Because the American agitator dispenses with such secondary labels, his methods of appeal are also more universal in scope, and are not bound to any specific national tradition or political situation. Despite his professions of Americanism, not a single one of his appeals refers to concerns of situations specific to the United States. The feelings that he stirs are in no sense limited to this country, for the social abscesses on which his invectives thrive can be found in any modern industrialized society.

The agitator seems aware of this when he declares that "I stand before you tonight, as I have stood before similar groups all over America, as a symbol of a state of mind that exists in America."[1] He does not tell us what this state of mind is, but on the basis of a study of his themes we can construct a portrait of the state of mind of his most susceptible kind of listener. This listener does not directly participate in the major fields of social production and is therefore always fearful that, given the slightest social maladjustment, his insignificant little job will vanish and with it will vanish his social status. He senses that in some way he cannot quite fathom life has cheated him. And yet he wonders why his fate should have been so unhappy. He abided by the rules, he never rebelled, he did what was expected of him. Bound and circumscribed by a series of uncontrollable circumstances, he becomes increasingly aware of how futile and desperately aimless his life is. And worst of all, he can no longer believe in any miraculous salvations, for no matter how much he hopes for them he is far too much the modern man really to place his faith in miracles. He is on the bottom, on the outside, and he fears that there is nothing he can do about it. Yet there are others, the intellectuals who talk about ideals and values and morals, and who make a living—a clean, comfortable living—by manipulating words. They are smart alecks who paint pictures of wonderful societies in the future and who live so comfortably in this one. Most of them are Jews, of course, who seem to have beaten the racket. And even more so, there is that secret and inaccessible gang that lives in air-conditioned penthouses, enjoys the favors of movie stars, and luxuriates on yachts, the lucky few, who tempt him with the possibility of success and the dream of escape from his own grimy and dreary life.

Sometimes openly, more often in the veiled areas of his daydreams, our listener admits to himself that in this world—and who can imagine any other?—all that counts is success. Only the successful are to be admired. It is a deadly struggle, and those who fall must be discarded. These standards are inculcated in him by every medium of mass amusement. The very places to which he goes for relaxation—the movies, the comics, the radio—provide him not with spiritual refreshment but with an exacerbated feeling that success is the all-essential fact of modern life, and that he is not successful.

And so the listener grumbles. He grumbles against bureaucrats, Jews, congressmen, plutocrats, communists—whatever political stereotype he can find to suggest to him concentrations of power. He grumbles against the foreigners who come to this country and get good jobs. He grumbles against the party in power, votes for the one out of power and then grumbles against it. But he knows no other means of venting his social dissatisfaction, and at one point or another he begins to become suspicious of the efficacy of his grumbling. And what is more, even grumbling has its dangers. One must be careful where one grumbles. A lot of it has to be kept inside one, repressed, barely touching the rims of consciousness.

The listener would like to do something about it, something drastic and decisive that will do away with the whole mess. Imagine—strike one blow on the table and everything is changed.

Rehearsal of Violence

How prevalent is the type that has been briefly sketched above? There is reason to believe that at least strands or aspects of this "ideal" personality type are widespread in modern life. The voluminous literature on psychic discontent, ranging from advice on how to keep friends and influence people to prescriptions for peace of mind, testifies to this fact. For a variety of historical circumstances, social and economic, the American agitator has not succeeded in gaining any large masses of adherents. Except for the early years of the New Deal and those preceding Pearl Harbor, the agitator's audience has been limited to a hard core of followers: disgruntled old people, cranks, toughies, unemployables, and certain undefined groups. Such audiences are often unkindly identified as the lunatic fringe.

The agitator must know that he can hardly expect to achieve significant results without reaching a wider audience; his ambitions are certainly not confined to his present groups, but he seems to sense that such initial audiences reflect on a small scale what might under certain social conditions characterize large masses of people. The beginnings of European fascism were equally modest, its original followers recruited from similar strata of the population. The American agitator tends to behave as if his present performance were merely a rehearsal and his audience merely paradigmatic. He can afford to be "unserious."

In an economic crisis the distinction between unemployables and unemployed merges, the middle class loses its security, and the youth its confidence in the future. The possibility that a situation will arise in which large numbers of people would be susceptible to his psychological manipulation seems to provide the agitator with the impetus to continue his present small-scale operations at the head of his legion of misfits and malcontents.

The Social Basis of Agitation

It is the deep and pervasive presence of the social malaise that we sketched in an earlier chapter that is both the origin of agitation and the field in which agitation flourishes. Malaise gives rise to agitation, and agitation battens on malaise. In some dim nook of his consciousness, the agitator seems aware of this; he has a keener sense of history than those of his critics who think he can be banished from history by showing that he is inconsistent. He claims to be issuing the "most important challenge that could be made to a bankrupt, blood-drenched, war-torn, hate-filled. Satan-run world,"[2] and he predicts that "unreasonable force will hold sway"[3] if the present intolerable situation persists. This prediction, it must be granted, is not entirely fantastic, and it is precisely because the agitator does refer to pressing realities, because he does touch on the most exposed and painful sores of our social body that he is able to meet with a response.

The agitator's themes are distorted versions of genuine social problems. When he encourages disaffection from all current loyalties, he takes advantage of a contemporary tendency to doubt either the sufficiency of efficacy of Western values. When he takes advantage of the anxiety and fears of his listeners, he is playing on very real anxieties and fears; there is something to be anxious and fearful about. When he offers them a sense of belonging, no matter how counterfeit it is, and a sense of participation in a worthy cause, his words find response only because men today feel homeless and need a new belief in the possibility of social harmony and well-being. And when he calls upon them to depend on him, he capitalizes on both their revolt against the restraints of civilization and their longing for some new symbol of authority. That which they utter under their breaths, the sub rosa thoughts that they are hardly ready to acknowledge to themselves become the themes flaunted in agitation.

What the agitator does, then, is to activate the most primitive and immediate, the most inchoate and dispersed reactions of his followers to the general trends of contemporary society.

After he has subtly awakened his adherents to a realization that in some inexplicable way they are being crushed, the agitator diverts them from a true consciousness of their troubles and from any possible solution to their problems by the following "reasoning": The forces that threaten to crush them are irresistible, inexorable, and uncontrollable by rational means. To oppose them with the "bare bodkin" of ideals would be sheer folly, a kind of utopian quixotism. Therefore the best thing to do is to join them, to become one of the policemen, one of the destroyers in the service of destruction. This proposal is essentially tantamount to a suggestion that the adherents destroy themselves. Because the forces against you are so overwhelming, join with them . . . and be overwhelmed. Like a cheater in solitaire, the adherent is to become a conqueror by defeating himself.

To recognize and play upon those disturbing sicknesses of modern life that the run-of-the-mill politicians ignore, and then to divert his followers from any rational attempt to regain health—this is the essential objective role of the agitator in society. The basic implication of his appeals is that submission to social coercion is to be more ready and unquestioning. Hence the basic implications of the themes—the charismatic glorification of the leader, the extinction of civil liberties, the police state, the unleashing of terror against helpless minority groups. For all his emphasis on and expression of discontent, the agitator functions objectively to perpetuate the conditions that give rise to that discontent.

A Dictionary of Agitation

The themes cannot be understood in terms of their manifest content. They rather constitute a kind of secret psychological language. The unimpressed listener may wave it aside as a kind of mania or a mere tissue of lies and nonsense. Yet some people succumbed to it: in the United States a few, but in Europe millions. Were there no other evidence at hand, this one fact would be sufficient to establish the conclusion that there are powerful psychological magnets within agitation that draw groups of people to the leader's orbit. But we now also have at our disposal the classification of agitational themes that has appeared in these pages—our attempt to translate the secret code of agitation into language accessible to all. As we analyze this material, we find that its essential meaning—that which attracts the followers—cannot be reached by means of the usual methods of logical inquiry but that it is a psychological Morse code tapped out by the agitator and picked up by the followers. How conscious the agitator is of the genuine meaning of his message is a moot question that we have not attempted to answer here; it is a job for another investigation. But for the purpose of finding the inner meaning and the recurrent patterns of agitation, the presence or absence of consciousness on the part of the agitator is ultimately of secondary importance.

In any case, the distinction between the manifest and latent meaning of an agitational text must be seen as crucial. Taken at their face value, agitational texts seem merely as indulgence in futile furies about vague disturbances. Translated into their psychological equivalents, agitational texts are seen as consistent, meaningful, and significantly related to the social world.

In all his output the agitator engages in an essentially ambiguous activity. He never merely says; he always hints. His suggestions manage to slip through the nets of rational meaning, those nets that seem unable to contain so many contemporary utterances. To know what he is and what he says, we have to follow him into the underground of meaning, the unexpressed or half-expressed content of his hints, allusions, doubletalk.

Always, then, the agitator appeals to those elements of the contemporary malaise that involve a rejection of traditional Western values. As we have seen in the previous chapter, he directs all of his themes to one ultimate aim: his followers are to place all their faith in his person, a new, externalized, and brutal superego. Except through translation into their psychological referents, it is impossible to understand modern agitational themes.

If we strip the agitator's message of its mystical grandiloquence and rhetoric, and present it in a rationally formulated version, we are in a position to understand the role and the basis of appeal of agitation. Such a translation lays bare the objective social consequences of agitation and the potential relationship between leader and follower. It does not in itself destroy the appeal of agitation for the followers or give a blueprint for opposing the agitator politically. But it does at the very least expose the true social and psychological content of agitation—the essential prerequisite for its prophylaxis.

The Agitator Means

My friends, we live in a world of inequity and injustice. But whoever believes that this state of affairs will ever be or can ever be changed is a fool or a liar. Oppression and injustice, as war and famine, are eternal accompaniments of human life. The idealists who claim otherwise are merely fooling themselves—and worse still, are merely fooling you. To indulge in gestures of human brotherhood is merely bait for suckers, the kind of thing that will prevent you from getting the share of loot available to you today. Doesn't your own experience tell you that whenever you were idealistic you had to pay for it? Be practical. The world is an arena of a grim struggle for survival. You might as well get your share of the gravy.

Instead of joining with the oppressed and suffering with them, come with me. I offer you no promise of peace or security or happiness. I hold before you no chimera of individuality—whatever that word may mean. I scorn even the catchwords that I use when convenient.

If you follow me, you will ally yourself with force, with might and power—the weapons that ultimately decide all disagreements. We will offer you scapegoats—Jews, radicals, plutocrats, and other creatures conjured by our imagination. These you will be able to berate and eventually persecute. What difference will it make whether they are your real enemies so long as you can plunder them and vent your spleen on them?

Not utopia but a realistic struggle to grab the bone from the other dog—that is our program. Not peace but incessant struggle for survival; not abundance but the lion's share of scarcity. Can you realistically expect more?

To win this much you will have to follow me. We will form an iron-bound movement of terror. We will ally ourselves with the powerful in order to gain part of their privilege. We will be the policemen rather than the prisoners. And I will be the leader. I will think for you, I will tell you what to do and when to do it. I will act out your lives for you in my public role as leader. But I will also protect you. In the shadow of my venom you will find a home.

Notes

1.   Smith, New York, Oct. 20, 1938, meeting.
2.   CF, Feb., 1946, p. 702.
3.   SJ, Mar. 21, 1938, p. 10.

Appendix I

Samples of Profascist or Anti-Semitic Statements by the Agitators Quoted in This Study

As we mentioned in the preface, in selecting a given agitator as object of this study we have been guided by his professed sympathy for European totalitarianism or avowed anti-Semitism. Below is a complete list of the agitators whose written or oral texts have served as the basis of our interpretations. Each name is accompanied by a sample anti-Semitic statement and in some cases by a profascist statement.

Profascist Statements	**Anti-Semitic Statements**
Court Asher	
"In Germany reigns unity of will and effort. In this country reigns disunity, approaching chaos and civil war. . . . The Germans are a people with a leader. We are a people without a leader." (*X-Ray*, December 6, 1941, p. 3)	But how, I pray you, can any intelligent person condemn the actions of the Nazis against the Jews in Europe and endorse the colossal crimes of the Communist-Jew controlled Russia who murdered millions of Christians. The Nazis murdered Jews. Surely, killing kikes is no worse than killing Gentiles." (*X-Ray*, September 1, 1946)
Father Coughlin	
"The ordinary citizen has neither time nor means at his disposal to correlate these things.	"It is time for Americans to recognize that Washington, D.C. is being dominated by a Jewish concept of life and that our people are being regimented into a totalitarianism which is best described as a 'Jewish democracy.'" (*Social Justice*, July 28, 1941, p. 4)
"If he suspects that a secret alliance exists between the so-called democracies of the world—America, France, Great Britain and Russia—is he sure that they are democracies?	

Profascist Statements

"Is he informed that the so-called totalitarian states, against which this alliance has been established, have rebelled against the dictators of money, the controllers of gold?

"Or, is this a fabulous assertion?" (*Why Leave Our Own*, "Foreign Relations—In Three Acts," February 5, 1939, pp. 61–62)

Leon De Aryan

"Democracy is mob rule. Do you want mob rule? Do you want to bring it to all the world and supplant orderly governments?

"Hitler said he did not want it. Mussolini said he did not want it.... Now if we all agree we do not want it, please, tell me, what is this war about?" (*The Broom*, June 16, 1941, p. 1)

Elizabeth Dilling

"The Germans were the best-fed, best-housed, most powerful, pinkcheeked, united and hopeful people in Europe while we were being told they were starving and ready to revolt. But now that they are holding down half the world, they menace the *British* empire but are less of a menace to us than ever before .. ." (*Round Table Letter*, February 1942, p. 1)

Charles Bartlett Hudson

"'Hate-Hitler' *CAMPAIGN* being used to prepare us for another World War. . . . Why the constant raps at 'fascism,' and the condoning by silence or excuses, the activities and threat of Anti-Christ Communism?" (*America in Danger!* July 24, 1938, p. 1)

Joseph P. Kamp

Anti-Semitic Statements

"Now these Jews don't like it that there are Americans who are Americans and really believe in what the Bill of Rights stands for.... They consider themselves a privileged superrace who may persecute those of a different mind and religion." (*The Broom*, December 4, 1944, p. 2)

"Instead of living and letting Gentiles live, organized Jewry continues to browbeat and extort from Jews huge funds 'to fight anti-Semitism' which they use to persecute Gentiles, to hire armies of snoopers, commit every sort of illegal conspiracy, terrorize, bully and engender indignation and anti-Semitism." (*Patriotic Research Bureau*, December 1944, p. 13)

"How would you like to have the bloodstream of your baby, or son, or husband, or daughter, or wife, polluted by dried blood collected from Jews, Negroes, and criminals?" (*America in Danger!* February 3, 1942, p. 2)

"Despite the smears, persecutions and libels, impugning my loyalty and patriotism, that I have suffered and endured at its hands, I have, up to now,

Profascist Statements	Anti-Semitic Statements
	been reluctant to name the Jewish Gestapo, not in fear of the consequences, not because it would be used to falsely brand me an anti-Semite, but for the very simple reason that such a truthful identification might be misunderstood and might unjustly reflect on good Americans of the Jewish Faith who, if they could know the truth, would be the first to condemn the vicious activities of this Gestapo, which presumes to act in their name and in their alleged interest. . . . It will not be an easy job to investigate and expose the Jewish Gestapo and the Smear Bund and their campaign. But Congress can succeed if it fully realizes the magnitude of the task and the difficulties involved." (*Open Letter to Congress*, 1948, p. 12)

Joseph E. McWilliams, and lieutenants

"Whatever man has destroyed Communism and Internationalism, if it is Mussolini, I stand with him. If it is Hitler in Germany, I stand with him, and again, if it is Franco in Spain." (New York street corner speech, July 29, 1940)

"I am Joseph E. McWilliams, the anti-Jewish candidate for Congress from this district." (New York street corner speech, July 13, 1940)

(Corresponding quotations are available from McWilliams' lieutenants at that time, Louis Helmond, Thomas Maloney, James Stewart, and Charles White.)

Carl H. Mote

"Is Hitler's barter system so objectionable to the money changers that we are fighting a global war to destroy it? . . ." (quoted in *Propaganda Battlefront,* February 28, 1945, p. 2)

"The Jews . . . are unwilling to share the fate of their fellowmen but they are demanding special consideration as a 'minority', a 'stateless' class, a 'homeless' race, a helpless people, a 'persecuted' religion . . ." (*America Preferred,* February, 1945, p. 10)

William Dudley Pelley

"It is a fact which posterity will attest, that Chief Pelley of The Silvershirts was the first man in the United States to step out openly in support of Adolph Hitler and his German Nazi program." (*Liberation*, July 28, 1938)

"Every student of international affairs knows that the economic conflicts and wars are caused by Jews." (*Liberation,* November 14, 1939, p. 5)

Profascist Statements	Anti-Semitic Statements

George Allison Phelps

"If you get them to talk, you'll find that they virtually bristle with hate because their pride has been hurt by Adolph Hitler. They have a persecution complex and they want America to go to war so that they can have their revenge . . . one racial group which Hitler doesn't like and which has a persecution complex. The latter group wants war even if it costs the lives of 10 million Americans, as long as they can have their revenge." (Speech, local radio station, Los Angeles, October 20, 1940)

E. N. Sanctuary

"He testified that he was opposed to democracy (s.m.p. 367,370) and that 'democracy has never succeeded and never will.' He testified that he did not feel either Fascism or Nazism was a threat to our government (s.m.p. 697) and was unable to point to a single place in which he criticized either Nazism or Fascism in all his voluminous writings (s.m.p. 405). (Respondent's brief, *E. N. Sanctuary Against D. S. and T. O. Thackerey*, Appellate Division, First Judicial Department, Supreme Court, 1947, p. 8)

"Yet the Jew, who is a product of the Talmud, is a liability rather than an asset." (Letter reprinted in *The Defender*, April 1947, p. 22)

Gerald L. K. Smith

"Communism is mainly a Jewish plot. It was thought up by Jews, originated by Jews. Its revolutions have been promoted by Jews and they have even been financed by Jewish bankers. This does not mean that all Jews are Communists, but it does mean that no one can understand the Communist problem unless he understands the plot of the Jewish extremist and the international Jews. (*Newsletter*, October 1947, p. 2)

Profascist Statements

Gerald B. Winrod

"With the rise of Hitlerism a new consciousness has developed in Germany and the hopes of its 67 million people have been revived." (*The Revealer*, February 15, 1935)

Anti-Semitic Statements

"International Jews are making the same mistake in the United States that they have made in Europe and Asia—namely the abuse of power possessed through the secret systems of control which they have invented." (*The Defender*, March 1940, p. 3)

Appendix II

Bibliography of Printed Source Material

Court Asher (editor and publisher)	*The X-Ray.* Muncie, Indiana (Weekly)
Charles E. Coughlin (publisher)	*Social Justice.* Royal Oak, Michigan (Weekly)
Charles E. Coughlin	*Father Couglin's Radio Discourses.* 1931–1932, Royal Oak, Mich.
Charles E. Couglin	*Why Leave Our Own?* Thirteen Addresses on Christianity and Americanism. January 8–April 2, 1939.
Leon de Aryan (editor)	*The Broom.* San Diego, California (Weekly)
Elizabeth Dilling	*Round Table Letter.* (Monthly)
Elizabeth Dilling (director)	*Patriotic Research Bureau.* For the Defense of Christianity and Americanism, Chicago, Ill. (Monthly)
Charles Bartlett Hudson (editor and distributor)	*America in Danger.* Newcastle, Wyoming (Weekly)
Joseph P. Kamp	*How to Win the War . . . and Lose What We Are Fighting For.* 1942 (Pamphlet)
Joseph P. Kamp	*Native Nazi Purge Plot.* 1942 (Pamphlet)
Joseph P. Kamp	*Famine in America, Home Grown by the Farmers from Union Square.* 1943 (Pamphlet)
Joseph P. Kamp	*Vote CIO . . . and Get a Soviet America.* 1944 (Pamphlet)
Joseph P. Kamp	*With Lotions of Love.* 1944 (Pamphlet)
Joseph E. McWilliams	*The Servicemen's Reconstruction Plan.* Barrington, Ill., 1942.

Carl H. Mote (editor and publisher)	*America Preferred—A Journal of Opinion.* A Monthly Journal of Opinion on Politics, Government, Finance, History, Current Affairs, Education, Agriculture, Labor, Religion, Business and Taxation. Indianapolis, Indiana.
Carl H. Mote	*Testimony Before the U.S. Senate Committee on Military Affairs of the United States.* June 30, 1941 on S. 1579 "The Property Seizure Bill."
Carl H. Mote	Address Before the Meeting of "The American Charter." Cleveland, Ohio, July 1, 1942
William Dudley Pelley (editor)	*Liberation.* (Irregular)
William Dudley Pelley	*Pelley's Weekly.* Asheville, North Carolina (Weekly)
William Dudley Pelley	*Roll-Call.* Indianapolis, Indiana (Weekly)
William Dudley Pelley	*What You Should Know About The Pelley Publications.* (Prospectus)
William Dudley Pelley	*Official Despatch,* "Silver Shirts of America are Mobilizing to Protect Your Life" Silver Shirts of America, Asheville, N.C. (Pamphlet)
George Allison Phelps	*An Appeal to Americans.* (Pamphlet)
George Allison Phelps	*An American's History of Hollywood.* 1940 (Pamphlet)
E. N. Sanctuary	*The New Deal is Marxian Sabotage.* (Leaflet)
E. N. Sanctuary	*Litvinoff, Foreign Commissar of U.S.S.R.* 1935 (Pamphlet)
E. N. Sanctuary (translator and publisher)	*Tearing Away the Veils.* 1940 (Pamphlet)
Gerald L. K. Smith (editor and publisher)	*The Cross and The Flag.* St. Louis, Missouri (Monthly)
Gerald L. K. Smith	Printed radio speeches: *Which Way, America; Why is America Afraid?; Dictatorship Comes With War; Labor on the Cross; Americans! Stop. Look. Listen; Mice or Men?; The Next President of the U.S.,* Aug., 1939; *Enemies Within Our Gates,* Sept., 1939; *Stop Treason!,* 1939. *Reds On The Run,* Nov., 1939.

Gerald L. K. Smith	*The Hoop of Steel*; An American's Definition of Victory. Published by the Committee of One Million. Detroit, Mich., 1942.
Gerald L. K. Smith	*The Plan*, as Prepared by the Post-War Recovery Commission, 1945.
Gerald L. K. Smith	*Letters.* (Irregular)
Guy C. Stephens	*The Individualist.* Danville, Virginia (Monthly)
Gerald B. Winrod (editor)	*The Defender.* Wichita, Kansas (Monthly)
Gerald B. Winrod (editor)	*The Defender.* Wichita, Kansas (Monthly)
Gerald B. Winrod	Radio speeches on War and Peace 1939 (Pamphlet)

The text of the unpublished speeches quoted in this book were recorded either by skilled court stenographers or trained reporters.

Part II

Terror's Dehumanizing Effects

11

Atomization of Man

There is a widely held opinion that the fascist terror was just an ephemeral episode in modern history, now happily behind us. That opinion I cannot share. I believe that it is deeply rooted in the trends of modern civilization, and especially in the pattern of modern economy.

Indeed the reluctance to face squarely and explore fully the phenomena of terror and their implications is itself a lingering phenomenon of the terror.

Those who live with terror are under powerful compulsion not to speculate about it or to increase their knowledge of it. But this does not explain the remarkable reserve and resignation displayed in the face of totalitarian terror by the fact-loving Western world. The West shrank from the facts of the fascist terror, though they were available from reliable sources, until they were forced upon it in the unmasked horrors of Buchenwald, Oswiecim, Belsen, and Dachau. It shrinks today from the facts of the terror that is succeeding the end of the military war. The self-preserving numbness of the terror-ridden countries seems to be matched by a psychological mass repression, an unconscious flight from truth, in the countries where civilization survives.

Essentially, the modern system of terror amounts to the atomization of the individual. We shudder at the tortures inflicted on the physical bodies of men; we should not be less appalled by its menace to the spirit of man. Terror accomplishes its work of dehumanization through the total integration of the population into collectivities, and then depriving them of the psychological means of direct communication in spite of—rather because of—the tremendous communications apparatus to which they are exposed. The individual under terrorist conditions is never alone and always alone. He becomes numb and rigid not only in relation to his neighbor but also in relation to himself; fear robs him of the power of spontaneous emotional or mental reaction. Thinking becomes a stupid crime; it endangers his life. The inevitable consequence is that stupidity spreads as a contagious disease among the terrorized population. Human beings live in a state of stupor, in a moral coma.

Let us examine more closely the main phenomena of terror in action.

Directness and Omnipotence

One of the basic functions of terror is to wipe out the rational connection between government decisions and individual fate. The wholesale arrest of people during the first stages of totalitarian terror, the mixing in the concentration camps of the most diverse elements of the population for the most diverse reasons, fulfills precisely this function of elimination of individual differences and claims before the apparatus of power. The qualitative difference between the imprisoned lawbreaker and the rest of the population does not exist between the victims of terror within the concentration camps and those outside. The principle of selection of the forced workers of the camps is direct terroristic calculation. They are in the majority trapped in mass arrests, with no question of individual guilt involved and no hope of limited punishment.

That the concentration camps are far more representative of the population at large than is the traditional penal institution is made ominously clear by the fact that they are supervised not by a specialized body of civil servants but by units of that same secret police that oppresses the population at large.

This interruption of the causal relation between what a person does and what happens to him fulfills one of the chief aims of modern terror, namely:

The Breakdown of the Continuum of Experience

With the breakdown of legal rationality and its clear relation to the individual fate, this fate itself becomes so enigmatic as to lose all meaning. The individual does not know what he may experience: and what he has already experienced is no longer important for his person or his future. The normal rhythm of youth, manhood, old age, of education, career, success or failure, is completely disrupted. The creative faculties of fantasy, imaginations, memory become meaningless and tend to atrophy where they can no longer bring about any desired change in the individual's fate.

Of course this transformation of a human being from an individual whose essence is continuity of experience and memory into a unit of atomized reactions is carried further among the trapped victims than among the population at large. But the difference is only in degree, and if we cite only examples from reports from the detention camps, it must always be remembered that the population at large was aware of both mass arrests and the terror within the concentration camps. Thus the terror actually visited upon the bodies of Jews, "radicals," Poles, and others terrorized the minds of all, which was indeed its primary function.

The breakdown of memory and experience has been described by a German psychologist, Kurt Bondy, who was himself in a concentration camp for a time:

"This uncertainty about the duration of the imprisonment is probably what unnerves the men most. . . . They try to forget. The past becomes uncertain and nebulous, the picture of their family and friends indistinct. . . . Here are the roots of hopelessness, apathy, indifference, despair, distrust, and egocentricity."[1]

Thus life becomes a chain of expected, avoided, or materialized shocks, and thus the atomized experiences heighten the atomization of the individual. Paradoxically, in a terrorist society, in which everything is most carefully planned, the plan for the individual is to have no plan; to become and to remain a mere object, a bundle of conditioned reflexes that amply respond to a series of manipulated and calculated shocks.

The Breakdown to Personality

In a system that reduces life to a chain of disconnected reactions to shock, personal communication tends to lose all meaning. The superego—the agency of conscience—in which people have stored the mechanism of moral decency, is repressed by what I may call a Hitler-ego. meaning that the inhibitions produced by conscience yield to inhibitions or drives produced by mechanical reactions and imitations. Neither the terrorized nor the terrorist is any longer a personality in the traditional sense. They are mere material conforming to situations created by a power utterly independent of themselves. An underground report by a prisoner escaped from Oswiecim tells how the camp system "destroyed every social tie in a victim and reduced his spiritual life to a fear-driven desire to prolong existence, be it only for a day or an hour." And a keen observer with personal experience in two camps, Dr. Bruno Bettelheim, now [1945] with the University of Chicago, has studied this deterioration to its end in loss of the vital passions:

"This outside world which continued to live as if nothing had happened was in the minds of the new prisoners represented by those whom they used to know, namely: by their relatives and friends. But even this hatred was very subdued in the old prisoners. It seemed that, as much as they had forgotten to love their kin, they had lost the ability to hate them . . . they were unable to feel strongly about anybody."[2]

A similar shrinking of the personality to a cluster of conditioned reflexes has been observed among the guards. In his report. *A Year in Treblinka,* Yankel Wiernik describes the practitioners of terror as automata devoid of passion or remorse, who performed their given tasks as soon as some higher-up pressed a button. Bettelheim describes their dehumanization in these words:

"Having been educated in a world which rejected brutality, they felt uneasy about what they were doing. It seemed that they, too, had an emotional attitude toward their acts of brutality which might be described as a feeling of unreality. After having been guards in the camp for some time, they got accustomed to inhuman behavior, they became 'conditioned' to it; it then became part of their 'real' life."

And there is, above all, the corroborating evidence provided by these automata themselves in the trials currently being held in Germany. They admit the most atrocious crimes but show not the slightest sense of guilt. Their inhuman conduct was justified, they maintain, because it was ordered by their superiors.

The Struggle for Survival

The old system of culture, from abstract philosophical metaphysics to the institutions of religion and education, had the result of permeating mankind with the idea that only rational behavior that included respect for the rights, claims, and needs of others could guarantee one's own survival. Under terror such behavior may be equivalent to self-annihilation. Terrorism wipes out the causal relation between social conduct and survival, and confronts the individual with the naked force of nature— that is, of denatured nature—in the form of the all-powerful terrorist machine. What the terror aims to bring about, and enforces through its tortures, is that people shall come to act in harmony with the law of terror, namely, that their whole calculation shall have but one aim: self-perpetuation. The more people become ruthless seekers after their own survival, the more they become psychological pawns and puppets of a system that knows no other purpose than to keep itself in power.

Former inmates of Nazi detention camps confirm this regression to sheer Darwinism—or perhaps one should say infantilism:

> The urge of self-preservation, bestial fear, hunger and thirst led to a complete transformation of the majority of the prisoners. . . . In

many cases the sense of responsibility towards others disappeared entirely, as well as the least feeling of consideration of their common lot. Many a prisoner carried on a wild, ruthless, and thoroughly senseless struggle for his individual survival.[3]

Reduction to Natural Material

What the terrorist masters fear most is that their victims may recover their awareness of belonging to a whole, to human history. The complete victory of totalitarianism would be identical with the complete forgetting of history, that is, with a mankind become void of reflection, or in other words with a mankind solely become natural material. To quote Hitler:

> A violently active, dominating, intrepid, brutal youth—that is what I am after. Youth must be all those things. It must be indifferent to pain. There must be no weakness or tenderness in it. I want to see once more in its eyes the gleam of pride and independence of the beast of prey. . . . I intend to have an athletic youth—that is the first and chief thing. In this way I shall eradicate the thousands of years of human domestication. Then I shall have in front of me the pure and noble natural material. With that I can create the new order.[4]

Here, if we discard the flowery adjectives, is a classic admission of fascist aims and ends. Mankind, having become domesticated again, becomes part of the overabundance of nature. It thus becomes material indeed, for exploitation where needed and for annihilation where not—in any case, mere material to be *processed.* Modern terror always looks at people with the eyes either of the big monopolist surveying raw materials or of the undertaker anticipating the disposal of the useless human corpse.

This attitude is perfectly illustrated in reports describing the initiation of inmates in the Nazi concentration camps of Eastern Europe:

> At the one side we surrendered our baggage; at the other side we had to undress and to surrender our clothing and pieces of value. Naked then, we went into another barrack, where our heads and beards were shaved and disinfected with lysol. When we walked out of this barrack each of us was given a number. . . . With these numbers in our hands we were chased into a third barrack where the reception took place. This "reception" consisted in that our numbers were tattooed on the left breast. Then they proceeded to take the data of each person and brought us, divided in groups of hundreds, into a cellar, later into another barrack, where we were given striped prisoners' clothes and wooden shoes.[5]

There is a striking analogy between this treatment of human beings and that of merchandise shipped into the inventory rooms of a large department store or factory. It is a planful handling of materials for certain purposes. According to the witnesses, the system became so streamlined that only the really useful human merchandise was tagged. He who got no number was a reject; he was disposed of. And as in any oversized administrative unit, no one cared to take the blame for mistakes. Even if the merchandise had been rejected by mistake, it was destroyed:

> Since the prisoners were checked according to numbers and not according to their names, an error could easily be made which would be disastrous. If the "block-writer" had marked "dead" a number which in reality was still alive—a thing which can happen in these extreme cases of great mortality—the mistake was corrected by putting to death the holder of the number.

Wiernik describes the reduction of the human being into nothing more significant or valuable than a potential cadaver:

> It was a continuous coming and going, and death without end. I learned to look at every live person as a prospective corpse in the nearest future. I appraised him with my eyes and thought of his weight; who was going to carry him to his grave; how severe a beating would he get while doing it? It was terrible, but nonetheless true. Would you believe that a human being, living under such conditions, could at times smile and jest?

These are hard facts, and they justify one's saying that within the logic of terror, man has himself become a fact of raw nature. And death gains the rationality of putting surplus human material to use: "The Germans carried out mass round-ups of Jews in the city. They spared neither men, women, nor children. The adults they simply murdered, while the children were given away to the Hitler Jugend squads as shooting targets."[6]

Assimilation to the Terrorists

Terror reaches its peak of success when the victim loses his awareness of the gulf between himself and his tormentors. With the complete breakdown of the personality the most primitive historical force, imitation, becomes openly prevalent in the dehumanized atmosphere of totalitarianism. This ultimate stage in regression is described by Bettelheim:

> A prisoner had reached the final stage of adjustment to the camp situation when he had changed his personality so as to accept as his own the values of the Gestapo. . . .

> Old prisoners who seemed to have a tendency to identify themselves with the Gestapo did so not only in respect to aggressive behavior. They would try to arrogate to themselves old pieces of Gestapo uniforms. . . . This identification with their torturers went so far as copying their leisure-time activities. One of the games played by the guards was to find out who could stand to be hit longest without uttering a complaint. This game was copied by the old prisoners, as though they had not been hit often enough without needing to repeat this experience as a game.

> Other problems in which most old prisoners made their peace with the values of the Gestapo included the race problem, although race discrimination had been alien to their scheme of values before they were brought into the camp.[7]

Can one imagine a greater triumph for any system than this adoption of its values and behavior by its powerless victims? When we again recall that the difference between the effect of terror upon the population within and without the concentration camp is one of degree rather than kind, we have here an appalling index to the magnitude of the so-called problem of reeducation in Central Europe.

So much for the atomization of the individual. What are some of the social consequences of a regime of terror?

It is characteristic of a terrorist regime that its tools and practices increase in efficiency, quantity, and cruelty. Terror grows by what it feeds on—its excesses beget the need for ever greater terror. Under this increasing oppression the victims cease to anticipate an end of terror; they hope only for its alleviation.

Thus terror, by its own inner dynamics, perpetuates its sovereignty. Its victims lose the power to envisage a different order of life. They become absolutely dependent, materially and spiritually. They are receivers of doles, from such rewards as the "Strength through Joy" benefits all the way down to the spoiled food and contaminated water of the concentration camp.

This, I think, explains the behavior of a good many Germans toward the Allied armies. It is a continuity of frozen reactions. The aloofness of some and the abject toadying of others to the military powers are alike the result of their long alienation from genuinely experienced values and convictions.

Another result is the emergence of an infantile collectivity. Terrorist atomization has resulted in almost complete destruction of the old institutions of society. Most important, because the family was the basic unit of society, is the weakening of family ties. The complete dependence of parents on the whims of the terrorist hierarchy; the state policy of training children to inform on their parents; the regimentation of youth; the "social engineering" that shifts masses of people about with a little respect for family ties as in the worst phases of chattel slavery; the creation of millions of orphans through mass extermination of adults; all these are practices that the totalitarian governments have made horribly familiar. And all these practices inevitably and designedly disrupt family relationships and deprive the young of reliance upon the warmth and security of family life.

The result is an upsurge of a feeling of adolescent collectivity, rootless and ruthless, in which the concept of the family is supplanted by the image of a cynical, tough, destructive, joyfully cruel, and extremely resentful community, frighteningly reminiscent of Hitler's vision of brutally domesticated and therefore brutal natural material.

Finally, the pattern of terrorist oppression has had its influence on the behavior of liberated groups and individuals. Without moralizing about the legitimacy or appropriateness of revenge, it must be said that reprisals that betray a resort to the means of the totalitarian enemy have a deep significance for the tasks of peace. It has been truly said that the system of terror that Mussolini introduced into Western Europe enjoyed a sinister triumph in the orgy of vengeance over the dead bodies of the fascist dictator and his mistress. It triumphed when French girls were paraded with shaved heads before a vituperative populace in punishment for intimate relations with German soldiers. The "humane and orderly" transfer of Germans from liberated Poland was foreshadowed in the remark made to Jan Karski by a girl member of the Polish underground: "The moment the Germans are defeated a ruthless mass terror must be organized. The imported Germans must be expelled from the vicinity by the same methods by which they were settled here—by force and ruthless extermination."

What is there in modern civilization that has set this terror loose among us? I should like to venture this thesis: Mankind today has so tremendously improved its technology as to render itself largely superfluous. Modern machinery and methods of organization have made it possible for a relatively small minority of managers, technicians, and skilled workers to keep the whole industrial apparatus going. Society has reached the stage of potential mass unemployment; and mass employment is increasingly a manipulated product of the state and state-like powers that channelize surplus mankind into public works, including armies and official or semiofficial political organizations, in order to keep it at once alive and under control.

This is to say that large masses of workers have lost all creative relation to the productive process. They live in a social and economic vacuum. Their dilemma is the precondition of terror. It provides the totalitarian forces with a road to power and an object for its exercise. For them, terror is the institutionalized administration of large strata of mankind as surplus.

Certain cultural tendencies emerging from the crisis of the liberal era may be cited as contributing to the rise of terror.

Under the impact of mass production, people have learned to live in patterns, not only material but also spiritual. They tend to accept uncritically entire systems of opinions and attitudes, as if ideological tie-in sales were forced upon them. To be a progressive is *ipso facto* to be for democracy, for the New Deal, for the Negroes, for the Jews, for Soviet Russia, and many other things. To be an isolationist is, or was, to be *ipso facto* against Great Britain, against Soviet Russia, against the intellectuals, against the Jews, and many other things.

It is not so much that people believe in these configurations of stereotypes as that they themselves become stereotyped appendages of this or that big cultural or political monopoly. Reason, consistency, personal experience no longer matter. One might say, for example, that there are no true anti-Semites any more, because anti-Semitism is not so much a reaction to anything experienced as specifically Jewish as it is a behavior pattern tied in with adherence to a certain cultural ticket. And this shrinking of genuine experience makes it all the more difficult to counteract distorted and fallacious stereotypes. The cultural monopoly, integrating a whole chain of attitudes, itself exercises a psychologically terroristic impact to which the individual yields.

The fearful discrepancy between the moral traditions of individualism and the mass crimes of modern collectivism has left modern man in a moral no-man's land. He still holds to the moral concepts of middle-class society—conscience, decency, self-respect, the dignity of man—but the social foundations of these concepts are crumbling. The overwhelming scale of power, size, destruction, extermination in the modern world make individual moral scruples, problems and conflict seem puny and irrelevant.

To cite a drastic example, the ethical issue involved in *Hamlet*, which may be considered a classical document of morality after the dissolution of medieval culture, is the question whether or not a time "out of joint" can be righted if Hamlet becomes the judge and executioner of his father's murderer. In the face of present-day physical and moral catastrophe this issue is almost ridiculous.

The individual today realizes, more or less consciously, that his moral values do not greatly matter, because not much depends any more, either materially or spiritually, upon his decisions. He feels alone, deprived of the material and moral heritage that was the basis of his existence in liberal society. He is exposed to tremendous fury and aggression. He had become a potential paranoiac. In this condition he is ready to accept the most insane ideologies and patterns of domination and persecution.

The facists were the first to spot the connection between potential material poverty and real spiritual poverty, and to exploit it rationally and systematically on a mass scale. They realize that in order to subjugate and control the surplus population it was necessary to burn into people's minds the awareness of physical and spiritual menace, and to extirpate the whole frame of moral and emotional reference within which people had traditionally attempted to survive personal calamity. Hitler himself, in a conversation with Rauschning, once expressed the fascist need of terror and brutality. According to Rauschning:

> He had not the slightest liking for concentration camps and secret police and the like but these things were simply necessities from which there was no getting away. "Unless you are prepared to be pitiless, you will get nowhere.... Domination is never founded on humanity, but, regarded from the narrow civilian angle, on crime. Terrorism is absolutely indispensable in every case of the founding of a new power.... Even more important than terrorism is the systematic modification of the ideas and feelings of the masses. We have to control those."[8]

Hegel once said. "How fortunate the institution which has no history." Our age of terror is history, and one of its blackest chapters. But the dreams of freedom and happiness that terror would destroy are also part of history.

It is only by applying the efforts of reason—in its theory and practice—to the phenomena of terror, their roots and their consequences, that mankind can hope to wrest itself from the most sinister threat and ultimately pathetic fate in which it has ever become involved.

The dreams of Western civilization may still become reality if mankind can free itself from its use of human beings as surplus or commodities or means. Otherwise we too may face the terror.

Notes

1. Kurt Bondy, "Problems of Internment Camps," *Journal of Abnormal and Social Psychology* (1943).
2. Bruno Bettelheim, "Individual and Mass Behavior in Extreme Situations," *Journal of Abnormal and Social Psychology* (1943).
3. Bondy, "Problems of Internment Camps."
4. Hermann Rauschning. *Hitler Speaks* (1939).
5. *Die Judenausrottung in Polen. Augenzeugenberichte. Dritte Serie* (Geneva, 1944).
6. Quoted in *News Bulletin* (Representation of Polish Jewry, American Division, 1945).
7. Bettelheim, "Individual and Mass Behavior in Extreme Situations."
8. Rauschning, *Hitler Speaks.*

Part III

Images of Prejudice: Anti-Semitism Among U.S. Workers During World War II

Prefatory Note

The study "Images of Prejudice" is an integral part of the project carried out by the Institute of Social Research between 1944 and 1945, "Anti-Semitism Among American Labor." The results of this project conceived by Max Horkheimer and essentially carried out by Arkadij R. Gurland, Paul Massing, Friedrich Pollock, and Leo Lowenthal have—despite several attempts—never been made accessible to a broader public. This first comprehensive and systematic examination of anti-Semitism, carried out by the exiled Institute of Social Research, was realized with the financial and organizational support of the Jewish Labor Committee and aimed at ascertaining the extent and dissemination of anti-Semitic attitudes among U.S. workers during World War II. When finished in 1945, the project report consisted of six individual studies and covered more than 1,300 pages. Almost all of these individual studies are, in their methodological type, qualitative content analyses. They were supplemented by extensive statistical analyses and reports given by the interviewers on their experiences. Especially noteworthy is the technique by which the data were collected. This technique represents an ingenious version of participant observation. The research group proceeded from the theoretical assumption that anti-Semitic remarks could be studied soundly only if they were provoked by indirect stimuli; to this end, with the help of various Jewish and labor organizations, 270 workers were persuaded to be trained as interviewers. These worker-interviewers then interviewed their own fellow workers in the workplace on the basis of a given set of questions. Between 1945 and 1953 several attempts were made to bring this extensive research project, which thus far had not been editorially organized, into a publishable form, but a number of methodological, editorial, and also political considerations kept the project from completion. Leo Lowenthal's monograph is one part of the entire project and has been edited for this publication.

From Helmut Dubiel's afterword to the German edition.

189

12

The Parasite

In most of the statements of the material evaluated for this study Jews stand out as disconnected from society as a whole. They appear as a group on the outside of the social structure and yet they exploit this very structure for their own purposes. They do not appear as an autonomous group that could exist by itself and might have peaceful or hostile relations with the rest of society. They appear as a group holding onto and feeding on the organized social unit whose geographical contemporaries they happen to be. They are useless and unproductive while making use of something that neither belongs to them nor was created by them. They are parasites.

Money is seen as the sole social product to which a Jew has any relation at all. But he wants something for nothing; he wants money without having to work for it. The intermediary between acquisition of money and eschewing work is the intellect. Mental agility is the Jew's tool in the same manner in which natural organs serve a parasitical animal. Avoiding exertion, this Jew-animal manages to penetrate into the warm fiber of the social texture. In their critique of the lazy Jew, the workers seem to express a need for confirmation and reaffirmation of their own social function. Although they question neither the objective necessity of this function in the contemporary social setup nor the desirability of a change of their own social situation, they display, in this context, ambiguous attitudes toward the intellect ranging from cautious distrust to outright contempt.

Who and what is here the object of perception and criticism? Is it the Jew as he actually lives among others in society? Or does the Jew merely serve as a triggering mechanism for the release of strongly repressed feelings and emotions? The social psychologist continues to wonder what might prompt the attacks on laziness and the praise of perpetual hard work. Might this be an expression of the worker's own rebellion against the lot he cannot evade lest he lose his livelihood? Is the aggressive stance against intellectual pursuits not a sign of unconscious longing for the release of one's own intellectual abilities? The righteousness that marks all resentment of the Jew as parasite seems barely to mask the accumulated fury and hostility against the existing social order, whose enemies the Jews are branded. The term *Jew* seems to function as expression of the notion that something is basically wrong with the status quo. "Jew" is a perverted revolutionary concept, a perverted, critical, even nihilistic reaction to an existing social organization.

> "People say . . . they [the Jews] have all the money, they won't work, but are parasites."

And the logical conclusion:

> "They have ruined every country they went to."

> "They have been run out of every country except this one."

Biological Foundations

Some of the interviewees believe they have discovered that the affinity of Jews and money has its roots in a biological disposition. It is simply that "they are born that way, they inherit it." Or, in the words of another: "They have an inborn business sense." Generalizing and stereotyping appears justified when allegedly based upon facts. Once the Jew is stigmatized by the facsimile of an experience, release of hostility is possible in an atmosphere of good conscience. In a way the Jew is as helpless as his critic. He is the way he is, and consequently cannot help being antagonistic toward society. But this also gives society—in the eyes of the anti-Semite—a justified claim to self-defense.

Continuing on the road of generalization, the anti-Semite finds that money is the only focus of Jewish interests:

> "All Jews worry about their money."

> "People say that they are geniuses in business and that they have a stronger love of money than any other race."

> "The majority of them are just looking for all the money they can make out of the increased spending by the public."

> "Yes, doing their share [in the war effort] to pile up all the money they can."

> "They are piling up the dough. But wait until the boys come back. We'll fix them!"

"They don't do anything except make piles of money while people get killed."

The psychoanalytically trained observer will notice the connection between the amassing of money and the production and accumulation of dirt. Later we will have an opportunity to analyze more closely the meaning of dirt as an anti-Jewish stereotype. Suffice it to say that the last of the above quotations presents interest in money as beyond decency. Consciously, the speaker affirms this by accusing Jews of lacking patriotism, and unconsciously, by his use of anal language. He, in fact, leads the chorus of voices that colorfully describe the busy little things rushing everywhere to grab their spoils and hoard them in their abodes.

There is the engineer who, upon commenting on the "sallowish skin" of the Jews, hastens to refer to their "money-hoarding, money-grabbing manner." There is the cannery worker exclaiming: "money-grabbers"; the machine operator who knows "first of all, they are money-grabbers." There is the sententious dressmaker who has taken a firm stand: "I for one am against the Jews. They are grabbers, and have a mad desire to rule." There is the unskilled laborer who talks himself into saying: "They always are grabbing, grabbing, grabbing, and use any method to gain their end."

The stereotype of grabbing has a double meaning. It refers not only to the purpose of the action, i.e. the treasures hoarded, but also to the gesture itself, i.e. aggressively reaching for something forbidden. The Jew appears like an oversized pickpocket.

"All they want is to make money at the expense of others."

"They connive at the expense of others to promote their selfish interests at the cost of anyone but themselves."

"They are taught from birth that their one aim in life must be to take constant economic advantage of the gentile."

The cliché of the "money-grabber" is but one item on the long list of behavioral stereotypes for the Jewish predator. The interviewees use many expressions symbolizing violence:

"The Jew is a 'robber.'"

"They need Gentiles only to rob and make money for them and fight for them."

"Jews are robbers and cheats and the worst people in the world to do business with."

"The Jew is a killer."

"If you work for them they want your last ounce of blood."

"They would cut your throat for a nickel."

"They'd slit your throat for a nickel if they had a chance."

"A Jew would cut your throat for a dollar."

"The Jew is a 'brute.'"

"They push, they squeeze, they tie your money if they feel like it."

"Jewish businessmen try to squeeze the most from you."

"Sure, they're Jews. Money-grabbers. Always get the last ounce of work out of you. Squeeze you to the bones."

"A Jew will do anything to push himself ahead. He'll step on anybody."

These statements project onto the Jew features of violence characteristics of present-day society as a whole, and they show to what extent the image of the Jew stands for a blurred theoretical concept of social phenomena and their dynamics. Needless to add that not a single interviewee ever attempted to connect the alleged Jewish practice of cruel manipulation of financial dealings to their well-known gentile counterparts in the development of U.S. finance capitalism during the era of "rugged individualism."

A last statement may illustrate the anthropological concept of the money-minded Jew: "If you take the Jew's money away, you might as well kill him." This remark is not just a cynical aphorism; it betrays the dynamics inherent in anti-Semitism. If "the Jew" is the force that prevents an adequate distribution of social wealth; if the Jew as grabber and hoarder drains the life stream of money to still ponds whence it does not flow back to fertilize the national economy, then he does not deserve any consideration. The unconscious meaning of a sentence connecting killings, money, and Jews is clear. The unjustified wealth should be taken away; the Jews should be "taken away" as well. Behind the psuedoanthropology lurks the specter of a pogrom.

To Live by Fraud

While allowing for possible exceptions to the rule because "some of them are all right," the interviewee nonetheless generalizes: "Most of them have that cheater in 'em. They always want to take advantage of you. They're grabby." Or, in a true spirit of self-righteousness: "Jews are all crooks. Gentiles are on the level." One interviewee may come close to the psychological meaning of such statements when he says: "People never get rich by working hard; all rich people got rich by crookedness." Less privileged groups in society naturally want to find a key to the puzzle of a social inequality, and especially of economic success. And it is in this context that the notion of the Jewish cheat is repeated monotonously and obsessively.

The idiomatic wealth of expressions to characterize Jewish dishonesty is impressive.

"A Jew will do his best to 'take you' for everything you've got."

"They'll 'do you' every chance they get."

"They'll always try to screw you."

"They have no principles, will do anything for money."

Repressed inclinations on the part of the accusers may very well be the driving force behind these charges leveled against dubious methods of money acquisition. In modern society the temptation to commit property offenses is as strong as the defenses set up to prevent such offenses. The Jew may symbolize crimes that the accuser himself commits in the realm of fantasy.

A peculiar situation is likely to arise when a worker has dealings with a storekeeper. The merchant is in a completely individual relationship to his merchandise; he has neither produced nor transported it, and represents merely the money barrier that separates the consumer from the uses of these necessary goods—exchange value compared to use value. There is something quite uncanny about this social relationship. The consumer's relation to what he needs to buy is different from the transparent relationship between a machine, the raw material, a worker, and his wages. The merchant seems to be nothing but an unnecessary, that is to say, parasitical intermediary between the working man and his means of reproduction. For well-known historical reasons a large percentage of Jews own or manage or help to run and manage a large percentage of stores serving workers and the lower middle classes in general. There is a thin factual foundation for identifying the Jew as the retailer. He then is stereotyped at once as the useless profiteer who feeds on the worker's vital needs.

Just as the general characterizations of the money-hungry parasite are neither confirmed nor refuted by genuine experiences, so incidental experiences, when they actually occur, immediately acquire the significance of generalizations. It is not the individual Goldberg who has done something that is not right, it is "the Jew." His being Jewish turns his action into the paradigm for all actions of all Jews. Or, to quote an interviewee:

"I've been cheated by one and I'll always remember it."

How it works has been well observed by an interviewee, a mechanical engineer, whom the interviewer describes as "a definitely good Christian who lives according to the teachings of Christ and has helped several people financially and otherwise." He says:

"There is little difference between the actions of Jews and those of others. Some people dislike Jews because of a disagreeable experience in a business deal that they have heard about or have had themselves. It seems that they are more apt to remember such things when a Jew is involved but that they forget them soon when a non-Jew is the culprit."

The competitive character of modern society thus finds an expression in all-embracing charges leveled against specific competitive abilities ascribed to the Jews. In numerous statements the caution and attention required in all competitive situations are said to be insufficient in dealings with Jews. An attitude of utmost distrust is recommended over and over again:

"They are not to be trusted."

"They cannot be trusted."
"I'm more careful when buying at a Jewish store."

"Has to be watched very closely or he will cheat you, he can't be trusted."

There is hardly a sentence in our material that occurs as frequently as "You cannot trust Jews." This phrase may give some hints on the psychological state of many workers. On one hand, it seems to say that the majority deserve trust and confidence; on the other hand, it betrays unconscious fear that the general standard of morals may prove unreliable and deceiving. It seems as if people jump at each opportunity to find a scapegoat for the general state of apprehension and the general lack of belief. Modern society has menacing aspects, but the notion of general disorientation finds an outlet and is quickly neutralized when expressed as distrust of the Jews. In fact, people do feel uneasy, and they do complain. The complaints indicate a helpless longing for a genuine change of moral climate. Ultimately, here as on all other points, the workers' charges against the Jews are nothing but misguided and distorted answers to genuinely experienced difficulties and conflicts.

False Friends

Whatever the Jew does is wrong. By instinct he is money-minded, by inheritance he is a cheater. What about pleasant traits? Are there not Jews who are polite or friendly or decent? Certainty, but there is always an ulterior motive:

> "They are polite but too slick. This niceness is just so they can make their way and get advantage over you in an economic way."

> "I worked as a salesman in a store and when people came in the Jewish boss would try to cheat the Christian customer in a nice way."

> "They have no heart, no conscience, they are nice if they need one [a friend]."

One has to harden oneself so as not to fall prey to Jewish friendliness:

> "You see, you expect a Jew to be a certain way and if he turns out to be a swell guy, then you're still a little suspicious because you think he's putting something over on you. You've heard the expression 'He was a Jew but a nice guy.' There's always that 'but,' because you don't expect them to be nice."

> "They will tell you anything to make a sale but you can't help liking them. They get very friendly and sociable as soon as you meet them."

The classical case perhaps is that of an electrical worker:

> "I have a Jewish lawyer. He's a good fellow. If I go down to see him and he puts his hand on my pocket and finds I have no money, he puts his hand in my pocket and puts in $10. But I know why he's doing that: he's handling my case."

This last quotation sheds significant light on the whole problem. To do something for its own sake, to be generous, friendly, and polite just for the sake of generosity, friendliness, and politeness, has hardly any place in the purposeful setup of modern society. These forms of human behavior turn into mere routine and are traits useful in the realm of business, but stripped of their functional meaning they tend to become suspect.

Of course, this routinization of emotions is not without a price. People learn to refrain from actions of individual solidarity. The scope of their personal development is mutilated and narrowed. In a world that requires one to be hard and unfeeling, it is intolerable that certain individuals should resist the trend of general petrification of man. The Jew inevitably has to be perceived as calculating and his apparent friendliness as deceptive.

Manipulative Language

A theoretical digression may be permitted at this point. Cheating and friendliness have one thing in common. They need the medium of language to materialize. Anti-Jewish attitudes to a large extent seem to adhere to an ambiguous concept of the role of language in modern society; gentiles are depicted as possessed by a fanatic love of truth so that their moral sensitivity must be hurt all the time by the Jewish betrayal of the godly gift of language. In reality, what we observe is an utter distrust of language, for which we see the following reasons:

1. The technological positivism of our era is increasingly replacing the cultural pattern that characterized Occidental culture from its inception down to the liberal era. Machines speak, man becomes mute. Language is needed only to express mathematical formulas. We note that many of our interviewees' sweeping statements are couched in pseudostatistical language: "majority," "minority," "many," "most," "always," "all of them," "none of them," and the like.

2. Next to the realm of technology, language is experienced mainly in the area of mass communication: press, radio, advertisement, political speeches. The individual exposed to a barrage of language resents the big powers of linguistic manipulation. He projects his irritation with the media onto the "cheating and lying Jew."

3. In a highly organized bureaucratic society the attempt to achieve personal success through intellectual means has become subject to suspicion. Repressed fear may be involved. The world is full of manipulated statements or, plainly speaking, lies, and everybody knows it. These lies generate fury and rage on the part of those who are their targets. The targets in turn point to the Jew as "the liar" because they neither detect nor eradicate the real causes of universal falsehood. But they also indict him lest he become the one to proclaim the truth and thus jeopardize the entire framework of our peaceful existence; the image of the Jew still reflects the Judeo-Christian origins of our civilization. The Jew unconsciously might even be venerated for being the witness to this tradition.

Moral sublimity and moral depravity merge to form the stereotype of the Jew. He is the paradigm of the eternal liar as well as of the bearer of the messianic message. Psychoanalytically, the Jew is the object both of projection and of reaction formation. As the former he reflects the rigid, inflexible, passive, resigned nature of modern man; as the latter he is the embodiment of man's hidden longings for a thorough change.

4. Language today functions mostly as a conveyor of orders and instructions: mathematical formulas are commands, prescriptions for how to achieve a given end. The fixed order of the working day, and even of leisure time, implies numerous commands to do this and that. Language as a conveyor of choices has become obsolete and dubious.

The Junk Man

The parasite who gnaws at society's structure from without is attracted to society's refuse. The Jew has predilection for junk. One interviewee remarks that the Jew "will do things for money which most other people won't do." Others elaborate:

> "These people will take jobs that a self-respecting man won't have, gathering rags, garbage, junk, etc. The type of work is not important, but getting ahead is. The Aryan, so to speak, has a pride beneath which he won't stoop."

> "Look at the type of work they'll do. They will collect junk or garbage and make a good living out of it. Go around the alleys and gather this stuff and eventually work themselves up to a good business."

The ideals of artisanship and craftmanship of former centuries still are alive in the minds of workers. To a certain extent workers still are under the spell of a hierarchical concept of the dignity of craft. The notion of the Jew as junk dealer identifies the agent with the matter with which he deals. The Jews deal with junk—are they social junk themselves? He who handles humble matter deserves to be humiliated; this may be the ultimate meaning of the harsh judgment of the Jews' predilection for society's detritus.

Work Habits. There is a marked tendency to think of the area of the exchange of commodities as socially superfluous. Although there is a plethora of statements that Jews are interested only in commerce, no objections are uttered with regard to managerial functions.

Workers seem to identify strongly with the most recent economic trends and to include managerial functions into their own orbit, merging them into the comprehensive technocratic image. At the same time they are inclined to accept a concept of productivity that is limited to working with one's hands and disparages any other social function or occupation. We encounter this tendency again in the workers' attitude toward intellectual pursuits. The identification of business with the lack of productivity and Jews is illustrated in statements like the following:

> "Yes, they never produce anything. They never work. They make a living through business or just conniving. They size you up to tell you just which way they can cheat you."

> "They will not work with their hands but try to go in business or open a store to make large profit but as an average they are non-productive."

> "Jewish people are all in business. They won't work in factories like other people."

Such statements seem to stem from a puritanic spirit of devotion to work, but they defy the very essence of historical Puritanism, which glorified business as a productive function at the service of God and humankind. It seems as if the workers have forced upon themselves the idea that only physical exertion, sweat and bodily strain, is socially useful. This appears to be self-glorification grown from need and necessity.

The self-image of the worker as a productive member of society finds a peculiar expression in the glorification of manual work, or negatively, in the castigation of the Jews' assumed aversion to it. We have heard "the witness for the prosecution," to whom it is a "proven fact" that the Jew never works with his hands, or at least that he, the witness, never "has seen a Jew work with his hands." (The involuntary retraction from "proven fact" to lack of evidence testifies to some twinges of conscience.)

> "They act like they think they are too good to work with their hands. They think only of making money."

Some interviewees admit that Jews work hard, but this concession is ambiguous. When the Jew works hard, he does it for one reason only: to be lazy afterward. No mention is made of the Jewish peddler, grocer, junk dealer, small businessman, who, as a rule, works endless hours and wears himself out without a chance of escaping his mediocre social lot. It is a point worth stressing. If anti-Jewish sentiments were really and predominantly caused by actual observations and experiences, the image of the industrious, tireless, and tired small merchant would stand out in relief. Instead, the image of laziness prevails.

If the Jew is not in business, where he usually makes money without expending labor, he transforms his situation as a working man into a business situation; thus he remains the parasite he always tends to be. He forces his share of work onto others, and he is particularly apt to use his mouth as a substitute for his hands.

> "They're lazy and are always trying to put their share of the work on someone elase."

The Jewish worker lives at the expense of the gentile worker, just as the Jewish businessman lives at the expense of the gentile community. Manipulating language, the Jew lies himself out of work into remunerative laziness.

> "They'll pull strings to get ahead and get overfriendly with anyone in a superior position."

> "They'll lie like hell and tell the boss how good they are and then he advances them."

The self-righteous portrayal of class solidarity is produced artificially. Competition within the ranks of labor and even within the individual plant is not admitted but perceived as a peculiar Jewish trait; the Jew "talks" his way into success. This gives a truly ironic slant to the American value of social mobility. Contrary to all accepted precepts, the striving for advancement, the attempt to use opportunities for success, is branded as improper. Jewish success—real or imagined—is the object of envy because most people cannot avail themselves of the chance to escape the worker's condition once and for all.

The pride in exhaustion and exertion, then, appears to be the result of frustration rather than a primary psychological force. The self-proclaimed proletarian suspects the Jew of being able to overcome this frustration through intellectual effort, i.e. through tricks. He resents the intellectual superiority he ascribes to the Jew because he feels impotent in his present situation, which to change would require intellectual, i.e. conscious, political activity.

13

Intellect and Education

Education, whether during childhood or during adult life, whether institutionalized or not, whether enforced by rational persuasion or authoritarian pressure, has the function of socializing the individual into a pattern of collectivity that the prevailing social order requires. Jews, however, are perceived and represented as a group within this collective that disregards the rules and requirements necessary for the collective's successful functioning. They offer— and represent—resistance and disturbance. They are not, as it were, a particular society's contemporaries but, rather, are seen as disobeying its accepted pattern. They escape or elude the conformism required from the subjects of modern society. They breathe the spirit of anticollectivity.

The anti-Semitism of the workers has a materialistic substratum. They seem to distrust all forms of life that cannot be verified as material or biophysical phenomena. Their outlook is biased toward a structure of reality in which human organs and extrahuman matter form an indissoluble yet transparent unity. The image of the Jew, who does not take part in this process of amalgamation, therefore acquires the features of uncanniness and depravedness.

> "They have developed their brains and energies to offset their social handicap."

> "They have good brains . . . and they'll get ahead of anybody if you let them."

> "Jews won't work. They use their heads."

> "You would never see a Jew on the labor gang. They live by their wits."

> "People usually don't like them, probably because they are smarter than the average run of people. . . ."

> "They are always first to expound some new idea."

A metal worker believes:

> "The two groups who are most dangerous to our way of life are the intellectuals and the stupid negroes."

> Jews are *Luftmenschen* and live in the air and off the air, they dwell in the invisible vacuum of the mind, they are ghostlike.

Idolatry of Education

The idea that it is the intellect that facilitates a parasitical way of life finds concrete evidence in the realm of education. Education is not looked upon as a process of guided human development but as a process of securing the means for ensuring a parasitical existence. The alleged Jewish emphasis on education often is tied up with other stereotypes of Jewish behavior. A laundress, for instance, says:

> "A Jew worships three things: money, education and clothes."

Clothing as a symbol of financial success is a device to acquire more of it by sheer outer appearance, or both.

A machinist has it all figured out:

> "The average, or rather all Jews, aim for three things: money, a good education and a family. And it is hard to choose [which desire is stronger] between education and money."

A steelworker who is not hostile to Jews states:

> "The Jews act more dignified than any other group of people, because more Jews today are highly educated. They are taught from childhood the value of education and money."

A garment worker is convinced that

> "Jewish people on the whole have more money, are well educated and act superior."

And a textile worker has this to say about the Jewish yearning for better intellectual training:

> "They try to get an education so that they don't have to do hard work."

The critique does not aim at practically applicable skills nor at professional knowledge required for managerial functions in the industrial organization. It is directed at education achievements that enable the individual "to get something for nothing."

It may be assumed that the critical emphasis on the Jewish devotion to education also contains an element of projection. The worker feels that he lacks something that would give him access to the world and provide an opportunity for his participation in the administration of this society. It is not without reasons that educational slogans and educational activity are closely connected with workers' organizations.

When workers refer to education with annoyance and irritation, they may be unconsciously expressing a strong desire for knowledge and learning. They may even be echoing the idea that desirable social change depends on the right kind of education. Jewish education, however, is seen as an instrument used to consolidate and reaffirm the status quo in privileges. The educated Jew is an irritant because he points to the possibility of improving conditions through intellectual analysis, i.e. education. The Jew is often perceived as if he were a member of a conspiracy to perpetuate by intellectual means the exploitation of non-Jews. An interviewee says:

> "Every Jewboy gets his three chances to make good. When any Jewish boy comes of age he is helped by rich Jews to go to school and to get into business. Only the inveterate failures are given up."

The Jewish family is alleged to do anything to save its children the trouble of actual work; therefore Jews emphasize and support education. Jews, according to the interviewee quoted above, "are taught from childhood the value of education and money. Jewish parents will make great sacrifices to educate their children." In the workers' image of the Jew the private and public spheres are closely linked. The family appears as the headquarters where the strategy of conquest is mapped out. This is an important aspect both with regard to a common stereotypical perception of Jews as well as a psychological explanation of persecution. In a psychological sense everything Jewish constitutes part of a totality; not even the most private area of Jewish life escapes stigmatization. Every aspect of Jewish existence becomes part of the ambivalent "enemy" image. People are thus conditioned to accept discriminatory action against Jews, their private life as well as their public functions. Although the whole pattern of the democratic way of life puts the greatest emphasis on the separation between the individual's privacy, which should be exempt, and his public functions, which have to fit in with the needs and demands of the community, the Jew is denied this private sphere. To put it differently: the critics of the Jew do not perceive him as standing in the democratic tradition but, rather, outside it. And as an outsider he is an outcast.

Jews, according to the stereotyped minds of our interviewees, have no problem children. Jewish children supposedly catch on to their parents' ideas of the value of education for the sinister ways of Jewish life. It is with fury that one man says: "They are trying to be the brightest kids in school. Have no right to. . . . "Jewish children are no children at all; they are intellectual robots.

> "They won't go into sports but instead will go home and study."

> "Jews are so ambitious. They go to any length to attain their goal. I mean beyond what a non-Jew would. If they are studying for an exam, for instance, they would study all night for days before, just to come out on top. A non-Jew will study and then decide there are other things in life more important."

> "They were the smartest ones in the class. They took advantage of everything that was free in education."

> "The Jewish boys and girls were not different than any other boys and girls, except they continued at school where they finally graduated from high school or college. I was forced to go to work at an early age and was deprived of greater power later on in life."

The emerging image is not that of a child but of a diminutive Jewish adult. At times, however, this stereotype is attenuated by genuine memories, and indeed some interviews are recorded that distinguish between young and adult Jews. Of all reported childhood experiences with Jewish children, more than half left a favorable imprint on the interviewees' minds; only a third of childhood experiences pertaining to Jewish adults were favorable. A few examples might illustrate this: A laborer who does not care "if they slice all Jews in two" and "some friends who are Jewish but they're just kids, American kids." The black cook to whom the Jews are "dirty all around, sexually and all," "went to school with Jewish kids. They were okay. A couple of them were pretty smart." The secretary who relays many unfriendly remarks that other people make about Jews, admits that she "knew Jews both at school and in her hometown" and that "they were very nice, just like the rest of the people."

Actual experience often is confined to young Jews with whom the workers came in contact in school. The anti-Semite who did not have unpleasant experiences with them, is likely to say that young Jews are just as American as other kids. As far as older Jews are concerned, in most cases no actual personal contact—or at best an occasional one—took place. The anti-Semite is very likely to extend to them the cliché of prejudice he has formed in later years.

The Professions

Of the prospects for easy living that Jews are said to secure through acquiring intellectual skills, the professions seem to offer especially favorable chances. Many interviewees claim that Jews monopolize the legal and medical professions. Jews are charged with using their hold on these professions as another means of getting ahead through intellectual manipulation. Considering their workers' view point, this assessment makes sense with regard to lawyers. The lawyer is viewed as one who knows how to make money out of his specialized knowledge of tricky rules and procedures; no one would have to pay him, if legal matters were not as complicated and impenetrable. The lawyer's work appears as socially unnecessary. This is what two of our interviewees, who both work in the same plant, indicate in their remarks:

> "They live by their wits. . . . Back home they have their little wagon with a bell on it and before long they own a whole damn store. They make good lawyers—a little Jew he can talk his way out of anything."

> "It's like a friend of mine told me: first the Jews were rag pickers, they they had their wagon, and now they're all doctors and lawyers."

Just as the Jewish merchant as middleman is suspect because he constitutes an unnecessary obstacle between productive work in the plant and reproduction of soul and body in the realm of consumption, so the lawyer's role as middleman is viewed with distrust. He keeps himself alive by intellectual means—a result of educational achievement. Whether a Jew makes money through business or through professional routine does not make much of a difference to the anti-Semite. "A Jew will beat you out of your money. . . . Jews are smart. The courthouse is full of Jewish lawyers and judges."

The physician, for reasons not easily explained, is also dragged into the same complex of charges. They may have to do with the lack of medical insurance [in the 1940s], which means that the worker in many cases incurs medical debts he can hardly meet. The physician is resented as a symbol of interruptions and disturbances in gainful employment. The worker in need of a physician stands to lose money in the factory as well as in the doctor's office. Jewish doctors are wedged into the pattern of the obnoxious parasite who has nothing in mind but to extract money and avoid work. No attempt is made to support the charge by reference to genuine experience. The stereotype takes care of everything.

> "They always try to get in a position to have other people work for them. They try to get into the professions like a doctor or a lawyer, so they don't have to do any dirty work. They don't like to work much. A Jew will beat you out of a dollar any time."

The derogatory remarks about Jewish physicians are not without irony. It is the physician function to free the body from alien matter, e.g. parasitelike bacteria and similar causes of ailment. The image of the Jewish physician as a blood sucker intent on using cutthroat methods strikingly expresses feelings of fear that underlie anti-Jewishness. The healer is exposed as the killer.

14

Manners and Mores

The Jew is not only rejected as a parasite but also denounced as a social outsider. As a parasite, he comes from the outside, attacking the solid structure of the societal order. As the unadjusted contemporary of this order he seems to be a source of trouble and disruption from within the community.

Many of the attacks on the Jews aim at their failure to adjust to community patterns and at their violations of established conventions of social order and private life. Charges of this nature are considerably more concrete than the furious generalizations based on the Jews' alleged social uselessness. Although the charges, too, are often generalizations of notions not founded on anything factual, they have more basis in fact and are thus more harmless than the paranoid image of the parasite.

The accusation of nonconventional behavior probably to a very high degree means what it says. With regard to behavior patterns, workers consider themselves a well-adjusted subgroup of society at large, with which they share essential standards and norms; there are, of course, standards and norms on which all groups agree—regardless of differences in social status. Jews allegedly do not fit into this pattern and are under attack for their lack of social conformity.

People are generally cooperative, but Jews are "aggressive." People usually follow an established pattern of advancement, but Jews are "upstarts" and disregard the conventions of climbing the social ladder. People generally behave modestly, but Jews act "superior" and are "arrogant." People tend to interact and associate freely with each other, both socially and professionally, but Jews tend to keep "clannishly" to themselves.

In psychological terms, the accusation of anticollectivity is yet another projection of the workers' repressed disappointment over the lack of genuine collectivity in contemporary society. Jews disturb the smooth functioning of social (and perhaps also private) life. The accusation against Jews that they lack solidarity and act against the needs and interests of a genuine social harmony brings out genuine social needs and awakens a longing for a life of interdependence and mutual cooperation. Workers express this yearning for a harmonious society through their attack on a socially highly diffuse group as the fictitious main cause and agent of social and economic inequality.

The images of the parasite and of anticollectivity merge into a contradictory pseudoimage of the Jews as a ruling class. They are both lazy and industrious, passively profiteering and actively exploiting. As parasites, they are a leisure class; as enemies, of the community they are reckless activists. In short, on all anti-Jewish fronts, the workers transform the Jews into a substitute for attacks on social domination.

Aggressiveness

The contention that Jews are aggressive and pushy permeates all our material. It frequently takes the form of an ascribed personality trait or a characteristic of physical behavior. In both versions it implies that the Jews have a tendency to acquire a status—economically, socially or publicly—that they do not deserve or that does not behoove them. The idiomatic formula "They should be put in their place" implies the accusation. As a group, they seem unaware that the frontiers of conquest no longer exist. The aggressive Jew seems to represent the eternal immigrant.

The Jew is portrayed as a modern version of the pioneer storming across the wide plains with his wagons and horses. The plains, however, have been replaced by the narrow confines of modern settlements, and the wagons and horses by the bodies of hurried subway riders. U.S. gentiles take the place of Indians—more or less defenseless against the ruthless omnipresence and ubiquity of would-be conquerers. Aggressiveness in the mere abstract sense is linked to forms of behavior perceived as typical for the ruthless, "pushy" Jew:

> "Yes, by religion and nature they are different: more aggressive, more ambitious, more determined."

> "Jews are usually more aggressive."

> "They are too aggressive, pushing themselves to the front, exhibitionists."

Jewish "aggressors" do not respect the pattern of order and restraint based on physical conditions:

> "They try to run over other people and think that other people should get out of their way when they are walking on the street."

"In New York they always walk across the street five in a row."

"They are all alike. They have one way that will make them known, and that is their lack of courtesy. A Jew will pass by you and almost knock you down and never apologize. They are so greedy and grasping."

And the list of examples to support this last allegation is long: In means of public transportation:

"And then in the subway and in the street they push and look around like crazy people, desperately looking for a place. And any place you go, if there is a line they just don't want to get in the line."

In restaurants and stores:

"If you go to a restaurant, they run to the table ahead of you. Shopping it's the same way."

"In the coffee shop they try to get to the head of the line of people waiting to walk in past everyone and grab a booth."

"Especially the way they push and shove in ahead of you in the market and in the stores. Only yesterday a big fat sloppy kike dame stepped all over me trying to get in ahead of me at the market."

The accusation of aggressiveness could be seen as a paradigmatic projection of the aggressiveness of the anti-Semite himself. The charge here is leveled at a competitor who is sized up as weak, and who therefore ought not to display attitudes reserved for the really powerful at the top. Jewish aggressiveness masks Jewish weakness. With the attenuation of Jewish economic influence at the end of the liberalist period, the anti-Jewish gentiles become aggressive themselves. They succumb to the ideology of a secluded "in-group." Rationalizing their desire to keep the competitor out, they find fault with his character and label him the intruder. The Jew who, on the one hand, is portrayed as aggressively demanding, is now exposed as begging for recognition and acceptance. Because, however, his request will be denied, this very desire for recognition has to be stigmatized first, and the psychological mechanism can operate all the more swiftly because the request in itself exposes the petitioner's weakness.

The Eternal Egoist

Jewish aggressiveness is also interpreted, by the anti-Semite, as an expression of extreme egoism. Here we encounter a perfect application of the just-described mechanism: people stigmatize their own repressed drives by calling them Jewish. Egoistic, egocentric, and monadic consideration of one's own interests is an original sin against the spirit of Christian ethics. Egoism, however, is also the foundation of bourgeois society. In the realm of economic behavior, cooperation and consideration are necessary by-products of egoistic needs rather than the prime motivation for actions and decisions. This is certainly a truism, but it powerfully promotes self-affirmation and self-glorification while debasing "the other fellow" who deviates from the ways of neighborly love.

Psychologically, the egoism of the Jews functions not only to exemplify man's moral conflict of self-interest and mutual respect but to make the Jews scapegoats for this conflict while exempting the non-Jew from facing it. In the realm of the unconscious, the attack on the egoistic, aggressive Jew is a crooked deal with religious commandments. This becomes clear when we take a closer look at statements that are visibly devoid of any justification in genuine experience:

> "A Jew may be recognized by his attitude toward his fellowmen and that he is primarily interested in himself."

> "They think only of themselves and what is in it for them."

The correlations of egoism and Jews, neighborly love and gentiles, are matched against each other. Pogrom looms on the horizon:

> "Jews haven't any use for us. . . . Why in hell should we love them? Jews are the cause of all evils, why not wipe them out?"

Part of this image of selfishness is yet another element at the basis of Jewish-gentile relationships:

> "They are always trying to push ahead of people, seeming to expect social favors. . . .When seated, they want all sorts of extra favors from the waitresses."

Comments on the special treatment Jews expect and the special favors they demand are frequent. They have a basis in reality, albeit a paradoxical one. The Jews, who never achieved the status of complete equality with others, were always compelled to ask for special consideration when they wanted to obtain what others enjoyed by birthright. It has indeed left a deep characterological impression on them, eagerly seized upon by anti-Semites, who denounce such "Jewish" character traits and, declaring themselves defenders of the equality of man, mount a campaign against the Jewish "privilege seeker." He who was not granted his share is branded as a shameless and arrogant applicant for special privileges and dispensation.

The underlying significance of aggression and egoism is conceived as wish for all-out domination: when the workers speak of these Jewish aspirations for domination they do so in collective terms. It is not this or that individual who aspires to power, but a whole group, "the" Jews. This is yet another version of the Jews as a substitute image for the ruling classes. In their daily life the workers face one or several individuals, the bosses and managers, as agents and members of the ruling social group. Corresponding to the bourgeois work and performance ethic, they represent for the workers what they would like to attain for themselves. Aggression and egoism on the part of those who hold such power positions, are usually perceived as the result of successful adjustment to the conditions of modern life. The Jews, however, do not fit into this picture, they are seen as usurpers of position of influence and power to which they are not entitled.

> "It appears to me that the Jewish race is out to control our country."

> "The majority of people think something should be done quickly or they'll rule this country."

> "They want to run the whole damn show."

From the notion of the Jewish attempt to dominate, it is but a small step to the notion that this attempt has been successful. Anti-Semitism demonstrates the mechanism of obsession. Fear of potential dangers turns into a hallucination wherein the potential danger has already materialized to the extent of a universal scourge. An interviewee who transposes his dread of future events into the contention that what he apprehends has already happened, says:

> "Their chief difference from other people is their desire to dominate . . . they are always dominating everywhere in everything."

And references to Jewish domination in different areas of life manifest this obsessive notion throughout:

> "If you let them go they'd have the upper hand. They're running the world now. They've got the money, ain't they?"

"They are dominating. . . . Everything is controlled by Jews . . . and Gentiles are compelled to abide by their rules and customs. . . ."

"They run this country, also are responsible for the war."

"Jews control the banking system, make profits from war."

Some remarks on the recurring phrases, such as "many people claim," "people say," and the like, are pertinent here. Over and over again interviewees have gladly jumped at the opportunity for such phrases offered by our questions. There is no doubt that in many instances people have used such phrases to rationalize feelings of their own. First, this is a form of evading individual responsibility for anti-Semitic attitudes, which some still regard as not respectable. Second, the individual justifies his prejudice by referring to a collective strength behind it and thus enjoys the conformity with general opinion.

The function of phrases like "people say" is particularly noteworthy with regard to violence, which is taboo but which may be looked upon differently as soon as it has acquired social approval. In most cases, it is safe to assume that the one who says, "People say" or "A friend said," is himself the anti-Semite.

The Upstart

The Jews violate the pattern of social adjustment by forcefully overcoming class barriers. They are regarded as people who in fact belong to the nonprivileged or underprivileged social groups but go out of their way to gain privileges, which earns them the label "upstart."

Interviewees displayed a contradictory and ambivalent attitude toward success. They equally adore and resent it. Consciously or unconsciously they have learned to become reconciled in principle to the differences and differentiations of social status, but when the Jews prove successful, they indict them. They are not granted the right to participate in the formulation of social commands, which is institutionalized and vested in the gentile management of society. They disturb the social compromise reached between the upper and lower strata. In the eyes of the anti-Semite, this disturbance is brought to the fore by the Jews' display of unjustly acquired power made apparent in their conspicuous consumption.

The accusations against the Jewish upstart reflect the need for an indictment of social injustice as well as the need to ignore is so as not to be constantly reminded of the desirability of change. Although the status quo can tolerate social adjustments, it must reject any notions of a fundamental transformation.

Wealth to the underprivileged is an irritant. Once the Jews are endowed with its symbols, the objective disturbance becomes a concrete and visible target of resentment and aggressions. The alleged malefactor is dragged out of his hiding place and exposed to public scrutiny. It is then that the diamonds that the Jews have retrieved from society's refuse are made to sparkle in the beam of manipulated vilification.

Jews are said to make tremendous efforts to climb the social ladder so as to escape the lot of the lower classes and establish a position of power. The upstarts, using any device to get ahead, is hard even against themselves:

> "They work hard, particularly when they are down."

> "They would do anything to get ahead of others."

They rise from ragpicker to doctor and lawyer. They are not reconciled to staying at the bottom. Are the workers? One may venture to say that their reconciliation with the present stage of social development, which practically precludes spectacular individual success on a large scale, is nourished by the belief that barriers of social status can be overcome only through a scavenger's shady and sinister devotion to junk and refuse. "Yes, they all had dirty characters," says the interviewee who blames the Jews for "pushing themselves ahead."

Some of the interviewees not only accept the social stratification by which Jews do not seem to abide but also adhere to the notion that social power and culture belong together. Jews appear to them as gate crashers invading the noble and stately mansions of those whom power entitles to refinement. The Jews are nouveaux-riches, and it is the element of novelty in their affluence for which they are indicted. That they are unworthy of success becomes evident through their inability to play by the rules of the game by which the legitimate upper class has played for generations. The gentile members of the upper classes react allergically to the newcomers and do not admit them to the "club."

People who live by the cultural standards of the upper class and want to emulate it, concur. We will find them among members of the lower middle class, white-collar workers, would-be upstarts themselves. A building superintendent says:

> "They are what I call the 'graduates from Grand Street', the ones that come very poor and move up to the Bronx when they have more."

A female cartoon painter in a Hollywood studio seconds:

> "It is also evident that they scrimp and live in extreme poverty for years—only to become extremely offensive to their neighbors when they have saved enough to be independent."

A laboratory technician relates an experience with a Jewish salesman:

> "He would pull his watch out of his pocket and tell me how much he paid for it. He would tell me how expensive his suit was or his shoes; even the handkerchief he blew his nose with he'd have to tell me how expensive it was."

A telephone operator gives the key to the interpretation of the Jew as alleged show-off. She thinks that "Jews often wish to shine because they feel sentiments against them and they have developed their brains and energies to offset their social handicap."

Jews apparently identify with the upper class. Their display of luxury is an attempt to demand the recognition and respect due them as legitimate practitioners of the capitalist system. This is an actual economic phenomenon. Although constantly threatened and ultimately unable to exercise social control, many Jews in business tend to conform to the established capitalist pattern of ruthless competition and thus can be rightly seen as merciless exploiters. This particular aspect of the phenomenon, although based in reality, nevertheless does not constitute the entire picture. The accusation of Jewish arrogance and ostentatiousness at the same time constitutes a projection of the envy of precisely those qualities that seem to make success possible and that the average worker does not seem to possess. Yet this allegedly typically "Jewish" arrogance is very much part of the mentality of the workers as it is of most members of modern society.

The workers' tendency to identify with bourgeois values, is the very cause for their resentment of Jewish manifestations of bourgeois attributes and attitudes. Their condemnation of this so-called "Jewish" behavior betrays their unconscious desire to affect precisely the same behavior. Furthermore, they sense that Jews are not really as successful in their identification with the upper social class. They sense that something is askew in the portrayal of Jews as rulers of society. As victims of anti-Semitic stereotypes, the workers always find new material in evidence of Jewish arrogance and superiority; through personal experience they know, however, that Jews may at times display sentiments of

216

inferiority and inadequacy. In the style of true Adlerians they declare a show of arrogance compensatory for actual feelings of inferiority:

> "They have an inferiority complex and so tend to want to out-do a Gentile."

> "Jewish people are often loud and tend to show off. If they have money, they obviously make a display of it. They often have an inferiority complex. They expect people not to accept them."

> "They have a chip on their shoulders and expect people to slight them."

> "They feel as though they are being picked on: that anything that is being done to them or that happens to them is because they are Jews."

> "Only for some funny reason they always tell you the minute they meet you: 'You know, I am Jewish', as if they expect to be hit in the face now or something."

> "They are more easily hurt. I knew a Jewish boy who quit his job because I told him just in fun to go to hell."

The last quotation bespeaks a certain insight into the deepest layer of the social dynamics between Jews and Jew-haters: they are afraid of each other. Both distrust the existing social order of which both are victims.

> "They are always in a hurry and always frightened someone will be somewhere before them."

15

The Clan

Jews are viewed as enemies of the collective. At the same time they are seen as the most solid form of a collective themselves. Numerous statements describe different areas of Jewish existence as manifestations of utmost coherence. In their economic activity, in their private life, as a race and as a religion, they comprise many self-sustaining, autarchic, exclusive units that are clannishly self-centered and that do not take any interest in other non-Jewish groups or individuals—and that even resist them.

Here again we observe a projection mechanism. Jews are accused of clannishness while the gentiles are the dominating in-group, the de facto clan. Because this clan does not accept Jews at all or only reluctantly, the out-group is being called an in-group, thus releasing the in-group from admitting the out-group into its community. The charge of clannishness betrays a bit of envy and longing on the part of the workers. The Jews are experienced as a model community permeated with the spirit of warmth, closeness, mutual support and identification, and genuine solidarity, adding up to the image of the utopian community. Although not openly expressed in workers' comments on Jewish clan life, that clan life seems to symbolize the redemption of frustration and hopes the workers experience in their daily lives and in their social destiny. The workers do not articulate it, but their attitudes toward Jewish clannishness clearly express their unconscious desires. This circumstance drastically demonstrates how utterly distorted, how falsified—socially and psychologically—a part the Jews are made to play in the workers' imagination. Jews are portrayed as responsible and trustworthy members of a giant partnership wherein everyone looks out for the interests of others. They do not compete among themselves; they act like brothers. But this utopian concept of Jewish solidarity is contrasted with the concept of a racket. They stand for one another's interests yet are ruthless in their actions outside the group. Helping one another, then, means refusing assistance to the out-group, or even exploiting it for the purposes of the Jewish in-group.

Once more the Jews are interpreted as a social class with commonly shared clear consciousness; they are aware of their interests and of the most effective means for their furtherance. In projective terms, the Jews are conceived as a group that has succeeded in attaining common goals in a hostile world of conflicting interests.

The Jews have made clear by their actions what their needs and wishes are. They seem to know how to deal with diverging needs and wishes when they encounter them. Either they demonstrate indifference toward non-Jews:

> "They have no respect for other people but are fanatically loyal to other Jews."

> "They live only to help one another and try not to help anyone else."

or they are outright hostile exploiters:

> "They think only of themselves and their own kind. They need Gentiles only to rob and make money for them."

> "Very clannish, help each other but knife Gentiles."

> "They will try to help one another to the detriment of any and all else. Gentiles are only to be used."

An electrical worker justifies his general statement "they were a bunch of swindlers" by giving an "illustration":

> "I was waiting outside of a liquor store—Jew store. A Christian walks in and tries to buy liquor. No go. The Jew refuses to sell him even the cheapest brand. Said he didn't have any on hand. Then later a Jew walks in. Walks over to the counter, picks himself a bottle of Calvert and J.P. Jones, and buys it. See, that's what I mean: they won't share anything."

In this anecdote the stereotype of Jewish clannishness reaches almost grotesque proportions. Not only is it alleged that a Jew will be immediately able to discern Jews from non-Jews—Jews are even able to perceive objects that remain hidden to a gentile eye. This is, of course, only a single instance, but it helps to highlight the element of uncanniness that is so characteristic of anti-Jewish imagery.

No mention is ever made of the fact that it was discrimination by non-Jews against Jews that originally prevented the social mixing of

Jews and non-Jews. On the contrary: bitter commentaries about the exclusivity of Jewish groups abound. One of the most blatant acts of discrimination against Jews, their exclusion from certain resort areas, is blamed on the Jews themselves:

> "No matter what resort you go to, Saratoga, Florida, Lakewood, they are all Jewish. Only a short time ago there were hardly any Jewish families there, but a few got in . . . and now there are none but Jews there. They don't want to mix with others."

That just the opposite is true does not matter. It does not occur to the critics that "the others" may have moved out because the Jews moved in. Quite otherwise, segregation of Jews is explained as a reaction to Jewish behavior:

> "They don't like the Gentiles much; otherwise they wouldn't stick together so much."

> "They are only interested in themselves and other Jews. People avoid them because they tend to keep apart anyway."

A connection is construed between the Jews' public and business activities and their private life, their alleged social aloofness and segregation evokes suspicion and distrust. It is assumed that such attitudes follow from the clan's determination to use the realm of private life for the preparation of public actions. The atmosphere of aversion and apprehension becomes more noticeable when endogamic tendencies ascribed to Jews are reported. Jewish family life is seen as representing numerous subdivisions of the big, all-embracing clan. A man married to a Jewish girl pretends that he is

> "excluded from the family councils. They get together in another room and I might as well be in China."

Other people are positive that Jews "won't marry Gentiles."

> "They keep their own language, marry only Jews, have special Jewish holidays. Naturally people notice they keep themselves apart."

> "Jews, when they talked about marriage, always thought of keeping the money in the family."

Attempts by gentiles to marry Jews seem to be painfully thwarted by the family clan. One interviewee remarks that

> "he was going with a Jewish girl for four years and wanted to marry her but her parents objected. He can't understand why they couldn't marry since the parents were not religious Jews."

Another adds:

> "Our landlady is Jewish and she is quite nice for a Jew. Their daughter went out with a Gentile, and you know the Jewish family across the street wouldn't have a thing to do with them. It's just like if we would go with niggers."

A chemist comes closer to facts when saying:

> "My friends would never go out with a Jewish boy. The reason appears to be that one might get to like a Jew too well and couldn't marry one."

Apparently puzzled by her own candor, she adds:

> "Jews always hang together and think of other Jews first."

Resentment and envy of the imaginary harmoniousness of Jewish life becomes apparent. The Jewish family assumes symbolic significance as a testimonial to the paternalistic family structure that is waning away, and this is painfully experienced by the lower middle classes. Their anti-Semitic members try to persuade themselves that Jews succeed in perpetuating this very structure, which is centered around the revered father who carefully handles the interests of this small group.

> "I've never seen a Jewish girl with runs in her stockings. The parents are usually very proud of their children and would do anything to see their children dressed well. . . . They also furnish their homes well."

> "The Jewish men are funny. They are wonderful to their wives, kind to them and give them everything."

> "People say that . . . Jews are indulgent to their families."

> "Jewish women will work hard to help their husbands get ahead. Just like Ann used to scrub the floor and work so hard in that store when some women would have hired a maid to do that hard work."

Another respondent is amazed about

> ". . . the devotion of Jews to their family, yet so hard and business-like to others."

The concept of the business clan and of the private clan rests upon the concept of a comprehensive unit whose constituents are effaced and indiscernible. Biological, religious, national, and traditional elements are thrown together into a cloudy, mysterious mixture called "the Jews," the "Jewish race," the "Jewish religion," the "chosen people," and so on. The vagueness prevailing in these hostile and ambiguous descriptions of Jews as a group indicates that this problem is more than just a minority problem like any other, for it is this vague conceptual pervasiveness that engenders the concept of the Jews as an anticollective entity.

To the average individual "the Jew" is hard to define within a conventional frame of reference. Jews display peculiar behavior in business, where they combine unique cooperation with unique competition. They behave strangely in personal relations, where they display a spirit of close association combined with a spirit of exclusion. This puzzles the onlooker. He then is prone to ascribe these peculiar traits to the fact that Jews belong to a social group that, in his interpretation, refuses to accept the prevailing cultural patterns of contemporary society and therefore should not be preserved within this society.

Fury, discoverable on all levels of anti-Semitism, is not missing from statements about the Jewish clan, either. Irrationality, the accidental character of the target, and helplessness that colors furious attacks are particularly characteristic for the outbursts against the clan, the Jews as a group. On this level, conscious acts of conspiracy, or religious obsession, as well as conspicuous biological or cultural race determinants are attributed to Jews. The common denominators are resentment and fear of a strange phenomenon that cannot be comprehended by means of everyday experience and language. As an interviewee puts it:

> "Theirs seems to be a different sort of emotional impulse which comes through heredity, tradition and clannishness."

In a way this resentment serves to rationalize the rejection of the perverted utopia that seems to be represented by "Jewish" activities in business and in private life. This particular utopia is rejected because it is not made up of clear, clean, understandable, desirable, modern, and efficient procedures or facts but emerges from the dark grounds of archaic reactions, emotions, and even biologically grounded traits.

The concept of the Jews as an atavistic group contains another psychologically relevant element. We encountered it before, but here it assumes special significance. Rejection of the Jews is connected with religious images. On the surface, the Jews are the people that repudiated Christ. On a deeper level, they are the people constantly pointing to the mission of Christianity and thus expose the failure of modern man to fulfill Christian commandments.

Statements reflecting the atmosphere of the Elders of Zion or similar propaganda nightmares are rare in the material evaluated in this study. However, there is evident a certain readiness to absorb paranoid ideas on deliberate organizational schemes underlying the structure of Jewish community life—with the implication that Jews want to manipulate gentiles. There are those who heard "that the Jews are taking over the government." Others were told of "secret special meetings for Jews only; no one knows what is discussed but the Jews." One interviewee was told that

> "the Jews are keeping records of what people say about them in archives and vaults. 'I-got-you-on-my-list' sort of thing. Now if that isn't Gestapo methods, I never heard of them."

The "conspiracy of the Jewish clan" is a notion more difficult to comprehend than the sterotype of aggressiveness and superiority, which in principle can be analyzed and explained psychologically. Those who are obsessed with the image of a secret and criminal conspiracy belong to the paranoid group. To them every attempt at explaining matters is seen as just another Jewish trick. Quite a few of those we interviewed considered religion the decisive criterion of Jewish clannishness. Overwhelmingly, comments on Jewish religious institutions and customs have a negative connotation. Vicious allusions are rather frequent. Alleged anti-gentile commands of the Old Testament are exposed, and the observance of Jewish holidays is considered detrimental to society as a whole.

In many cases these allusions refer to areas of economic conflict and aim at special advantages and privileges that the Jews are said to enjoy through observing religious laws. Other aspects, however, seem equally important. The essence of Christian teachings is transcendental. For a true Christian, expectation of fulfillment is outside the realm of earthly life. An anti-Judaic concept of Judaism may be determined by those elements of the Jewish religion that indeed imply promises of potential fulfillment of desires during the lifetime of this or another generation. But it also may contain the expression of wavering Christians' unconscious objections to Christian teachings, an anti-Christian protest of the mortal who resents that the fulfillment of his hopes and dreams should be deferred until after his death.

Judaism is experienced as an obscure and sinister guide to happiness through powerful religious arrangements. It is contrasted with the Christian doctrine, which stresses the impotence and fragility of individual life on earth and is not concerned with an individual's happiness in a materialistic way. This ambivalence toward religion touches upon the limits of democracy in our society. Democracy is reduced to a mere sterotype and does not necessarily enforce respect for and tolerance of all religions. Many who profess to accept the principles of democracy do not hesitate to deny democratic safeguards.

A worker who believes "in economic equality for Negroes" is convinced

> "that Jews are different by religion and nature, more aggressive, and will do things for money which most other people won't do . . . and that God willed it that Jews are to be persecuted."

Another who deplores and condemns the anti-Semitic measures of the Nazis says

> "The Jews observe their cultural and religious customs very closely to the exclusion of all else. They refuse to become absorbed as a part of the New World community . . . . Gentiles are only 'to be used.'"

Yet another, who is convinced that Hilter's measures "are a disgrace to any human tolerance," and that the Jews contribute their share to the American war effort "as much as anyone else," believes that

> "Jewish people are different from others, and it's due to their philosophical outlook as a religious group. That also makes them act differently."

His ambivalence is revealed when he adds:

> "The historical question of the killing of Christ is one of the reasons that people will always feel that way about them."

Another interviewee remarks,

> "I do not believe in persecutions and atrocities as they are going on in Europe."

And expresses this at another point in the interview:

> "I have heard that Jewish religious laws show the Jews how to cheat others."

He gets support from a coworker who says:

> "The Jewish Bible tells them to commit adultery on Christian women."

The observance of Jewish holidays serves as an especially obvious manifestation of anticollective behavior:

> "I don't see why Jews can keep stores open on Sunday while Christians would get a ticket if they did that."

A Cuban worker is convinced that anti-Jewish feelings in his homeland were created by "Polish Jews who came over between 1920 and 1921" and who closed their stores on Saturdays but not on Sundays. Even stronger accusations are contained in statements like the following:

> "They don't keep Sabbath laws. They are open Sundays, closed on Saturday. If they are Americans, they should keep the law."

> "When at the last Jewish New Year almost all Jews celebrated a few holidays while none of the Gentiles was allowed to stay home on Christian holidays or state holidays it showed that Jews esteem their religious traditions much more than the welfare of America."

One of the interviewees tries to justify the Nazi persecution of the Jews by alluding to the Jewish holidays:

> "The sons of bitches asked for it and they got it. That's what's going to happen in this country. They just go off and close up their stores on their holidays without giving you any warning and then you can't get anything anywhere."

The fact that Jewish and Christian holidays usually do not coincide inspires peculiar hostility. The strict regulation of work and leisure seems to be violated by the Jewish holidays. Religious Jews do not work when gentiles work, and vice versa. The entire relationship between work and leisure seems involved. It has cost society a considerable psychological effort to stabilize this relationship, so that anyone disrupting the fixed order is seen as violating the rules of civilization. The Jew is bitterly resented because unconsciously everybody would like to break the rules. Rationalization for this resentment is offered by religious heritage. Alleged Jewish contempt for Christian holidays is a reminder that the Jews have rejected Christ. Sometimes the notion that Jews violate the collective pattern of modern society grows into furious outbursts against the group regarded as the promoter of a segregative religious mythology. The Jews are said to perpetuate their clannish seclusiveness by their adherence to the arrogant dogma of being a "chosen people."

> "They think they are God's chosen people and the world owes them a living and they are going to get it regardless whom they hurt in life to achieve their goal."

> "Hell, haven't they always regarded themselves as a 'chosen Jew'? They have always been a lousy lot."

The Jews' alleged belief that they are religious favorites mobilizes strong emotional forces of revenge. Jewish religious doctrine is taken as the justification for the punishment to be inflicted upon the Jews.

> "They have their 'chosen people' complex believing that all Jews go to 'heaven' and all Gentiles go to 'hell.' I appreciate that they have been mistreated in lots of ways but they brought it on themselves to a large extent by such ideas."

> "Why I hate the Jews most is because they always brag so about being God's chosen people."

Unaware of the contradiction in his statement, another interviewee says:

> "Outside of their religious beliefs they no doubt feel as others do but their conceited religious ideas make them conceited. Most of the people I know don't like them because of their conceit and their crooked business practices."

This is the final verdict about the anticollective character of the Jews. The charge is that their immutable religious doctrines and mentality are tied up with their actual role in society and that they combine belief in an exclusive godly grace bestowed on them with their everyday business routine. The image blends together aloofness and activity, segregation and omnipresence, spiritual vanity and materialistic efficiency, allegiance to the loftiest symbols of mankind and indulgence in its lowest urges. The amalgamation of such contradictory ideas into one comprehensive image strengthens the fear of the "uncanny" Jew who had better be eliminated.

16

Unpunished Enjoyment

In an ambiguous manner Jews are conceived as a "free" people—free from those conventions that ensure the continuous function of the social mechanism. This notion of perverted freedom seems to entail exemption not only from all moral obligations but also from the whole set of mores guiding the conduct of social life.

By virtue of their alleged renunciation of institutionalized social duties, the Jews are seen as creating a sphere of their own, a living space within—or rather outside—the genuine living space of the community. They have created a sphere of independence in a world of interdependence, a sphere of autarchy in a world of mutual dependency, a sphere of license in a world of restrictions. Breathing a social air of their own, they attempt to live by moral standards of their own making. They disregard the generally accepted restraints imposed on individual behavior and try to escape the punishment for their infringement.

The moral code, which the Jews allegedly disregard, is of wide scope. It not only covers ethical concepts in the true sense of the word but extends to aesthetic and sanitary standards. The Jews seem to be offenders against both moral and hygienic sanitation, refusing allegiance to the rules governing these areas. The idea of the disorderly Jew—implying every kind of disorder—comes to the surface. The image of the outsider changes into the image of the outcast. The profiteer who hoards goods and money also spurns moral and other social values. Fantasies of specific forbidden Jewish enjoyments definitely have a projective character. They represent jealous participation in pleasures that are taboo for the community. Such pleasures can be experienced in vicarious excursions only. Then they become permissible because the offender expiates his dream by castigating the moral depravity of those whom he envies. Although this applies to all kinds of accusations, it is especially true of alleged offenses in the sexual sphere. The outcast seems to be at liberty to develop more drives, more energy, more vitality toward enjoyment of all kinds, toward infringements of rules and regulations, and toward overstepping conventional boundaries than the in-group may dare to do. The image of the joyful Jew has a quasi-playful connotation. He has his pleasures for pleasures' sake; he cheats because he likes to cheat; he bosses others around because he likes bossing around; he runs after women because he likes to play around; he dresses and eats sloppily because he enjoys sloppiness; he is dirty because he likes filth.

Dirt and Food

The complex of alleged violations of the hygienic code may well be illustrated by the following two statements:

> "The Jews up around 12th Street are coarse, dirty, and the women immodest."

> "They're dirty as hell. I've worked for them and I know . . . I mean dirty all around, sexually and all."

Both remarks reveal the psychological function of accusations of the Jewish lack of cleanliness and lack of sexual restraint.

Quite a few statements aim at dirt plain and simple. Interviewees sometimes refer to neighborhoods that become filthy as soon as Jews start moving in:

> "We knew where they came from [the Jewish East side], and besides in a few years the clean section became filthy."

> ". . . who aren't used to our way of living and they are dirty. They leave their garbage around and have roaches and all sorts of bugs in the house."

Another statement:

> "I will have to move out of my present neighborhood if Jews move in because they are dirty. They never keep their lawns clean."

Another interviewee mentions Jewish gesticulations and—as an afterthought—adds:

> "And they are dirty."

A coworker agrees and says:

> "They are dirty about their persons and about their homes."

Dirtiness often serves as a stereotype for Jewish character in general. One interviewee speaks of the "dirty little storekeepers"; another refers to the Jews as "filthy"; a third says that "most people I know do not want to have anything to do with them because of their filth, lying."

Sometimes improper and sloppy clothing is drawn into focus. A nurse relates some of her hospital experiences:

> "All Jewish women, regardless of how expensive the outer clothing was, always had dirty underclothes."

Other testimonials:

> "They are either overdressed or in short sleeves."

> "Having their relatives spreading all over the terrace with food and the men in their shirtsleeves and they just don't act like white people."

> "It's the way they dress that you can tell them. The men's pants are always low down, the tie is knotted wrong or is to one side. They're sloppy."

Criticisms of Jewish eating habits are numerous:

> "They eat too much."

> "In restaurants especially one can always tell a Jew by the way they eat as if they were starving. They gobble their food down in a mouthful."

> "They eat fast, large mouthfuls. And lean towards their plates."

> "They spit on the floor; when a Jew eats he will belch as if he were going to vomit."

It may be noted in passing that the issue of Jewish eating manners is very complex. Statements about poor Jewish eating habits are often mere rationalizations of misgivings about kosher food. After all, the most crucial and most cruel anti-Semitic accusations from the Middle Ages down to the turn of the century referred to the area of food—from well-poisoning to ritual murder. It seems more than a coincidence, that those in our sample, who commented on poor Jewish eating habits, also turned out to be openly anti-Semitic.

The baker according to whom "every Jew belches after his meal" also cannot "blame Hitler. I think it is the Jews' own fault." The textile worker, who says. "Jews eat as if they were always starved," sometimes thinks that "any country would be better off without them." The waitress who seems to have noticed that "Jews eat large mouthfuls and lean toward their plates" also mentions that

> "it is well-known around here that a lot of Jewish boys . . . have gotten deferments because they claim their mothers as dependents when the old men have plenty of money. The government does not check up on this to find the truth."

From a psychological point of view there is not much difference between those who blame the Jews for their lack of adjustment to conventional eating mores and those who admit to liking Jewish food in spite of their anti-Semitic attitudes. The truck driver who believes "Nazi actions against Jews in Germany were justified," who thinks that "New York employers are mostly Jewish," and who is convinced that "Jews will do anything to stay out of the army" likes to frequent Jewish restaurants. "I like the way they put up their salads and I sure go for their rye bread and their sandwich meat." The California steelworker who does not "think it was such a bad idea what they do to the Jews in Germany" used to go over to a Jewish schoolmate's home "and eat the best foods. I like their food." When the same truck driver says of alleged Jewish draft dodgers that "they go to doctors and get treatments and everything," and when the same steelworker remarks, "You can't kill off the damn Jews," the interpretation suggests itself that a taste for Jewish food masks an unconscious attempt to unveil the secrets of Jewish power, and—at the deepest layer—to participate in them.

The accusation of uncleanliness and sloppiness is yet another version of the image of the Jews as archaic. The archaic is identified with the dirty. Old clothes become the symbol of uncleanliness. The outer appearance of an orthodox Eastern-European Jew sporting a beard or even a caftan evokes associations of dirtiness. Corresponding behavior attracts great attention. Jews practice that which is forbidden. They indulge in restrained laxities and depravities. They refuse to forgo anything that may be pleasure but they do not want to pay in self-imposed restrictions. Sexual life, which is referred to in some instances, is the highlight of such unrestricted enjoyment.

Sex

Some of our interviewees accuse Jews of violating the prevailing code of sexual mores. Unlike the usual Nazi propaganda on this subject, the most common accusations against Jews in the area of sexual behavior are not those of attacks on the virtue of gentile womanhood, yet this Nazi line is not completely absent. Those who express such accusations, however, do not represent the typical factory worker. A woman worker who was not a worker in peacetime, says:

> "The Jewish men are always inclined to hold Jewish girls in high esteem and show a complete lack of respect for a non-Jewish girl. I thought about this fact in regard to improper sexual intimacies because I have known Jewish men who carried on with non-Jewish girls whereas they would not consider bringing disgrace to a girl of their own religion."

A forewoman in a laundry who refuses to be considered a worker declares:

> "They go off on sex orgies, attack white women."

A DuPont worker who approves of paternalism in labor relations, elaborates:

> "The Jewish Bible tells them to commit adultery on Christian women. They think our women are pigs and that if they steal from Christians or rape Christian women it is a good deed."

Accusations of alleged Jewish sexual depravity are frequently tied to professed obedience to sexual taboos and reveal considerable resentment of self-denial of illicit enjoyment. This is naively expressed by a woman office worker:

> "If you want an obscene picture or some 'French' picture postcards, you'll always get them among the Jews."

The resentment expressed in these accusations, in a few instances, is accompanied by fantasies of revenge. An Italian barber says that "once he beat up a kike for trying to date his sister." Of a small businessman now working as a toolmaker, the person who interviewed him says his "real idea" was "to castrate all Jewish males, render all Jewish women sterile, so as to exterminate the race."

The furious reaction to alleged "Jewish rape." though this reaction is not typical of workers, is engendered by present-day society. It requires a more thorough explanation. Resentment of Jewish sexual depravity is but one element of the general repression of desire. The tremendous pressures of modern society have forced upon its members a utilitarian concept and practice of recreation. They play or watch others play merely because it fulfills the need for relaxation and replenishment of their physical and mental capacities. The more or less planned utilitarian character of leisure makes it necessary to suppress the drives and instincts that aim at playing, loafing, and pure enjoyment as biologically rooted objectives. Regression into the mental stage of childhood and its various forms of relaxation is no longer socially permissible unless it is coordinated with progression into the adult stage; it is not permissible unless leisure time is made an indisputable part of working time.

Against the background of domesticated pleasures at the service of social usefulness, Jews are resented as people who seem to have broken the inescapable circle of work and leisure. They seem to know how to enjoy themselves without accepting the restraints imposed by social conventions, by which pleasure is perceived only in its recharging function for useful work. Jews are seen as living in a paradise of pleasure, in a utopian state of freedom from cares and worries, while non-Jews are expelled from the pastures of pleasure and sweat in the dust of labor. These unconscious fantasies betray the deep longings of toiling humanity. They become perverted projections when they are consciously released under the label "Jewish." Pleasure becomes depravity; freedom from care, carelessness; freedom from conventional restraints, shameless offense against the accepted standards of morality.

All accusations of a sexual nature imply sexual promiscuity, albeit rarely verbalized. Psychologically, however, it is the culmination of the three main features of the anti-Semitic image. As parasite, the Jew claims sexual prerogatives without giving or paying anything, without compensating for his pleasures by social usefulness. As enemy of collectivity, he disturbs the pattern of sexual conventions. And as the beneficiary of unpunished enjoyment, he ignores the institutionalized responsibility of marriage and the moral responsibility of resignation or repentence, and instead playfully and irresponsibly uses and abuses the other sex.

Loose Morals

Many statements of workers interviewed make the moral behavior of Jews appear as a background against which the high moral standards of the business world stand out in relief. Jews either lack the tools for differentiating between good and bad, or are indifferent to these values when they make their decisions, or are eager to play along with the bad and the low and often enjoy partnership with the devil. It sometimes seems as though they are obsessed with the delight of playing bad tricks. They seem to indulge in them even when the economic advantages obtained are ridiculously insignificant. Some declare that Jews have an original lust for amorality:

> "In a choice between an honest and dishonest method of obtaining money profit, the Jew will choose the dishonest method."

> "They are domineering when their inner desire is strong enough and then they have no compunctions."

> "They feel that it's a matter of pride within themselves to get the best of people."

> "They think it's smart and clever to cheat someone."

The Jew is sometimes seen as dominated by the one desire to violate moral standards just for the pleasure of offending and even hurting Gentiles.

> "They are taught from birth that their one aim in life must be to take a constant economic advantage of the Gentile."

> "They are cornering all the wealth and would starve the Gentiles to death if they could."

Anti-Semitism in action is organized sadism in action. The manipulated image of the Jew in totalitarian countries always emphasized sadistic impulses that people are capable of releasing when protected and justified by collective behavior. The Jew as common enemy functions to unite a disparate group and to motivate it to joint action. The potential readiness to violent persecution of particular groups is psychologically fostered when such groups are turned into targets of projection; more specifically, when they are perceived as endowed with the very sadistic impulses harbored by the in-groups on the offensive.

Boisterous, joyous, playful, joking, and at the same time bloody and cruel pamphlets, poems, and songs are common in anti-Semitic propaganda. They serve as psychological stimuli when the ground has been prepared by the image of the Jews as a boisterous, joyous, playful, and at the same time bloody and cruel group of outcasts finding special satisfaction in acts of cheating, exploitation, destruction, just for the sake of cheating, exploitation, and destruction. Where this image of the

Jew prevails, moral concepts developed in the philosophical doctrine of Western civilization, namely, that good should be done for its own sake are reversed. When Jews are accused as evildoers for evil's sake, the stereotypes pertaining to the image of the Jews, money, intellect, laziness, aggressiveness, clannishness, and the like, are also experienced as expressions of evil in society.

Ultimately, anti-Semitism among workers is thus a condensed, perverted, manipulated concept of all social conditions that they resent or reject. However, distorted by a partly sick and crazed imagination, this critique can produce sick and crazed reactions: nihilism, rage, and finally, the demand for the extermination of the Jews.

Body and Gestures

Various representations of alleged Jewish characteristics—i.e. that of the parasite, the enemy of collectivity, and unbridled, excessive hedonist—find tangible expression in the portrayal of the Jewish physiognomy. The topic of the body-image itself is of great importance, for it embraces the entire corpus of idiosyncrasies directed against the Jews. Intensity and color of anti-Jewish reactions may be largely determined by these idiosyncrasies. Remarks about "Jewish" facial characteristics or gestures are often immediately preceded or followed by quasi-rational attacks upon "Jewish character traits" and "Jewish behavior."

The bulk of the statements on Jewish body characteristics refers to the face, especially the nose and lips, to gestures, and to motions of the hands. "Typical" lips probably are seen as indicating sexual desire, and frequent mention of the "Jewish" nose may have similar unconscious sources. The nose and gesticulating hands appear to have related functions. The long, large hook nose seems to be more than a static part of the face. To the unconscious, it is an organ in motion, intruding, sniffing, drilling into the living space of other people, extending the physical range of an individual in a similar manner as gesticulating hands. Some interviewees translate this nose-concept into symbolic language by speaking of Jewish "nosiness."

> "They always start to ask questions right away the minute they see you and they interfere in other people's business—stick their nose into everything."

> "You can recognize them mostly by look and action—they are too nosey and very insistent about getting information from other people and reluctant to give about themselves."

"They are lazy on the job and love to nose into people's conversations."

The nose and its function are assimilated to the Jew's social functions. As an organ of exploration, the nose takes on intellectual significance, which, by virtue of its agility, assists the parasite in its parasitical activities.

Connections between physiognomical and verbal stereotypes are impressively illustrated by statements on gesticulation. A sentence such as "They gesticulate when speaking" is immediately followed by "They are pushy and aggressive. A person who says, "They shrug their shoulders and use their hands quite a bit," instantly adds, "and they are dirty." In one breath an interviewee enumerates these Jewish characteristics: "Facial features, e.g. moving of hands, discussion of money" One might ask whether the image of the gesticulating and agitated Jew possibly indicates the worker's fear of jeopardizing his own emotional stability and losing the precarious inner balance the work discipline requires?

The resentment of Jewish expressiveness requires closer study. Analysis here relies on conscious as well as unconscious elements of the testimony. Consciously, all aspects of verbal and physical expressiveness are resented. What remains unconscious is the desire to imitate Jewish expressiveness. Quite a few of our interviewees did so in the course of conversations that took place between them and our volunteer interviewers. In some instances direct reference was made to the expressive nature of "Jewish speech," which was termed objectionable:

> "I can tell them sometimes by talking to them. Often they are found to be hysterical or rather very emotional."

> "They converse differently from a Gentile. "They become excited and the manner in which they speak is different."

In other instances criticism is more general:

> "They have their own way of talking and expressing themselves."

In most cases, however, objections are raised against loud talk. It should be noted that this specific form of expressiveness is closely associated by the interviewees with other Jewish traits that seem equally unacceptable. One characteristic incident will illustrate the point.

One of the interviewees, a female sewing operator, began to gesture with her hands while criticizing Jews. Noticing it herself, she self-consciously remarked:

> "Here I am—talking with my hands. I have worked for them so long. I get to act like them."

The unconscious desire to imitate that which is seen represented by Jewish expressions is legitimized by social conventions inasmuch as it is nothing but "acting." The Gentile docs not turn into a Jew; he *imitates* him, he "acts" Jewish. Quite a few episodes of mimicry can be found in our material. One interviewee relates in detail a particular childhood experience. He reports that Jews "always" made motions such as scratching or pulling their chin. They had one Jewish boy in class who used those gestures, and the Gentile children were given to mimicking him. This bothered the sensitive Jewish child very much. He then tells the interviewer that when the offenders, one of whom was the interviewee, were punished, they blamed the Jewish child for complaining about their behavior and thus the antagonism was intensified.

Most likely the problem of imitation is of far-reaching importance. Archaic drives are released in those who "act" or "pretend." Closer psychological analysis probably may reveal a good deal of fear and bad conscience in the minds of the actors who imitate Jews; in many instances the "acting," who then might turn against the Jews for having been instrumental in releasing the forbidden and repressed in the "actor's" psyche.

17

Totalitarian Aspects

In the course of this analysis we have repeatedly stressed a specific quality of many individual anti-Semitic charges. The interviewees presented each particular action or behavior on the part of a Jewish individual as a poignant case in point in the context of generalizing observations and experiences that serve to characterize the specific individual as a member of the Jewish group.

Overimpressed by generalities, people become blind to the specific and particular. This reflects a most significant and dangerous trend of recent history: the ability to perceive individuals or individual traits is impaired. Individuals and individual traits are seen through the medium of stereotypes, thus stripping them of their individual significance. New and genuine experience is stymied. Sensations are conveyed to the mind in a distorted, deindividualized, stereotyped version.

Contemporary anti-Semitism in the form of generalizing stereotypes, has become a tremendous force that poisons the democratic way of life in this country as elsewhere. The onslaught on the Jew is the onslaught on the individual, more precisely on the individual's specific and particular nature, on his rights in a free society. The great danger of reaction by stereotypes becomes powerfully apparent when we analyze the statements of those interviewees who identify Jews in the most general and vaguest of terms, or who maintain this vagueness in spite of or in contrast to the detailed and concrete remarks they make to rationalize their vague prejudices or aversions.

People who plead the elimination of Jews from society almost always claim the ability to unmistakably spot a Jew: he is different and therefore easily recognizable. Ninety-one percent of those interviewees who approved of the Nazi's treatment of Jews, considered Jews as different; of those who qualified their disapproval of Nazi terror, 84 percent agreed that Jews are basically different from other people. Conversely, of those who saw Jews as not different from others, only 1.9 percent definitely approved of Nazi terror against Jews. The proportion increases to

4.6 percent among those who see some Jews of certain types or Jews as different, and it jumps to 25.8 percent among those who consider all Jews different. These totalitarian "spotters" are most susceptible to totalitarian tendencies. In many instances they involuntarily betray a lack of resistance to attacks on democratic institutions and a tendency to relinquish the prerogatives of reason by analyzing the merits of a case. Instead, they show a tendency to revert to a quasi-tribal pattern of behavior: they can "smell" a Jew a mile away.

Ambivalent Spotters

The following statements express considerable ambivalence or reservation with regard to the extermination of Jews.

What to do with Jews	How to recognize Jews
The economic condition was in the hands of the Jews, and the German people had to get it back but they took the wrong methods.	Nearly always, either by features or actions. The way they act—if you can't tell by their looks, watch their actions.
The Jews more or less brought it on but certainly don't deserve what Hitler did.	Oh, yes, you can tell by their man-nerism. which has definite charac-teristics. . . . They are just different.
Hitler's methods are pretty rough, in some cases justified.	They do act differently. I can tell them nine times out of ten by their way and actions.
The Nazis made the innocent suffer with the guilty.	Eighty percent of the time they are recognized by their physical and racial characteristics.
The interviewed person does not know about crimes committed by Hitler against the Jews.	Jews are cheaters. . . . You can smell them twelve miles away.
The interviewee does not like what the Nazis did to the Jews in Ger- many but felt that the Jews were responsible for some things—he is not sure what they are—and should have been punished for them but not killed.	I can tell the difference simply by their behavior. If a person is rude and has an accent, he is likely Jewish.
Extermination of the Jews is not the solution but economic and social control. . . . Hitler was correct at least in defining the Jews as a reason for Germany's impoverishedposi tion after the last war.	A sure way to tell a Jew is in any discussion of the problem: anyone who will defend a Jew is either a Jew, or has some Jewish blood in him.

What to do with Jews	*How to recognize Jews*
If the Jews chose to live there [in Germany], then they certainly have no right to kick at the treatment they receive.	Usually by their features, dialect or money traits.
[Hitler's measures] were somewhat justified but they shouldn't have been so cruel. They should just have taken control of the money out of their hands. We should do the same.	Just by their outlook on things.
It [Nazi persecution] was carried too far.	By their actions, movements, way they go about doing things.
Hitler went too far . . . But we have to do something to keep Jews in their place . . . Probably everybody except the Jews are very sick of Jews.	Usually by their features.
If the German people felt something had to be done they should do it but they went to too much of an extreme.	Of course you can tell them. I don't know exactly how, but I can tell them.
[Hitler] should just have chased them back to Jerusalem and kept them there.	I can tell them a mile off . . . I can smell them a mile off.
We'd be a lot better off if we would get rid of them here. Where? Back to Jerusalem.	You can always tell. You'd be surprised but you can. I can't describe it exactly.
I don't believe in killing any one, but I think the Jews should be driven out of this good old USA.	Yes, you can tell them apart: by their appearance.

These statements all attest a willingness to "understand" extermination, although the endorsement of genocide is mitigated by varying degrees of scruples. Some interviewees show the formation of a stereotype in the making. They already are exposed to the compulsory connection between stereotypical perception and stereotypical reaction, between the spotting of the Jew and potential killing. Yet they still are susceptible to genuine experience and reasonable reaction when facing actual everyday events. At the same time they show some inconsistency because the violent hostility in the abstract frequently in is contrast to the genuine, frank, and honest reactions in particular instances. These people might be called borderline cases: on the verge of falling prey to totalitarian reactions, they are still capable of genuine individual experience.

The Spotter-Killer

Another group of interviewees are no longer in a state of ambivalence. They openly combine inarticulate, animal-like, quasi-mythological spotting with the desire for extermination. Quite a few of them, while endorsing Hitler, advocate deportation of Jews to Palestine. But their pseudo-Zionism is a mere rationalization of their desire for pogroms:

"The Jews will kill each other."

The language used by some of the interviewees in this group is that of fury, with total disregard for the usual levelheadedness otherwise characteristic of Anglo-Saxon idiomatics. Those who speak of Jewish stinkers, of Jews not being human, are virtually practicing fascists.

What to do with Jews	How to recognize Jews
[Asked about Nazi persecution:] It was OK.	You can always tell a Jew from a Gentile. It is instinct that tells a Jew from a Gentile.
Hitler did the right thing in Germany and we ought to do the same thing here.	I know a kike when I see one.
What the Nazis did to the Jews was right.	First, I can smell them. [Qu.: Cer-tainly not all of them?] Well, you can look at him and tell he's a Jew. He's going to let you know it some way.
[On Nazi persecution:] They got just what they deserved.	My wife can spot one a block away.
The Jews didn't want to obey orders of the Nazi government. The result is what they're getting.	By their appearance and their accent and by the way they act.
Hitler didn't do a good enough job. He left 3 million living. There were 7 million to begin with. He killed 4 million.	By looks . . . and action.
[Nazi persecution] served them right. They asked for it. The Germans were the only ones who had guts enough to get rid of them. . . . Most of my friends would like to see us get up enough nerve to run them back to Jerusalem because we would be better off without them.	How can they feel like us? They are not people—just Jews.

What to do with Jews	*How to recognize Jews*
If there is one good thing Hitler did, it was to get rid of the Jews. He ought to be commended and not condemned for it. . . . All decent people would like to be rid of them. There might be a chance then for other people to live.	They are always different.
Sometimes I think that [what the Nazis did] is the only way you can handle them. If they are not careful and if they keep on trying to run things the same thing will happen to them here.	I can always tell a Jew from a Gen-tile. Sort of hawk-like look aboutthem. Gets my back up just to lookat one of 'em.
I fell that the Nazis were justified because the Jews were beginning toforget that they were born Jews and must die Jews.	By their physical features andmannerisms.
I don't like Jews, they are the lowest thing on earth, especially the kikes. . . . I think they should all be annihilated. What we should have here is a pogrom. One good thing Hitler did.	Hell yes, you can see a Jew a mile away. They act different, they aredifferent.
We need a Hitler here to chase them out.	Actions. Speech. Dress.
They [the Nazis] did not finish the job.	And how [I can tell a Jew]! As soonas they open their mouth. . . . Met Jews at school—riff-raff.
Treatment by Nazis justified.	They are selfish, money grabbers. and the lowest type of people. Long nose, aggressive, talk loud.
All Jews are good for nothing and should be done away with . . . Hitler did a good job, he should put all the Jews on a big ship and dump them in the middle of the ocean.	Can tell a Jew from a non-Jew by the way he acts and eats and talks.
Burning one million at Lublin: probably lying propaganda and in any case was of no importance because the victims were only Jews.	What do you think. I'm blind? They stink. . . . All crooks, thieves and robbers. No decent people could compete or live with them.

(Continued)

(Continued)

What to do with Jews	How to recognize Jews
[Complete agreement with what Hitler did to the Jews.] If Hitler hadn't started the war, he would have gone down as the greatest man in history.	I can always spot them.
[About Nazi terror:] Well, that's one way to get rid of them. Might be a little harsh but it sure works. Course, it would be best to ship them all back to Palestine, then they could jew each other to death.	Certainly they do [act differently]..... They have always been a lousy lot. Read the Old Testament; it proves what a lot of riff-raff they have been and are. Most of them have a Jew nose, talk funny and are loud-mouthed.

The above statements are amplifications of the preceding images of prejudice. They serve to illustrate the danger of contemporary anti-Semitic manifestations. From harmless jokes about the Jewish manner of speech and gesticulation, of dress and behavior, from expressions of discomfort with Jewish clans is but a small step to the acceptance of Nazi-measures and "the final solution." Adulation for the "cradle of Christianity" leads to the choice of Palestine as giant concentration and extermination camp. Dislike of "Jewish noses" turns into rejection and condemnation of the Jews. Irony and sarcasm turn to bloody rage.

The Danger

Contemporary anti-Semitism is characterized by this coherent inconsistency, this amorphous image of the rejected, this vague inarticulateness of articulate details, this obscure generalization of hazy recollection of experiences. All this makes anti-Semitism into a tool for expressing the helplessness—rational, emotional, political, cultural—that threatens humankind in its last democratic refuges. Anti-Semitism then can be seen as a perverted, irrational, aimless expression of the need for help.

The various facets of the image of anti-Semitism as it unfolds through the interviews evaluated in this study, shows U.S. labor—and, one is tempted to add, U.S. society—at the crossroads, and the danger signals should not be ignored. To be sure, there still is inherited tradition, there still is the willingness to confront and assess experiences open-mindedly, there still is the spirit of common sense intent on respecting humanistic values, and some interviewees clearly attest an inner struggle between reason and prejudice.

We see workers who approve of Hitler and his measures, but do not object to working with Jews. We see others whose attitudes and behavior are characterized by pervasive ambivalence. There is, for instance, the female electrical worker, a college graduate, who cannot help but call "typically Jewish" a Jewish woman who "would work you to death for little or nothing," but who is willing to admit that another "was lovely—and had none of the objectionable traits about her at all."

There is the engine tester who says that the "Nazi-way of handling the Jews was brutal . . . but in a way the Jews asked for it," who thinks "a Jew is still a Jew no matter what he does," and who nevertheless admits, "I suppose they are the same as other people."

Awareness of such a split in the mental makeup of people of pronounced anti-Jewish responses is the first and basic condition for the discussion of countervailing policies. Some of these people, to be sure, are almost inaccessible. Others, however, might still be open to the language of experience, of genuine rational and emotional reorientation. On a certain level of consciousness, the worker knows that anti-Semitism is the wrong solution to legitimate issues and problems. Somehow, he senses that his grievances are deflected toward the image of a race instead of being focused on the reality of social inequalities. A steelworker who always ends up discovering that every person he dislikes is a Jew, thinks that "it was not such a bad idea what they did to the Jews in Germany." But repeatedly he says in his conversation with a coworker: "You can't kill off the damn Jews." At first glance this man seems to be the incorporation of all-out vicious anti-Semitism. He is in the clutches of a mythological fear of the Jews, who, indestructible as they are, assume a supernatural quality. A closer look at his inner struggles reveals that he, in the words of one of his coworkers, "worries about most everything; is afraid someone else will get ahead of him, is not efficient and is generally afraid of other people." Asked whether the extermination of Jews would mean more opportunities for him, this worrier replies. "Oh well, I guess, if it weren't the Jews, it would be someone else." His fury turns to helpless despair and reveals the specific background of anti-Jewish feelings among workers. Filled with anxiety and rage, they accusingly call "a Jew" what in actuality is the psychological consequence of their legitimate social concerns. They could call it fate as well. If these workers could be encouraged to recognize the implications of their image of the Jew in the context of their complaints and grievances, they might ultimately be able to articulate their legitimate demands and hopes in adequate and rational terms.

Part IV

Toward a Psychology of Authoritarianism

18

Authority and Culture

Human beings in society are not governed by coercion alone. Only in quite extraordinary cases, often of very limited duration, are relations of groups and individuals based on physical power relationships alone. Even periods such as Asiatic Despotism or ancient slave society, in which a clear master-slave relationship is present, cannot be explained solely by reference to the power apparatus the rules had at their disposal. Such a theory would remain purely mechanistic.

This viewpoint, according to which human beings resemble the blind being dragged on a rope along a precipice without the possibility of any orientation of their own, stands in opposition to another thesis that is no less extreme. According to it, history, social order, or social change can be explained by conscious reasoning. Human beings possess allegedly inherent abilities—psychic dispositions and drives as well as mental capacities—that allow them to reach their social and personal goals. Thus history presents itself as a series of increasingly higher social orders; society steadily attends to its business in a manner ever nearer a state of perfection. While the mechanistic model fails to consider the factor of goal-oriented behavior in its explanation of history, the rationalistic point of view underestimates not only truly "blind" elements in history but also a wealth of psychic and institutional facts that are present in every phenomenon of social life.

Every step taken by members of a certain social order is conditioned by an extraordinary number of concrete institutions and psychic factors. These in turn have either been produced by this society or have been adopted from previous ages and developed further. We will refer to "culture" as the embodiment of all factors that transcend physical compulsion and purely economic elements of social life. Culture also includes all organizations and structures, such as governmental and legal institutions, the educational system, and the psychic makeup of the individual members of society.

The effectiveness of a particular cultural system may be studied most precisely by regarding the history of the great Asiatic societies. In the professional literature it is universally accepted that ancestor worship was of decisive significance for the development of China. Certainly the reasons for this cult and for the place it originally occupied in the total social structure can be found in the material causes of the ancient Chinese mode of production in which the lessons handed down from distant ancestors were an important productive force. In the course of time this cult and its power over the mental and cultural constitution of the individual member of the society became a factor that assisted the preservation and static reproduction of the society. The cultural aspect of the ancestor cult, constantly inculcated by education may have originally been a necessary and fruitful aspect of the production process. In time, however, it assumes the function of preserving this fixed mode of production as well as the social networks that arise from it.

To understand the awe and respect with which the village clan, the strict hierarchy in the family, and the quasi-divine power of the sovereign are revered within the classical Chinese social order, to understand by what means people repeatedly adjust themselves to an existing social order, it is neither sufficient to study the purely material conditions of production nor to register the power apparatus that the dominant groups of this society had at their disposal. Rather, to explain this phenomenon properly, it is necessary to take into consideration the great cultural power of the ancestor cult as it is reproduced in the character structure of members of this society.

Indian society may be similarly examined. Here, too, one may suppose that certain conditions of production originally caused a rigorous division of social functions. The development and retention of the caste principle, however, have lost a direct relation to these conditions. Its transformation into an immutable sacral institution whose commandments determine the spirit of Hindu upbringing and mold conscious and unconscious character traits of its members in early youth serves decisively to reproduce both the established mode of production as well as the related class conditions.

The power of cultural mechanisms influences just as well the private behavior of members of a society. A particularly instructive example is the encounter of Asiatic societies with modern Euro-American methods of production methods. In his studies on the sociology of religion, Max Weber asked in what way Indian religion was responsible for the absence of capitalist development. Clearly, culture in this sense can become a fetter to the development of productive forces. By becoming so deeply rooted as a psychic factor in the life of a society, culture helps to perpetuate the existing order while resisting any development of the productive forces and wealth of that society. The literature in the field constantly points out how the caste system as well as the ancestor cult hinder the revolutionizing of social conditions and subjugate countless masses to an order that they would have to destroy if they understood their true interests and the latent technical potential of the society.

Sociology and the philosophy of history have been aware of the problem that social power may cause productive forces to remain fixed at a certain level. The real difficulty arises in trying to explain how the totality of culture develops on the basis of a certain mode of production, how it unfolds in the most dissimilar manner, and reproduces itself in people's minds so as to favor the preservation of this social order. Neither the infrastructure alone nor the cultural factors that reinforce it can explain permanence or change in a given society. It is, rather, the reciprocal relationship between these two forces that explains this dynamic.

Culture integrates people into a given historical order and has different functions, depending on the degree of maturity of a given society. In a situation where the material mode of production is at the peak of its possibilities, the economy basically produces for the "economic subjects" a maximum of available resources. At this point culture, institutionally and psychologically, contributes to social stability. Culture, to use a metaphor from the building trade, is the mortar of society at this stage. In contrast, we encounter historical conditions in which the cultural sphere helps to maintain a mode of production that is out of line with the forces of production that are present. In this case culture acts in the interest of maintaining an obsolete social order. Under such conditions culture becomes a regressive factor. It serves, to retain the metaphor, no longer as mortar but rather as mere putty, trying to keep whole a brittle order that threatens to fall apart.

Thus, the term *culture* designates factors that help to strengthen an existing order through certain institutions and that help its members adjust to it. These factors can drive a certain order forward to its highest level of development and maintain it at this high level. On the other hand, these factors may laboriously keep a sinking organization "afloat." We regard these cultural factors from a dynamic point of view. We stand opposed to a positivistic theory for which facts appear in accidental isolation. The isolation of a social fact, unavoidable in research, must not lead to the erroneous conclusion that the social process itself is constituted by adding up such isolated moments. In reality all individual facts are woven into the dialectic of totality, and in a certain way each fact, when expressed in conceptual isolation, must bear the characteristics of the whole. Society is present in every single aspect of culture, including its economic infrastructure.

In bourgeois society a person lives in two dimensions: he is a public being with a certain career, with a certain position in the state or the military, endowed with certain public rights and duties, and so forth. At the same time he leads a private existence, above all in the family. This existence is carried out in relative independence from the person's public life. To be sure, the separation of these two spheres is more appearance than reality. To speak of a private human existence, completely divorced from social functions, is a mere illusion. Such illusions are widely propagated and have often in history performed a compensatory function for groups whose life circumstances were depressing and unpleasant. In reality, the processes that occur in the so-called private human sphere—for example, how a person uses free time, his specific position within the family, more complicated matters such as his emotional reactions in love, pleasure, and ill-humor, apparently trivial characteristics such as his taste in clothing and food—all have an essential effect in determining the way in which his public existence is shaped. Conversely the events of private life, in their every detail, bear traits of that "public" existence as it is prescribed for the individual by his position in the production process. The maintenance of a certain form of social organization is equally dependent on two factors. First, the effects that a person's public existence have on his private life must not be brought into total conflict with the individual's social functions. Second, everything important in private life makes a person more malleable, as it were, for the social mechanism.

The way in which the cultural mechanism functions, its different function in different groups, its rate of change in relation to that of material production, all depend essentially on the fact that it represents a certain unity; but this unity arises by means of the mutual interaction of very different and heterogenous strata. There are social functions that wholly serve the purpose of social cohesion. Institutions of the state make order their primary function: financial administration, military and public transport, the educational system, and public health agencies are organizations that directly guarantee the dynamic functioning of this order; they are necessary prerequisites of production and aid the economic process by providing external coercion and sanctioned rules. Yet, this structure as a whole fulfills a relatively independent task as well. It brings about the continual psychological recognition of a given order, and it is precisely the illusion of its far-reaching independence from the economy that invites people to accept this order as necessary and fundamentally unchangeable. A miniature picture of this rational social mechanism is reproduced in each person's psyche and provides for a perpetually renewed emotional interest in the maintenance of the status quo.

Sociological literature frequently distinguishes civilization from culture. By *civilization* one refers to all functions that represent the mechanical and organizational conditions of life in a society. *Culture* suggests those forms by which people expresses their values in religious, artistic, erotic, or other more or less private commitments. Because civilization concerns direct conditions of production, its elements change in close correlation with production. Cultural factors, however, have an incomparably greater power of resistance. Cultural phenomena are extraordinarily differentiated and stratified. If one tries to classify them, one could start with a series of facts beginning with those having yet a very close relationship to civilization and ending with those linked closely to the biological and physiological processes of life. One could perhaps start with the church as an institution and could end with sexual life. In this cultural stratum also belong religious and philosophical beliefs as well as attitudes toward art and literature, the conventions of social intercourse, participation in sports, ideas about the meaning of life as well as manners. All these factors are historically laden; a historical tradition of nations, races, social groups, and religions, reaching far back into the past, has been incorporated into them. At the same time the power of the historical lends them a particular weight, and endows them with a resistance to change. Change will take place only relatively slowly and only under the pressure of material compulsion.

Paradoxical as it may seem, this concept of culture is largely synonymous with that of human nature. What is referred to as the nature or essence of the human being is by no means an invariant structure divorced from social life processes, merely conditioning or limiting social life to a certain degree but impervious to historical influence. In truth, human "nature" is subject to historical development; and it is a legitimate enterprise to study human nature within the confines of the social sciences.

Whenever we speak of human nature we touch on history. Indeed, it is an impossible task to separate neatly those human elements that are historical from those that are not. Even human hunger as a natural need cannot be satisfactorily understood if one abstracts it from the time-bound situation in which a person finds himself, from prevailing concepts of human needs and necessities, from the mode of production, and the place that this person occupies in the social order.

The concept of human nature incorporates not only individual factors but also relatively unchangeable or slowly evolving forms of community. The family provides us with an excellent example of such a "natural" community. Like the physiological qualities and psychic dispositions associated with the individual, the family does not change at the same speed as material production. It exhibits a certain resistance to the process of history.

One trait that runs through all previous human history is the fact that existing institutions, traditions, and persons become recognized as legitimate in one manner: through voluntary subjection of oneself to the symbols, notions, or commandments of the institutions, traditions, or persons. It is simply impossible to imagine a form of social existence in history that could have developed without this process of voluntary approval of persons or institutions that are regarded as superior. Here the decisive point is not whether during certain periods or within individual social groups a consciousness exists, nor is the extent to which the approval of the existing structures is alive in these groups decisive. The power of authority stands firm as a cultural factor, independent of all ideological concepts, and forms an indispensable mechanism of human history. Because it runs through all of history, it may indeed be considered part of human nature. This does not mean, however, that its manifestation does not change. But change does not affect its function in maintaining and preserving society and its meaning as an important and indispensable precondition of social life.

19

Authority as a Social Relationship

According to a conventional view the modern age differs from the medieval period in that all life in the latter age was dominated by authority, whereas since the Renaissance, rational reflection, the self-awareness of the critical, autonomous individual has supplanted mere belief. This idealistic outlook places authority and reason in brusque contrast to each other. The Middle Ages appear as a pyramid whose contours were firmly established by dogma, so that not only no thought outside the autoritarian belief could be conceived but the rules determining economic life as well as the particular features of political organization were formed by the canonical teachings of the Catholic church. At the same time there arose a social world that, while not free from human suffering and affliction induced by the new order, nonetheless, as a result of attenuation of the power of religious authority, by posit reason as the final criterion for decisions, could claim to hold the key to resolving all difficulties in human life. This view, which today [1934] has been threatened by totalitarian countries, has been a major power in the history of thought. The dominant motif of classical bourgeois philosophy and the beginnings of modern science is the declaration of war against all belief in traditional authority for having retarded progress in social and individual life. Belief in authority per se is considered by the modern period to be a mere opinion, superstition, emotional bias, mere habit—in sum, an unproductive adherence to tradition that continually threatens the development of culture. At the beginning of the bourgeois age Decartes's philosophy, through the category of doubt, endeavored to ban authoritative factors controlling thought and history.

The struggle against forms of authority at the end of the Middle Ages was certainly a powerful productive force for the development of the capitalist age. This struggle was an indispensable condition for the invention of new scientific methods of dominating nature, for creative imagination, and for the administration of all organizational forms: state bureaucracy, urban society, manufacture, and commerce. The name of Francis Bacon suggests itself in this context. Machiavelli and his school discuss the problem of state organization of the basis of a theory of human nature, which they strive to study with the aid of scientific methods and knowledge. We are not dealing merely with new schools of writers. Nor is it sufficient to point out that in these times of transition ideological reflections of certain social relationships stand in opposition to one another. It makes considerable difference whether modes of thought aim to reinforce the existing order or to upset and change it. Where everything aims to view the future and its possibilities in terms of the past, where expectations can be only variations on what already exists or what did exist, progressive forces of humanity are in constant danger of atrophy. Conversely, the effort to order society from a rational point of view necessitates the development of ways of life directed toward general human interests. Although with the struggle against authoritarian thinking we certainly touch on an important trait of modern history, it would be absurd to characterize the age of capitalism as free of authoritarian elements.

The political literature of the bourgeois age itself possessed a well-developed consciousness of the meaning of authority. Above all, when it is a question of supplying practical formulas for the political leader and promoting the tangible interests of certain personages or classes, a mass of prescriptions appear with advice on how to shore up the government's power of authority or how best to tie subjects to the existing order. Machiavelli—the classic example of postfeudal politics and the most extreme representative of a powerful authoritarian state order—carries the principle to its most extreme conclusion at the beginning of this *Discorsi*. There he points out that now is the time not only to act in accordance with ancient ideals in the fields of justice and medicine but also to follow the models of the ancients as authorities "in the establishing of republics, the maintenance of the state, the government of the rich, the development of the military and the art of warfare, in the administration of justice to subjects, and the expansion of the realm." Statecraft in both its absolutist and constitutional variants is essentially concerned with the legitimation of state authority and the subjection of the citizen's will to state sovereignty.

Modern social consciousness of authority is contradictory: on one hand, the struggle, proclaimed in philosophy and science, against the authoritarian principle; on the other hand, not only political literature but also pedagogical and theological literature bear witness to the power of authority in the present—not infrequently amounting to professions of faith.

A mere enumeration and typology of authoritarian relationships is open to two kinds of misunderstandings. The impression can arise that these relationships appeared arbitrarily and that there is no possibility of describing a structure upon which authoritarian relations rested and from which they were formed. However, no generally valid criterion exists according to which one could conclusively decide for all history how a relationship of authority must be constituted so that its observation would coincide with the concrete interests of those who observe its rules. First, the judgment of a concrete situation of groups or individuals is rendered more difficult by the fact that a plethora of authoritarian relationships is constantly present. Further, determining objective suitability demands first of all the total analysis of a given historical moment. To be sure, the authority of a surgeon, a ship captain, or an engineer assigning jobs to workers on a construction project is in closer proximity to objective social interests than the authoritarian acceptance of a certain taste in art or fashion. In the first examples, subjection to authority corresponds at least potentially to the objective level of knowledge in a certain situation. True, in an individual case the physician may be unqualified, the ship may not reach its destination owing to unfavorable circumstances, and an error may be found in the engineer's blueprints. A person who wishes to act appropriately in such situations can nonetheless do no other than to comply with the authorities at hand in spite of the possible risks. Conversely, in other cases one is more likely to assume that due to the mechanisms of conformism and the desire to be "with it," attitudes are accepted that may be at odds with the demands or independent thought, the promotion of health, or the proper management of income.

Now, in order to have a certain standard by means of which one can distinguish various authoritarian relationships from one another, we introduce at this point the concept of rationality in an objective and in a subjective sense. Imagine a scale that at one end lists behavior submitting to an authority in a completely irrational manner, merely out of admiration, love, fear, or a combination of these feelings, while at the opposite end the act of submission to an authority is based on a reasoned consciousness about the motives of one's subordination; a behavior that even while forgoing the prerogative of independent thought and action, knows itself to be guided by reason—we call it rational behavior. When the savage submits to the medicine man, when the small child yields unquestioningly to the alleged total superiority of his father, when, in the intoxication of emotion, a group allows itself to be persuaded by insidious persons to commit deeds that can result in grief for themselves and for others, then in such cases we speak of an irrational submission to authority. When a patient, after careful consideration, allows himself to be treated by a specific doctor, when on the basis of experience and study a group of people complies with the leaderships of a certain political party, when a young scientist is inclined to follow the teachings of a mature and experienced representative of his field, then we speak of a rational submission to authority. But the party leadership may turn out to be a group of decivers. The patient may pay for his trust of the carefully selected doctor with his health. The student may be mistaken; his mentor may be just a dilettante. Conversely, the savage may perhaps do very well to follow tradition and "primitive" reasoning, for he might forfeit his life if he were to try to cure himself independent of the traditions linked to the medicine man.

Contemporary relationships of authority cannot be measured by being tested in isolation. It would be fruitless positivism to analyze individually such relationships and apply to each one the criterion of subjective or objective rationality, for one would only end up with a profusion of positively or negatively evaluated structures. The question of how they relate to each other, how they affect the social dynamic as a whole, in short, an outline of the fundamental relationships and tendencies of an existing order that one expects from social research, can never come into being through this method.

For the judgment of the authority relationships in a certain historical epoch it is necessary to find the key to the decisive and fundamental relationship present in all other authoritarian relations.

> All combined labour on a large scale requires, more or less, a directing authority, in order to secure the harmonious working of the individual activities, and to perform the general functions that have their origin in the action of the combined organism, as distinguished from the action of its separate organs. A single violin player is his own conductor; an orchestra requires a separate one. The work of directing, superintending, and adjusting, becomes one of the functions of capital, from the moment that labour under the control of capital, becomes co-operative.[1]

These are Marx's introductory comments on the specific form of the division of labor in capitalist society. The new methods of production, the advancing complexity of the technical apparatus, the continual development of special mechanical work processes, the necessity to bring about the most varied forms of cooperation between workers in a manner appropriate to the composition of organic capital, all demand controlling authority. However, the capitalist modes of production differ from those of previous epochs not only in the former's infinitely more complex status of the production tools but also in the specific skills and characteristics that are demanded of people and without which the rational work process of machine production could not be managed. The relative stability of work methods and work tempo in medieval production, (i.e. artisan manufacture and agriculture) is incompatible with the amount of diligence, order, and punctuality needed to adapt to the continually changing conditions of the industrial apparatus and demands of the new economic system. Indeed, a new type of authority is needed. At the beginning of capitalist society one finds authoritarian forms of education geared to the requirements of the machine, some of which have taken on terroristic forms in their production of discipline, punctuality, and work intensity. The authoritarian measures that have been used in the history of capitalism are directly related to the economic process. They extend from brutal punishment on the bottom of the scale to the products of the fine arts and poetry, in which orderly and disciplined labor is celebrated as the essential human core. Out of the nature of capitalist society arises the objective necessity for people to submit to a certain regulation of work that does not of itself correspond to their will or needs.

The authority relationship by means of which one group regulates the work process for the majority is, however, not established for the objective interests of all members of society in equal measure. Certainly, in the new economy a rational work process determines the manufacture of products needed by society as a whole, but this process also simultaneously serves capitalist exploitation. The authority required in the process of production is exerted by the owners of the means of production, the capitalists, in their own interest. Capitalist management of production is "in substance two-fold."[2] If one wanted to regard the authoritarian control of the modern economy only as a function of the necessities of the technical work process, one would fail to understand even the earliest stages of capitalism, for even there economic authority revealed itself as a class relationship. Those who exert authority or in whose name it is exerted are always and regularly the owners of the means of production and "the authority of the . . . capitalist, in the shape of the powerful will of another . . .subjects their activity to his aims."[3] In all social orders to date, relations of production were at the same time interspersed with relationships of authority and the latter were molded by the former. In the medieval order the feudal lord was both strict father and provider to the peasants, who accepted and revered him in fear and respect. His authority as the child's providing parent was present. In capitalist society, the authority of the rulers produced by the relations of production is invisible, inaccessible, and alien. This social development would have been unthinkable without the educational authority of early capitalism, and the continued authoritarian organization of production remains the basis of the existing order. If in general we understand authority as the voluntary submission to an "alien" power embodied in persons or institutions, then authority relationships become in the last analysis synonymous with the acceptance of the order itself.

The relationship between class and structures of authority permeates indeed all areas of culture. Not only are *governmental branches* such as the legislature or judiciary inextricably linked with an existing economic order but these links exist for the state itself as a result of its demand for recognition by the citizen. For the history of all modern states the constant adaptation of administrative practices to the economy is more characteristic than the repercussions of official regulations on the processes of production and distribution themselves. Mercantilism demands an absolutist state, for entrepreneurs cannot function without government protection. But this relation between state and the economy does not occur only in the former's adapting to the latter; all state functions generally promote the acceptance of the economic order. Friedrich von Gentz referred to this in an astonishingly naive manner:

> It is the basis of a correctly organized state and the triumph of its constitution . . . that a great amount of rights and powers, abilities and education thereof, of inherited and acquired possessions of extremely unequal persons coexist through common laws and government so happily with each other that no one could arbitrarily infringe into his neighbor's sphere, and a poor man's cottage and field belong to him in precisely the same absolute sense as the palace and the power belong to the richest man.[4]

Basing an existing order on the institution of private property in such a direct manner does not occur too frequently in literature; in any case in modern German philosophy the "world-existence of man" appears as "bound to property" and thus as "bound to the totality of the order of society."[5]

Education may be everywhere colored by authoritarian aspects, and we must certainly not overlook the objectively rational moment in the recognition of the teacher and his expertise. But these pedagogical relationships of authority are two-sided. Both the prerequisites for the educational process as such and the submission to the authority of educational institutions are necessary conditions for the incorporation of the individual into the economic process itself. In recent decades we have seen many debates on whether schools should be authoritarian institutions of learning or should instead encourage, as much as possible, the creative powers of the child. Although these discussions are certainly significant, the fact remains that in spite of the life consequences the two educational methods may have, in either case the educational organization as a whole serves to integrate young people into the status quo. Whether this takes place in a despotic or liberal way often reflects the economic situation. In a time when the ruling groups feel themselves particularly obliged to solicit recognition and acceptance of the social order as a result of general economic uncertainty, the methods of instruction are less strict than in a situation in which acceptance is enforced with all possible severity as is at present [1934] the case in totalitarian states.

In all cases the fundamental authority structure is visible in the teacher's authority and in the willingness, in spite of impulses to the contrary, to follow his orders, that is, to obey and to learn. The learning of skills, the acquisition of knowledge, the acquisition of modes of behavior, and character traits necessary for economic success—all these achievements of the pedagogical authority structure form a direct and important condition for later incorporation into economic life. The social role of pedagogical authority is understandable only in terms of the relationship of this authority to the social totality.

Another example of the manner in which individual relationships are determined through the prevailing order is the *relations between the sexes.* In practically all bourgeois states the overwhelming majority of women are obliged to seek the economic help of men. The fact that most social institutions and public opinion are formed by men is crucially related to the fact that men possess economic predominance over women. The tendency in popular speech to distinguish, for example, marriages of love from marriages of convenience may indeed, in individual cases, emphasize certain features of human relations, but it ignores the fact that feelings themselves already undergo a process of formation by existing social relations along the lines of a predisposition for authoritarian relationships. When dealing with emotions a clear distinction between what is individually and what is socially conditioned is impossible. Even Romeo and Juliet's relationship is subjugated to the laws of patriarchal marriage, and it is the male who initiates this relationship. This couple does not perish for immanent emotional causes but, rather, in their conflict with social institutions whose power, based on property, is sufficient to stifle a relationship that tries to place itself outside the social structure.

Scientific work too cannot be understood outside the fundamental twofold relationship of bourgeois society. Although on the one hand it is a powerful productive force for the development of the economy, it nonetheless contributes to the maintenance of the social organization as a whole, both with regard to the methods and approaches of the individual disciplines and with regard to their professional organization. In the history of science, whenever results are produced that are not in the interests of the existing social structure, or tend to conflict with it, the results and its supporters are denied social prestige.

The development of modern natural science is very closely tied to the beginnings of bourgeois society. The laws of mechanics, the views held on the motion of heavenly bodies, and the refutation of ptolemaic geocentric theory contributed greatly to the disruption of the medieval social organization. The proponents of these theories were originally persecuted for these attacks on a declining society, which was nonetheless economically and politically still secure. Modern natural science itself becomes an authority only when its results can be used in machine production and transport technology by the new dominant bourgeois strata. Similarly, only at this moment do the proponents of these scientific disciplines find themselves in an economic situation where they both contribute to and benefit from the fruits of the new order and its authority. When new scientific theories run up against severe opposition, such hostility is connected with the fact that powerful groups feel threatened. In the history of the social sciences, however, one may frequently observe the condemnation of theories whose implications threatened traditional authoritarian values. Thus, the radical wing of the French philosophers of the eighteenth century or Karl Marx and his followers in the nineteenth century experienced literally the power of the ruling authorities.

Positive religions promote and reinforce the immutability of the status quo. Their theme and practice to a great extent is the reconciliation of the majority to their lack of social power. *Religious conceptions* reflect existing social life insofar as man is confronted with a being independent of him and who demands that he accept his fate as just. Religion repeats, as it were, the entire ideological process by making it its business to confer on prevailing authority the character of its justice and legitimacy. Authority gains the ideological appearance of legitimacy through religion because the uniform submission demanded of all human beings by the powers of transcendence conjures an appearance of equality. "In other words and because there is only God above men: the rulers and the ruled become and remain free and safe from each other only by submitting to one and the same law, not human, but divine, or by serving one and the same God."[6]

In the most recent past the contradictions of the social order have become so obvious that interest in their preservation seems to demand an extraordinary exertion and strengthening of authoritarian social mechanisms. In some countries today [1934] in all areas of life, authority is becoming the guiding principle of all modes of action, thought, and feeling to such an extent that it no longer seems to matter *what* is ordered and *what* demands recognition but, rather, that orders continue to be given and to demand submission. It is clear, then, that irrationality is reaching its apex. The velocity and extent of this process at the same time point to the moment of its potential subversion of existing authority, and although authoritarian institutions may very well deteriorate into sheer physical oppression, and finally into terror, this very process generates the tendencies for the totalitarian system's final collapse.

Notes

1. Karl Marx. *Capital,* vol. 1 (New York, 1967), pp. 330–31.
2. Ibid., p. 332.
3. Ibid.
4. *Fragmente aus der neuesten Geschichte des politischen Gleichgewichts in Europa, 1806. Staatsschriften und Briefe,* vol. 1 (Munich, 1921), p. 119.
5. Karl Jaspers, *Philosophie,* vol. 2 (Berlin, 1932), pp. 364f.
6. Franz von Baader. *Sämtliche Werke,* vol. 5, *Über den Begriff der Autorität* (Leipzig, 1854), p. 295.

20

Authority in the Course of History

In his *German History in the Age of the Reformation* Leopold von Ranke remarks: "The secret of power lies in the fact that power is only capable of utilizing all of its resources when all forces voluntarily follow her command."[1] Here Ranke points out a fundamental relationship between power and authority: power, the indispensable ingredient of authority, is at the same time dependent on its voluntary recognition. Power relationships themselves are founded on specific material relationships. The direct preservation of power relationships is largely tied to the material base; and as soon as the latter becomes shaky, the maintenance of its supporting authority is likewise threatened. Ranke's statement is found in the introductory remarks to his portrayal of the reign of Charles V; it is of great significance for the entire historical situation of the fifteenth and sixteenth centuries. The events of that time, out of which decisive traits of modern history developed, are themselves a classical example for the connection of power and authority; "authoritarian" ages such as the Middle Ages are not superseded by ages in which bare power triumphs or where to a great extent a lack of authority dominates. Rather, out of the battle with the obsolete authorities, new authorities develop and consolidate their position. These new powers need new sanctions.

For the Middle Ages, consistently viewed by historians in light of their authoritarian restrictiveness, one need not comment on authoritarian relationships. We are accustomed to judging the decisive struggles of this period as an aspect of opposing powers competing internally within a closed authority system. The empire and the papacy, royal central power and individual feudal lords, the pope and demanding church princes were indeed forces that were in an almost constant struggle with each other: in their totality they formed a solid power structure to which both the broad urban and peasant masses and also the lesser lords and dignitaries submitted. But aside from these obvious political forms, the entire economic-technical apparatus, education, childbearing and science, and, above all, religious life appeared as firmly established orders of authoritarian validity.

The hierarchically organized authoritarian structure of feudalism became increasingly unstable with the beginnings of the new scientific discoveries, early industries, the newly forming concentrations of capital; with the extension of trade through development of international trade routes and the opening of new lands; with the introduction of new production methods on the basis of the natural sciences, the radical change in war technology through firearms, the broadening of the horizon of knowledge through the rediscovery of the classical Greek and Roman tradition. Such entirely new societal conditions of life in all areas, such new material foundations of power undermined the previous leading groups.[2] When neither the Roman church nor the empire seemed capable of asserting themselves any longer against the new national states with their efforts to expand economically and politically in both the domestic and the international spheres; when the core of medieval armies, the knights, was declining and dying out as a result of its now obsolete and impractical weapons and its pitiful methods of agrarian production, and the resulting high indebtedness; when the various monastic orders, in view of the new needs and possibilities, could no longer play an important societal role in the raising of children, the care of the poor, and the instruction of the peasants in the cultivation of the land, then was not only the power of these groups threatened but also the authority rooted in it.

The struggle between the typical authority structures of the Middle Ages and those of the modern era was particularly well represented in the great reform councils during the first half of the fifteenth century. At that time three historical periods and three different methods of ruling arose. The papal and the imperial central power backed by large groups of ecclesiastic and secular feudality all endeavored, through appeals to the dignity of a long historical tradition and eternal statutes, to keep a system alive, against which all progressive forces of the time rebelled. These claims were opposed above all by the territorial princes, whose economic and political interests were coming into ever greater irreconcilable contradiction with an apparatus that was no longer able to satisfy the interests of the new ruling classes. As the control of the old central powers decayed, their authority was also threatened; and as the economic and political order of the national states arose, they claimed the recognition of a new authority structure. At the same time, along with absolutism, its opposite also developed. The old powers had a negative influence on not only the economic interests of the future ruling groups but also the needs of life of the broad masses (which, after all, would become the future object of domination by the new powers). There came into being—particularly in the Italian and Bohemian uprisings—a dynamic by which the authority of absolutism was already affected in its beginning: the protests of exploited masses.

The events of the councils faithfully reproduced this struggle between historical claims. A unanimous posture developed, aware of the danger that, under the banner of religious freedom and social justice, could threaten the old as well as the new powers. The leaders of this movement, and with them the movement itself, were exterminated, explicitly in the name of authority. This was done in the name of secular power and also in the name of the authority of the church; in defense against the common enemy, the hostile forces once again united. In this type of battle, the not yet clearly distinct struggle of the old and the new orders was expressed. "The synod, which wrested dominion over the church *(Kirchenregiment)* from the pope's hands, implemented it in his place and thoroughly in his spirit according to the principle of authority."[3] When Walser in his analysis of the legitimization of the struggle against the dangerous subjectivity of Hus makes the observation that by its actions the council remained stuck in the Middle Ages, he is exaggerating. By the authority that the council assumed for its resolutions, which were arrived at on the basis of a national division of votes, the claims that hitherto had been directly associated with the person of the pope now went over to other more up-to-date authorities. Nonetheless, the fact that the content of this authority as ecclesiastic dogma remained essentially unchanged indicates that the power struggle was not yet clearly decided, as the contemporary recovery of the papal central power under Martin showed.

At the Council of Basel the power constellation was still quite similar; the fronts just became more clearly defined. Although the church assembly still stressed the principle of its own absolute authority, and the worldly rulers *(Landesfürsten)* thereby availed themselves of a traditional form, nonetheless this form itself had been affected so greatly by the actually existing structure of power of the national state that, due to the reform decisions, the pope reigned in his "church state" like any secular ruler, but as regards his duties to Christendom had to carry out the function of a "higher church bureaucrat . . . who every year gives an account to his voters and judges of his carrying-out of the duties of his office."[4] Of course, both council assemblies still were representative of a transitional period in which both the old and the new powers tried, as it were, to outsmart the authoritarian pretensions of the other party and to lay claim to the same authority from the same sources and dogma.

In the great historical battles and wars in the first half of the sixteenth century, absolutism achieved a clear victory; the authority of pope and emperor, feudal nobility and the monasteries[5] was in decay, and there arose the first forms of a new authority that was coming into its own. When the absolutist order raised the claims of rationality and religious dignity through the territorial High Church, it was not authority itself but, rather, its social content that had shifted. This became particularly evident in the country where the bourgeois-capitalist nature of the modern era attained one of its most precise expressions: England. Although the struggle against the papacy was fought there largely alongside a demand for freedom of thought and belief, there then arose an authority structure, well represented by Puritanism, in which the rational elements in the struggle against the old order carried through by means of religion. This authority structure was to prove useful in the maintenance of the new order. The social teachings of Protestantism, Puritanism, and Calvinism served to justify the new bourgeois lifestyle.[6]

The problem arises whether and to what extent an existing authoritarian structure survives longer on the strength of its psychological hold than the actual social conditions of life would demand. In any case, this is true only for a certain transitional period. When the new power relationships are finally stabilized on the basis of the changed mode of production, then a clear-cut situation arises: the thoughts, feelings, and intrinsic dispositions prevailing in a certain period function decisively in the interests of the ruling minorities. To be sure, it is a particular historical problem to ascertain in which social classes the different forms of authoritarian behavior are developed (this must not, by any means, be the case in only the upper class), but they function in the interest of the ruling minorities' desire to preserve the status quo.

When in an era certain conceptions of authority have triumphed, they correspond to the interests of the dominant classes. The two-sword theory of the Middle Ages, the images of the papal sun and the imperial moon, the pyramid of the feudal order, did not serve merely as a codification of existing power relationships but, rather, at the same time to "anchor" psychologically these relationships in European humanity. Later, the doctrines of divine right and the territorial prince's freedom from popular accountability were significant for the personal protection of the monarch and also as a precise expression of the authority of the absolutist system, including its dignitaries and bureaucracy. If these two types of authoritarian conceptions seem particularly static, this was related to the fact that the production methods during this period were developing at a very slow tempo. If these change completely and an agrarian or artisan production is supplanted by modern industry, the power of the leading groups in the relatively static system is itself threatened.

As local and national self-sufficiency was supplanted by the world economy, the conception that ruled people as an authoritarian law was very closely connected with the principle of achievement: thenceforth, certain groups and individuals were not legitimized in assuming control of society by the grace of eternal divine laws; rather, the legimation of leading groups and individuals occurred in such a way that economic success also included the justification of their social position. An individual's success appeared as the honor that in principle anyone can attain under apparently free and equal social conditions; it was an order to which he who, because of his own behavior had failed, must submit. Here, the human being must continually struggle and slave; if his exertions are not in vain, then this is a sign that he belongs to the chosen. This connection between economic success and justification of social position, originally developed in Calvinism, forms the basis for the entire history of bourgeois consciousness.

Although the conceptions of authority prevailing in a given period are at the service of the ruling groups, nonetheless, it is necessary to avoid the overly simplistic view that the underlying strata did not take part in the formation of the authoritarian structure. It is certainly true for history up to now that those groups and individuals who set forth a claim to authoritative validity for the institutions that they controlled acquired privileges from this claim: economic goods, social prestige. However, insofar as the authoritarian ruling power still, albeit in an unsatisfying manner, insured the reproduction of society as a whole, the particular social manifestations of authoritarian structures were affected to a certain extent by the interests of those classes that were the object of the authoritarian claim.

The form of this participation and its extent depend on the constellation of society as a whole. Let us take two marginal cases. The irrational component—the safeguarding of the power to rule—can so obscure the rational component—the safeguarding of the work process—that absolutely no material, cultural, or spiritual interests continue to bind the subordinate gorups to the antiquated, shattered order. At such times, the ruling power may indeed still be able to develop a cruel system of physical oppression and terror, and it may thereby at least lengthen itself for a time, but it no longer possesses authority: the situation is revolutionary. In the last third of the eighteenth century French absolutism, along with its feudal appendages, the first and second estates, had lost all authority over the broad urban classes and, to a large extent, also over the rural population. The history of all revolutions basically shows that when the old order receives its death blow, it has long since lost all power support. On the other hand, where the social conditions are formed so that the great majority of people can simply not imagine an existence outside the given order, the given authority structure tends to be accepted absolutely. The question is whether this absolute acceptance is based on a relative degree of rationality justifying the existing conditions of life or whether a more effective societal organization would be possible in view of the level of knowledge and the production apparatus. For the first situation, the Middle Ages are particularly representative. The artisan or the peasant was bound to authority in a objectively reasonable manner, in view of the inadequate technology and scientific organization. Hence, the range and importance of authoritative behavior was practically unlimited. At present, however, in many areas of Europe not only are ideas of authority often propagated that consciously imitate medieval conditions but such ideas have also found widespread acceptance. This authority structure has, nonetheless, many more false aspects than in the medieval case and must also leave broad areas (above all, that of personal existence) outside its "jurisdiction," or, at best, must very energetically endeavor to subordinate these areas to its power. Such authority functions are essentially irrational.

Between these two extreme cases of the relation of dominated groups to societal authority, there exists a multitude of other possibilities. Where a system appears to be very fluid, that is, where in fact or in the collective imagination a relatively free play of forces prevails and most groups and individuals are convinced that the prevailing authorities in their epoch serve the general good, then its effect is conceived as being neither absolutely unjustified nor as a superior power to be accepted without question. Rather, the tendency arises to regard this voluntary submission to the forms of authority as an act that is both obligatory and useful for all members of the social order. In such situations it may well be that this identification with authority is largely founded on rational premises; it can, however, be an illusion.

Examples of volatile historical periods where the ruled identify with authority abound in bourgeois society. To whatever degree this thought may or may not have been justified, in any case it is one of the characteristics of liberalism that many groups are firmly convinced of the possibility of their own social advancement. Economics, politics, and culture are all experienced as fundamentally rational; and however this order may be enforced in the last analysis by a real power apparatus, nonetheless, it is not seen by the societal consciousness as intimately connected with the recognition of the system. Rather, it tends more likely to become a symbol of the whole that equally protects and promotes everyone. In situations where authority is imposing itself as such, it essentially calls on reason for support. The best guarantor in these historical situations was the ideology of upward mobility, which itself puts forth the greatest claim to authority. In actual periods of civil disorder, a considerable unity of interests seems to exist among all groups that oppose an obsolete order. Nevertheless, the outcome of bourgeois revolutions has shown how one group actually benefits from the new order and leaves the great majority with their more extreme demands unsatisfied.

The history of all bourgeois revolutions repeatedly exhibits the same process: at the end, those forces who wish to carry the struggle further, who had been comrades-in-arms, are declared rebels by their former allies who have now come to power.

> It is ... the nature of all parties or classes which have come to power to demand that the newly found (by the revolution) legal basis must now be accepted unconditionally, must be looked upon as sacred. The right of revolution *existed*—otherwise, after all, those presently in power would not be justified, but from now on, it must no longer exist.[7]

This mechanism came to bear in an equal manner on the radical trends in the Reformation, on the Levellers after the Puritan Revolution, and on the Hébertistes in the French Revolution.

Authority does not affect social relationships in only a general way; rather, in every detail the existing societal conditions influence the authoritarian mechanism. The history of constitutional governments in modern times, the establishment and prestige of parliaments and of the entire political apparatus, is an important source for state and social authority in general. In German history before World War I, when large landed property still played a political role over and against the interests of almost all other groups, the political system enjoyed a considerable amount of authority in the bourgeois classes, but with some reservations. The possibility of abandoning this respect for authority as soon as the situation became somewhat critical was always present.

A much more exact example is offered by the relationship of the French bourgeoisie to Napoleon I, who for a period of many years possessed quasi-absolute power and then lost it suddenly. At first, his policies restrained the shocks of the revolution and safeguarded the development of trade and industry. With the Napoleonic wars hope for economic expansion was aroused, the blockage was an extraordinary inducement for French industry, and the reform of the national administration assured the security of the capitalist economy through legal and commercial norms. As long as the bourgeoisie did not feel itself able to create on its own a political system suited to its interests, it made do with Napoleon's political authority. However, the moment that the political system threatened to become independent, that wars impeded production, and the blockage turned out to be a cause of crises,[8] Napoleon's authority also fell to pieces. No change in the role of the leading groups took place during his years in power; rather, the history of the consolidation and dissolution of his authority reflects precisely the economic and social processes.

> Napoleon came to an impasse because he acted exactly according to the protectionist views of the capitalist bourgeoisie. On the other hand, this very bourgeoisie was forced, in consideration of their interests and their future, to withdraw their support from their ruler who continually brought about new causes of political and economic crises.[9]

Benjamin Constant is especially representative of the development of concepts of authority in the leading bourgeois groups since the French Revolution. To be sure, Constant wrote a draft of a constitution for Napoleon when he returned from Elba, but it was an attempt to further the interests of the leading bourgeois groups. For Constant, the existing level of development of the bourgeois mode of production seemed to depend on accelerating, as much as possible, the development of economic forces. Thus, his continual praise of peace as a necessity for present society and his warning against granting political rights to the nonproperties classes. However—and this is the crux of his political ideology—all of his thought stands under the sign of the struggle against paternalism, against authority. In the introduction to a later collection of essays he wrote:

> For forty years I have defended the same principle, freedom in every-thing, in religion, in philosophy, in literature, in industry, in politics: and by the word liberty I understand the triumph of individuality, both over the authority which would like to govern by despotism and over the masses who demand the right to subject the minority to the majority. Despotism has no rights.[10]

Constant's antiauthoritarian program does indeed contain all those elements that are crucial for the liberal bourgeoisie's own authority: on the one hand, the program of unlimited individualistic action; on the other hand, resistance to the demands of the proletariat. The conscious authoritarian reverence of the absolutist state power is replaced, as it were, by the authoritative pretensions of private property. Although at approximately the same time a philosophical proponent of the Restoration defined the problem as how to attain a clear understanding of the essence of authority,[11] such statements merely reflect the consciousness of groups that were behind the times. The liberalism of the reign of the *roi bourgeois,* the self-consciousness of the bourgeoisie of the time as the consciousness of the authority of its own power, are the most vivid examples of the authority structure of this relatively uninterrupted and unchallenged period of bourgeois rule. However, the further this development proceeds, the more bourgeois society comes to understand the maintenance of an existing order as the uninhibited unfolding of production and the need to anchor it in a conscious demand for its eternal validity.

In his later years. Nietzsche once remarked: "The esteem for authority increases proportionately to the decrease of creative powers."[12] And indeed his statement does indicate the direction that authority was to take in the process of bourgeois development. Out of an originally conscious rejection arises, in the end, the highest recognition of authority. Although a sentence like Arthur Vierkandt's that authority brings out the best in a man[13] is still limited to the individual, gradually the conviction that the maintenance and rebuilding of authoritative power was a vital question of the existing system generally become realized politically. G. Ferrero wrote, "Political anarchy, which could bring about the collapse of all principles of authority in Europe, would coincide with the most complete spiritual and intellectual anarchy which has ever existed in Europe."[14] The liberal Italian historian, having opposed states ruled by authoritarian means, when confronted by the present became the herald of authoritarian forms of society because giving them up would endanger the order: "The state, the ethical view of the world, the concepts of beauty, the family, property."[15] The last word makes clear that for the early bourgeois Constant, just as for this later bourgeois thinker, it was in both cases the same order whose defense demanded different means in accordance to the situation as a whole.

The arguments previous in this section essentially were intended to show the nature of the dynamics involved in the formation of new relationships of authority. It has already been pointed out that a certain authority structure that connects antagonistically the social requisites of production with the unilateral promotion of the interests of the leading groups necessarily reaches beyond itself. Certainly, during long periods (e.g. the High Middle Ages and early capitalism) authority, linked with the power of the reigning minority, nonetheless in a certain way provided for the affairs of society as a whole. However, as a consequence of authority's contradictory origin, this provision took place in a growing tension toward the large groups of society. Periods of history in which the fundamental authority relationship is marked by increasing irrationality continually vacillate between open violence and the exaggeration of the threatened authority's claims to legitimacy.

The history of the Middle Ages is just as full of polemics and disputations as of bloody persecutions. The Stuarts, struggling in vain to prevent their downfall in the first half of the seventeenth century, and the English aristocracy, whose interests were intimately linked to the Stuarts, waged their struggle against Parliament and the middle class sometimes with appeals to their own authority, protected by the most holy traditions, and sometimes by violent dissolution of the legislative bodies and rigorous sentences for the leaders and representatives of the oppositional movement. In a complicated way this process was repeated just before the French Revolution, in which, however, yet another defense mechanism of a declining authority was operative. This consisted of trying to outsmart, as it were, the new authority, already recognizable in its contours and demands, by attempting to capture it for the interests of the old order in a progressively thicker net of concessions.[16] The halfhearted consideration of bourgeois wishes when appointing ministers, and the ambiguous attempts to appear to satisfy these demands in the Assembly of Notables while in fact quashing them serve to supplement the examples of the administrative use of power and of legitimist justifications that accumulated directly before and during the first stage of the Revolution.

The history of the post-Napoleonic Restoration contains, so to speak, a catalogue of the various means by which a societal order attempts to guard its own threatened authority against decay. From the constitutional promises of the Viennese *Bundesakte* and its very limited fulfillment of the promise to allow many members of the bourgeois intelligentsia to participate in the government for the purposes of a reactionary administration to the half-liberal Prussian cabinets and the concessions of Friedrich Wilhelm IV at the burial at the *Märzgefallene,* the attempt is continually repeated to safeguard one's own authority over the system through concessions to new groups on their way to social and political power. Hand in hand with this go efforts to lend the regime necessary dignity by making it appear sometimes as a natural, organic entity and at other times as the fulfillment of a heavenly plan. The founding of the Holy Alliance became, among other things, a visible symbol for the authority demands of legitimacy. The claim to the inseparable proximity of throne and altar, the doctrine disseminated in universities and in official publications of the superiority of monarchy, the apparent proof of their direct historical link to the medieval feudal order, whose justification applied to present conditions, was forced on the opposition with an iron discipline and—if necessary—with violence from the Wartburg festival to the trial of the Göttingen Seven. These were all important means of protection for the threatened authority of the ruling classes.

These palliatives are used by statesmen to supplement other means. The doctrines developed in the heyday of early national states and absolutism on the well-being of the state and how this can be promoted by a refined technique of the art of psychological control had a certain productive meaning while these authoritarian, centrally governed state systems were still the relatively most advanced means of promoting the development of the capitalist mode of production. However, with the advancing increase and development of production, this technique became reactionary. In an almost cynical manner, Friedrich von Gentz, one of the most effective publicists of the Restoration, dealt with this denunciation of the future in the interests of an existing distribution of power:

> When . . . as in our century, the destruction of everything old becomes the prevailing, the overwhelming tendency, then outstanding persons must become orthodox *(altglaübig)* to the point of obstinacy. . . . Even

> now, even in these times of dissolution, many must, it goes without saying, work for the culture of the human race; but some must dedicate themselves absolutely to the difficult, the thankless, the more dangerous business of opposing this excess of culture . . . ; [one must] retain the exalted spark of an eternal opposition against the fury and decay of world-ravaging innovations.[17]

At times a group whose power is threatened attempts to prop up its authority in such a way that the existing order essentially has to be accepted only out of historical or religious tradition. It thereby aims to obfuscate existing historical contradictions; and then the concept of justice comes to embody the protest of the repressed interests of society as a whole, or at least the interests of the great majorities. Thus, the slogan "justice" has been placed on the banner of many revolutionaries in the modern age. This word adorned the banners of the Roman people's tribune Cola de Rienzo,[18] which—to be sure, in a situation not yet ripe for real revolutionary change and without a clear consciousness of its political aims—represented to a large degree the interests of the urban population of Rome against the unlimited demands of the economically unproductive nobility.[19] The same slogan was heard at all decisive steps taken by the English middle class in its struggle against the medieval social order at the juncture of the fifteenth and sixteenth centuries:

> The slogan of divine justice as the epitome of all programs which one must not request but demand flew from mouth to mouth. All the small complaints of the tax-paying peasants, the tears of the dispossessed, the crude demands of the urban proletariat, the industrial ambition of the journeyman, the quiet pleas of the beggar, the silent wishes of the patriot for truly monarchical rule, for domestic peace, for international standing—they soon found their reflection . . . in one great word, in the demand for God's justice. . . . The educated and the illiterate, rich and poor alike spoke of divine justice when political and social wishes were being formulated; already in the 1502 uprising on the Upper Rhine the inscription of the banner raised there read: "Nothing but God's justice."[20]

Justice is the name of the protest against a bad old order; however, as a new social order is formed, new minority interests tend to override the interests of the majority, and the slogan of justice begins to include an additional connotation that is derived from those interests that become dominant in the new order. In the motto of divine justice, on the one hand, the theological framework of the Middle Ages lives on and is used against the age itself. On the other hand, theology rein-forces the authority and "justice" of the absolutist bureaucratic state against further demands for reform. The declaration of justice in the French Revolution is inseparably linked with a liberalism that rejects any attacks on the order of private property as not corresponding to its concept of justice.[21]

In history to date, the end of a certain system of government has by no means resulted in a situation lacking all authority, unless one understands *authority* to mean state power. In such moments the form of authority that, due to more fundamental conditions, has already gained wide influence comes into a position of political dominance. The period of terror in the French Revolution essentially unleashed the principles of a petty-bourgeois morality: absolute severity toward powerlessness while simultaneously respecting power and the cru-elty of the thrifty and "respectable" individual. In the battle with his own drives, this individual becomes sadistic and begins to envy those who—in fact or only apparently—are capable of pleasure (bourgeois resentment of the nobility and anti-Semitism have similar psychologi-cal functions). The belief that one must conform to existing conditions and that blind necessity knows no other considerations is what led to the idea of the guillotine. The guillotine symbolized total indifference to individual fate and values, and corresponded to the system that the petty-bourgeois masses of the cities had already previously embraced and that had, through their efforts, won general power. In this system societal necessity was carried out blindly and without respect—not, however, without authority. The slogan "la nation" did not designate a rational and classless social organizatioan but rather a system of dependency that necessarily produced cruelty in human beings.

In a similar form this order has expressed itself not only in the mass murders after Napoleon's fall but also in an entire series of so-called uprisings up to the present day. Real dependency, insofar as it is felt to be inevitable and external, causes discontent. In the French Revolution and even more strikingly in the terror of the counterrevolution, the necessity of economic ranks, of poverty, and difficult conditions of existence was for the most part never questioned. Those struggles did, however, also point beyond this entire period; they already contained hope for an epoch free from oppression. In light of such far-reaching tendencies, terror loses its moral meaning. Insofar as terror is necessary for defense, however, it ceases to satisfy feelings of comradery. Rather, it serves only to fight and intimidate the opposition. In the French

Revolution both of these aspects were mixed together. At times, the terror seemed to be calculated more toward satisfying the bloodlust of its supporters than toward the oppression of its enemies. The feeling of hopeless dependence and of a *vie manquée;* the conviction that oppression is objectively necessary and that if one cannot avoid it oneself, then others should also be subject to it; the idea of a natural process as the model for human society and the strongest expression of this process, death—all seemingly justify the fact that in society happiness and talent perish meaninglessly. This bourgeois trust in authority, bound to the feelings of spite and egotism, experiences satisfaction at the sight of the suffering of others. The policeman Dutard declared, according to Mathiez's report, on the execution of twelve condemned men at the beginning of the Reign of Terror:

> I must tell you that these executions produce the greatest effects politically, the most important of which is that they calm the resentment of the people at the ills which it is enduring. In them its vengeance is satisfied. The wife who has lost her husband, the father who has lost his son, the tradesman whose business has gone, the workman who pays such high prices for everything that his wages are reduced to practically nothing, perhaps consent to reconcile themselves to the ills which they endure only when they see men whom they believe to be their enemies more unfortunate than themselves.[22]

This observation is pertinent not only for the French Revolution.

The struggling order is supported in its attempt to consolidate its authority neither exclusively by violence nor by conscious propaganda. Rather, it has at its disposal the internal disposition toward an authoritarian cast of mind, which it produces ever anew by means of education and the process of character formation. By acting in a retarding manner, these instinctual dispositions (*Triebstrukturen*) are one of the most differentiated and effective means of delaying decline for a relatively long time. When in situations of decay it comes to a long struggle between old and new power, when a method of ruling that uses the device of strict authority has no prospect of effectiveness, then this is intimately connected with that psychological anchoring and reinforcement of authoritative behavior. The establishment of a new order and its authority are crucially affected in speed and extent by the transformation of those psychic structures.

Notes

1. L. von Ranke, *Deutsche Geschichte im Zeitalter der Reformation,* Akademie-Ausgabe, vol. 1, (Munich, 1925), p. 339.
2. Cf. here in Excursus I the exemplary account of the crisis of the ancient authority structure.
3. Ernst Walser, "Die Konzilien von Konstanz und Basel," *Gesammelte Studien zur Geistesgeschichte der Renaissance* (Basel, 1932), p. 4. This essay by Walser portrays in a particularly instructive manner the world-historical meaning of the reform councils and gives an analysis of both the material, economic, and political foundations and the ideological battles centered on the concept of authority.
4. Ibid., p. 18.
5. "The subversive tendencies show themselves all the way up to the highest reaches of the old secular-religious hierarchy. The future of Europe depends on whether these achieve complete power or whether the conservative powers inhibiting change which were, after all, still strong and powerful, will gain the upper hand." Ranke, *Deutsche Geschichte im Zeitalter der Reformation,* vol. 4, p. 9.
6. Cf., besides the well-known analyses in the works of Ernst Troeltsch and Max Weber above all the following: Levin L. Schücking, Studien über die Familie und Literatur in England im 16., 7. und 18. Jahrhundert (Leipzig and Berlin, 1929).
7. Letter from Friedrich Engels to August Bebel, November 18, 1884, *Briefe an A. Bebel und andere,* vol. 1 (Leningrad, 1933), p. 374.
8. Cf. above all Benjamin Constant's attacks on Napoleon's war policy, which, Constant claims, was ruining business life, while industry and trade depend on peace. See in particular his essay "L'esprit de conquête" (Paris, 1918; foreword by Albert Thomas).
9. G. Bourgin, *Napoleon und seine Zeit* (Stuttgart und Gotha, 1925), p. 144.
10. Benjamin Constant, *Mélanges de littérature et de politique* (Paris, 1829), p. vi.
11. Franz von Baader, *Sämtliche Werke,* vol. 1, (Leipzig, 1852), p. 76.
12. Friedrich Nietzsche, *Sämtliche Werke,* vol. 13 (Nachlass), p. 217.
13. Arthur Vierkandt, *Gesellschaftslehre,* p. 231.
14. G. Ferrero, *Der Untergang der Zivilisation des Altertums* (Stuttgart, 1922), p. 189.
15. Ibid. Similar formulations are used frequently today by leading statesmen, specifically even in those countries with a great liberal tradition. A more recent demand by Cailloux was already mentioned. A particularly interesting propagation of the principle of authority as the necessary condition for the continued existence of the hitherto existing societal order is found in a collection of speeches by the former French President Domergue, *Discours à la nation française.* Cf. above all pp. 12, 45, 69.
16. There is much material on this, above all in A. de Tocqueville's classical work *L'ancien régime et la révolution,* vol. 4 of *Oeuvres complètes* (Paris, no date). In English: *The Old Regime and the French Revolution.*

17. Friedrich von Gentz, *Staatsschriften und Briefe*, vol. 1 (Munich, 1921), p. 294.

18. Cf. Ferdinand Gregorovius, *Geschichte der Stadt Rom im Mittelalter*, vol. 2 (Stuttgart, 1871), p. 245.

19. Ibid., pp. 241f. Likewise Konrad Burdach's investigations, especially in: *Rienzo und die geistige Wandlung seiner Zeit* (Berlin 1913–28), p. 167 and passim.

20. Karl Lamprecht, *Deutsche Geschichte*, vol. 1, first half (Berlin, 1921), p. 128.

21. Cf. the social analysis of liberal mottos in Marx's *Capital* (Meissner).

22. Albert Mathiez, *The French Revolution*, trans. Catherine Alison Phillips (New York, 1962), pp. 396–97.

21

Authority and Family

Among the cultural structures that are conditioned by the manner in which society fulfills the needs of life, the family assumes a place of particular importance. In the course of history it developed its own historical dynamic; a family per se does not exist. This dynamic has constantly exerted an influence on social conditions as a whole. In the course of history and particularly in the bourgeois era the family has fulfilled various functions. In sociological literature general agreement exists that this is the place where biological propagation and maintenance of the human species is ensured, and where the upbringing of the younger generation is carried out, preparing it for incorporation into existing the society. For this latter task many important means are used: the cultivation of religious traditions, the awakening of the feeling of piety, guidance that encourages a harmonious compromising of one's own interests in face of those of other family members, and the educational value of leisure time spent together. In addition to these functions, the family in bourgeois society is entrusted with the duty of maintaining and increasing individual property, i.e. family property, a duty that finds juridical expression in laws of inheritance. Above all, it is characteristic for the family in bourgeois society that, in contrast to earlier periods, it increasingly ceases to be a place of production and becomes increasingly a community of consumption. In this context we will regard the family purely from the perspective of its relationship to authority. This must not, however, be taken as meaning that a new, previously ignored aspect of the family is being presented. Two main points will be made. First, how are character types produced in the bourgeois family that adapt to existing society in an authoritarian manner and thereby aid the reproduction of this society? Conversely, how does society as a whole continually produce the family as an institution that is capable of carrying out the function of creating this authoritarian character type?

Aside from the changes that the bourgeois family has undergone, one factor remains constant: the relations between the generations and between spouses are essentially based on forms of domination and submission. Although in sociological literature this theme is modified to suggest that rigid family authority and discipline become progressively more relaxed, this does not affect the family in its essentials. Undoubtedly, there have been periods when women appeared emancipated, if not superior to men. There have even existed tendencies that would allow the wishes of the younger generation relatively free rein in the family as a whole. Nonetheless, the fundamental form of the bourgeois nuclear family, led by the *paterfamilias,* in which specific concrete social duties are demanded from the individual members, remains unchanged.

In the Middle Ages not only agrarian production but also trade and industry was essentially carried out in the family. Today, however, work takes place outside the home and employs labor sources in such a way that the contribution of family members no longer plays an essential role, as it did in the past. Of course, the role of the family in bourgeois society is not limited to that of an organ of consumption. If this were true, it would be difficult to understand why the beginnings of capitalism in Western Europe coincided precisely with the emergence of an unusually disciplined family organization. Especially in the Protestant countries the view arose that the *paterfamilias* was entrusted by God and society with an important task, namely, to create out of his family an upright community that would find in order and hierarchy, love of work, and self-denial and true, ecclesiastically sanctioned goals of life.[1] This absolute "superior rank" of the father over the woman, children, and servants, along with his right to mete out physical punishment, cannot be explained on the basis of the distribution of consumer goods alone. Rather, it indicates other important functions of the bourgeois family.

One may speak of a public and a private existence in the modern era to the extent that work takes place in the free market under the conditions of competition while the family becomes a place of consumption, rest, and the development of emotional life. This separation must not, however, be understood too narrowly. The "outside" of the career and the "inside" of the family are interrelated insofar as the family represents the sphere for which paid work is consciously carried out. The egotism of individuals that goads them into productivity is not limited to the pursuit of individual interests but, as a rule, also those of the nuclear family. As individuals produce for the market, they ensure, without knowing or desiring it, the reproduction of society as a whole and simultaneously the interests of limited individual families that are mutually exclusive economically.

The relationship between society and family may appear to be an external one. Indeed, to a certain extent, this authoritarian form is also characteristic of previous periods. In reality, the separation of the family from the sphere of actual production considerably increased its importance in society. As is clearly shown even today in backward agrarian modes of production, strong relationships of authority are formed in all cases where the family is also the basic unit of production. The father knows the business of production better than his children, and the demand to respect his authority is, from a practical perspective, rational. This respect becomes transformed, without great difficulty, into a character structure that respects the authoritarian basis of society per se. On the other hand, where the separation of production and consumption has occurred, as is generally characteristic of the bourgeois family, the education of authoritarian characters, that is, of people who sincerely accept given social conditions and thus reproduce these conditions in their social behavior, becomes an important social task. The capitalist process of production, which takes place outside the home, demands authority in a twofold manner. It demands that a person adapt himself to a regulated, diligent, exact mode of work, to order and punctuality, to manual and verbal precision. On the other hand, it demands the acceptance as a natural and unchangeable fact of the separation of those who own the means of production and those who do not. Herein lies the actual social task of the bourgeois family. Having ceased to produce directly, the bourgeois family now acquires the important role of establishing one of the most crucial conditions of production, namely, reinforcing the authority necessary for the maintenance and reproduction of bourgeois society.

The family is subject to this function in a twofold manner. On one hand it is created by society as a whole, as a cultural entity in which authoritarian character types are produced. At the same time, these character types conversely influence society and thereby reinforce its authoritarian character. Just as the family and the services rendered by it for authority must be understood from the perspective of the mode of production, this mode itself is continually reproduced anew by those people whose characters were molded on the foundation of this production mode.

We begin by speaking about paternal authority in the family but not only because the power of paternal authority became so clearly visible in the initial period of bourgeois society; the crucial factor for understanding the father's role is that his authority derives directly from the man's role in production. He is the one who, by providing the family with the means of sustenance through his activity in the sphere of production, also comes to represent power in the sphere associated with the acquisition of goods in bourgeois society. That the father in the bourgeois family procures the "means of consumption" and both establishes and increases the inheritable property of the family has profound effects on the emotional relationships of family members. Because he possesses this authoritarian position in the family by virtue of this economic function, and the other family members are directly dependent on his role as producer, the feelings of love and affection, respect and attachment, are affected in an essential way by the father's economic supremacy. The psychological structure of love in the family is dependent on an economically decisive, superior figure; this love cannot be explained as a social phenomenon without its authoritarian aspects.

The dual character of authority is reproduced in a specific way in the paternal role. On the one hand, the objective function of the father is his family's powers of consumption through his activities in the sphere of production, in which he himself is subject to the general law of social authority. His authority bears witness to his necessary role in protecting the family's interests under the given circumstances. On the other hand, his services for the family bring with them a position of dominance within the family. This dominance is expressed not only in legal terms but above all in the prestige and respect that the father enjoys within the family. In child rearing, the processes that serve to create authority and to form authoritarian characters converge. This is not to say that the content of upbringing and education is meaningless; nor are the emotional processes that are characteristic of the father as "child rearer" always consciously carried out as authoritarian measures. However, the knowledge imparted in upbringing is essentially a knowledge of relationships of hierarchy in history and nature. The entire conscious and unconscious atmosphere in which the child rearing takes place, i.e. the family, especially in the relationship of the father to the children, is itself authoritarian both in its own structure and in what it teaches.

However punishment is grounded in pedagogical theory and practice, whether simply as an expression of the blind obedience or as the rational consequence of irresponsible behavior, it remains a crucial part of bourgeois child rearing that achievement and reward, failure and punishment, are directly linked. When the child is made to carry out assigned tasks, to refrain from certain actions, and to perform other less pleasant ones, this familial demand on the child reproduces the consciousness of bourgeois society and its laws of life. Just as the father must concern himself with success in the sphere of production, and the degree to which he realizes this success is considered a result of his achievement, likewise in upbringing itself the association of effort and success is presented as the authoritatively highest standard. In the initial periods of capitalist development it was particularly necessary to proclaim labor the highest virtue, and economic success as labor's just reward. If this motto is no longer continually propagated openly, this is not because it has become less necessary for the reproduction of capitalist class relationships but rather, above all, because the fulfillment of this condition for bourgeois production has been taken over by familial upbringing in an increasingly automatic way.

As a direct result of this association of effort and success, bourgeois society expects the acceptance of the unequal distribution of social wealth among various classes and groups. This necessary clement of bourgeois ideology is also based on authoritarian, paternal upbringing. The rules of good behavior, the demand on the child to be "good," that is, either to identify with the behavior of adults or to modify his own behavior so that it does not appear as disruptive to the adults' life, promotes the development of a character that in later life will require a respect for the status quo from itself and its subordinates.

Situations in which the father represents a society that demands recognition are, of course, not limited to the examples given above. The fact that he is decisive in determining the religion and often the child's profession is the most obvious and palpable way in which the father subjects the child to societal authority.

The family has at its disposal means to maintain authority that are other than conscious. The child growing up in the nuclear family is brought up to believe in authority simply due to the fact that the child perceives adults as bigger, older, indeed, all-powerful. The extent to which authority is established as natural at an early stage in the child's character due to the fact that the child is dependent on the power and will of adults is a psychological question. In any case the child experiences the power and demands of economic relationships through the father and indirectly through the respect that is shown the father by other family members.

The conscious and unconscious methods of child rearing in the patriarchical bourgeois family contribute to the formation of a character that is disposed to see in the status quo the authoritative dignity necessary for its own existence. People of the present historical era have learned to view the world essentially from a perspective of domination and subordination. This begins with the views of God contained in the positive religions and the "ethical paradises" of idealistic philosophy, in the division of people into those who accomplish something and those who fail. Here it is unimportant whether this division is expressed either in the historical schema of great men and great peoples or in the enthusiasm over the biographies of well-known personalities; or in the more or less conscious association of a happy or unhappy fate of people or groups with merit or blame. This perspective is also suggested by the fact that questions of personal and social prestige play a role in emotional life, in the relation of the state and its organs to the citizens, and in the hierarchy in business life manifested in competitive battles between companies, but equally present in the smallest office. From the foregoing discussion of relations between social and private forms of intercourse that derive from family organization, it is clear that in bourgeois society the real and ideal worlds are constantly experienced in categories of domination and subordination.

Because a person in bourgeois society does not develop his life in society on the basis of planned, collective action, organizational forms of this society are constructed so that the individual does not, in working together with other individuals, consciously subject extrahuman nature to the control of society (that is, does not consciously adapt nature to the real interests of humankind); rather, it is the fate of the isolated individual to adapt and subordinate himself to reality. Indeed, it is only through this act of subordination, that is, by accepting the existing class structure of society as the only means of social reproduction, that the bourgeois individual has any possibility whatsoever of asserting himself in life. The child learns to subordinate himself to his father's authority as part of a process of adaptation to the conditions of bourgeois life.

The instilling of this "proper perspective of reality," which is brought about through the father's authoritative role, also pertains to the cultural and ethical values that have developed in the course of modern history and are connected with the dynamics of bourgeois society. Certainly, in family life the values stressed are those that were developed in the early periods of the capitalist order as slogans opposed to obsolete and retrograde forms of life. The slogans were taken so seriously that the rising bourgeois strata, largely embattled, sacrificed much—both goods and lives—for them. Freedom and justice, veracity and courage, moral consistency in deed and thought are the ethical ideals that originally exerted their influence. They were also passed down as values in the upbringing of children.

When the child experiences repeatedly that adults contradict the ideals that they profess so authoritatively, when the child can observe that the father, who seemed to personify unconditionally the world of values, relativizes this world through petty injustices, bad moods, and insincerity, then it is not a question of mere coincidence. Instead, the inculcation of perspectives necessarily involves making the child aware of the highly relative validity of ethical ideals vis-à-vis the reality of social relations. During puberty the merely relative authority of accepted values is manifested in striking fashion, for when the adolescent attempts to act on the basis of his own drives, wishes, and impulses in the name of those values learned from his parents, he does this in opposition to his parents and especially his father. In the course of this process, the child experiences in an often very severe and drastic manner the situation that is known as adapting to the facts, as a result of the so-called impossibility of changing the existing world. All of the "relativities" connected with bourgeois society, whether known by the catchword of reasons of state, social morality, the factual bottom-line, the white lie, the natural limitations of human wants and plans, or the unalterable nature of destiny, belong to this concept of "proper perspective of reality" (*Realitätsgerechtigkeit*), which enters into the formation of bourgeois personalities through the authority of the patriarchal nuclear family. Clearly, a bourgeois education is not oriented toward rearing revolutionary individuals.

The process of child rearing contains two aspects: it is an expression of a social order that is socially contradictory, and it promotes the reproduction of necessary social functions. Without the acceptance of the social tradition, societal operation of society would cease to function. However, in bourgeois processes of socialization that side of authority is reproduced that helps confirm the negative aspects of order through the necessary acceptance of the order as natural and unchangeable. Furthermore, the authoritarian relationship between father and son does not function clearly as a breach between the two generations. Certainly, the possession of authority signifies for the father a strengthening of his own interests and desires, an increase in prestige, self-confidence, and power. On the other hand, the son certainly experiences his passive role, the disciplining of his actions and reactions, as a wrong done to him, indeed, an injustice. Nonetheless, there arise directly overlapping interests. By rearing the son by authoritarian methods and thereby inculcating a "realistic" attitude—that is, an acceptance of reigning societal authority, relations including the prevailing relationships of dominance and subordination—the father hopes at the same time to create the successor to his own position in the sphere of production. He is thus raising his own future partner, his own future breadwinner. But the father is simultaneously attending to the real social interests of the son as his heir, an authoritarian character (an important and necessary condition for the bourgeois position in production) who is capable of looking out for the father's personal interests. The father reproduces in his family an identical class interest for the next generation. When, as we have observed, in the last great economic crisis a loss of authority occurred principally in those families where the bourgeois *paterfamilias* lost his leading function in the economy or sank into unemployment and poverty, then this negative phenomenon shows that the positive subordination to paternal authority—characteristic for the bourgeois family in earlier epochs—stands in direct relation to the father's actual social position.

At present [1934] in totalitarian states tendencies are becoming evident that amount to a *conscious* promotion of the authoritarian structure of the family. This situation is similar to the one that prevailed at the beginning of the bourgeois epoch. Then as well, under the direct pressure of state and ecclesiastic authorities, the maintenance of family authority and in particular paternal authority was raised to a social and ethical duty. At that time the son's subordination to paternal authority was compensated by material and social rewards. Now, however, the same demands occur in a fundamentally different social context, insofar as the critical economic stiuation has made it necessary to demand respect by all means possible for an order that functions only for the benefit of special interests. The increasing indications of rebellious impulses on the part of the younger generation of the bourgeoisie and its members' increasing embitterment point to the breach that exists between what paternal authority demands and what it has to offer. It seems that W. H. Riehl's prescription should be applied to these late bourgeois groups. In his book on the family, an illuminating objective lesson on the significance of authority in the bourgeois family, Riehl formulates this in an almost prophetic manner:

> At present [in 1865] the recognition of the authority of the prince, the administration, public legislation, the church, in sum, of all public powers of life, is demanded more urgently than at previous times. This can mean none other than that the conscious or instinctive bending of one's will is demanded in the interest of the whole. This spirit of respect for authority only becomes prevalent among the masses when a generation is imbued with a feeling of respect for the complete authority of the family. The apparently restored authority of public powers will remain completely tenuous and fragile as long as the authority of the family structure is not restored within the home. In the civilized Europe of today, a patriarchal state structure, based purely on a relationship of authority and piety, can no longer exist. However, a patriarchal family structure can and must exist where a genuinely conservative spirit is to reign among citizens. Only in the home, moreover, can our people attain the spirit of authority and piety, in the home they can learn how discipline and freedom go hand in hand, how the individual must sacrifice himself for a higher moral collective personality—the family. And in state life, although it is built on a different idea than the family, the fruits of this home will be harvested.[2]

In the "classical" bourgeois family, no breach exists either between the father's authority and his social position or between his demands and his son's interests. These conditions are very different in the proletarian family. Certainly here, too, one finds a strong tendency to raise children according to the model of the bourgeois family, but this is true only for certain periods and certain strata that are dominated by ideologies of social mobility. However, insofar as these families are conscious of the social situation of nonpropertied groups, authoritarian forms of child rearing are not found in such a pronounced manner. Due to the harsh compulsion of reality—want, poverty, the insecurity of employment, the constant threat of accident, hunger, or other severe reverses of fate—the proletarian family, in which not only the father but also the mother and children must work, presents a much less rigid structure than the bourgeois family.

The strict separation of the public and professional sphere from the private sphere of existence of family members does not arise out of the actual situation of the proletarian family. When, for example, the father advances, in the same authoritarian manner as does the father in the bourgeois family, his demands in the child's upbringing, thereby identifying himself with interests that are not relevant to the actual social life of his class, then in fact there exists the same breach between his authority and his children as exists between his authority within the family and his position in society. In the more developed proletarian families the relations between the generations tend to be ruled not by authority but by a feeling of comradery and solidarity against a world of hostile interests.

In earlier stages of bourgeois development the accusation of prodigality, luxury, and overly refined pleasures was continually leveled by rising groups against the court and all those who profited directly from the absolutist regime. Conversely, one of the measures used by the absolutist state, whenever it found itself in conscious battle with the bourgeoisie, was to vanquish the ascetic and rational morality of the oppositional groups through the promotion of pomp and splendor, and through offering various sensual pleasures. The relativization of pleasure belongs to the regulation of bourgeois society. On the one hand, an upbringing that stresses a strict work ethic and the recognition of duty as the highest virtue is a means of dominating the broad masses. On the other hand, the production and increase of profit, the accumulation of the means and products of production, the investment of liquid capital in organic capital in order to assure constantly increased production, all demand an extensive limiting of consumption and of material pleasures. The state of the productive forces in itself allows for a considerable increase in the potential for cultural and material pleasures. However, the conditions of production, geared solely for profit, become obstacles to the conception of the many possible forms of pleasure and happiness open to human beings. These conditions also cause people to discipline their wishes and to deceive themselves about their wishes in the interest of the sphere of production. The family developed its own particular sexual morality and at the same time, in the interests of material welfare, social standing, and the future of individual family members, obliged those family members, but especially the economically decisive father, continually to make do with modest comforts and to limit their own pleasures. In this way, through the family, society as a whole exerts a strong authoritative influence over individual interests and needs. Thus the family becomes the place of both the development and the limitation of consumption.

Society's authority over the bourgeois family is directly asserted over women. Owing to the dominant position occupied by the male because of his role as breadwinner, the female is a subordinate. Beginning with education at home and in school, the prospects of her intellectual and emotional development are fundamentally less favorable than the male's. As a rule, her life takes place outside the actual sphere of production, although, to be sure, she is indirectly dependent on that sphere through the man. Just as the father's authority stems not only from his natural aptitudes, age, and experience, but also from the reification of a social relationship, i.e. his position in production, reified traits are also present in the woman's position. It is impossible to determine what role is played by purely economic interests in the emotional relationships that link her to her husband and children, but it is precisely in the woman's economically subordinate and dependent position that the demands of society as a whole are manifested in her.

From a social standpoint, the woman's role is a conservative one. Her life takes place in the narrow confines of the family, which results in her dependency. On the other hand, this dependency is at the same time the basis of her existence, and it is her powerlessness that makes her the guarantor of the family's interests and thereby also of the authority produced in it. In a time of economic instability the petty bourgeoisie defends its threatened position stubbornly and clings to a rigid social situation. Similarly, women hold onto a form of life that is often diametrically opposed to their potential for self-development. The behavior of women in society is that of an oppressed group who, if they wish to live, have no other choice but to adapt themselves to existing conditions.

Women are subordinate to the social authority represented by the male, but they also encourage this situation by adopting their position. In this reciprocal process of passive subjugation to authority and its active encouragement, women themselves assume authoritative traits. Out of the limiting precepts and prohibitions of sexual morality arises the ideal of the housewife and mother—of the special dignity afforded her in the family organism as a whole. She becomes the guarantor of feelings of tenderness and affection that are evinced her by family members and are encouraged by her within the family. If the father's authority is the material prerequisite for the reproduction of the family, then its emotional security is essentially assured by the social elevation of the feminine and maternal role. In the hierarchy of socially recognized values neither her sexual partnership with the husband nor her biological functions as mother appear as the reason for the respect and reverence felt toward her. The former is considered nothing more than a duty based on religion or law, the latter remains the natural foundation which, to be sure, appears to be self-evident and unchangeable for the care and upbringing of children.

In bourgeois art and literature the motive of subordination and the trivialization of sexual and natural functions is transformed and adapted in favor of certain recognized emotional values. To be sure, the direct connection between the family and the underlying economic order is not always expressed so naively as in the classic family novel of the liberal German bourgeoisie, that is, Gustav Freytag's *Soll und Haben,* where the way to the girl's heart is through the prayer on the first page of the "T. O. Schröter & Co. secret ledger" and where the father, beaming with joy, says to his new son-in-law: "When you left us, I angrily saw my fondest hopes destroyed. Now we hold you, you dreamer, in the pages of the 'secret ledger' and in our arms."[4]

In the classical period of the rise of the bourgeoisie two literary themes were developed in which the connection of restrained and devalued sexual pleasure in the family and the irreconcilability of an uninhibited life of pleasure with the existing societal values are clearly portrayed. In *Don Juan* the principle of sensuality finds its embodiment. His obsession with his sexual desires is paired with his lack of faithfulness and change without end of sexual partners. The pleasure principle is irreconcilable with the world whose law of production demands self-denial and restriction. The figure of Don Juan has, as it were, a negative ideological significance: it teaches that the relation of sexuality and monogamy is a necessity of nature simply because the drive for pleasure, seeking change and variety, diminishes the spiritual quality of those people who give free rein to this drive.

The devaluation of sexual pleasure in bourgeois society was justified by means of the converse devaluation of higher spiritual values that in principle must occur when their unconditional superiority is not accepted in the form prescribed by society. *Romeo and Juliet* satisfy this norm: the bourgeois ideal of marriage is suggested by the exclusivity of their relationship of romantic love. The relationship between the two is felt to be eternal; it is not primarily grounded in sensuality but rather in the wish for exclusive possession and community. The entire social consciousness of the bourgeoisie is reproduced in the conviction of the permanence of marriage. Just as in production, the distribution of social wealth, the relations between competing groups, the division between the haves and the have-nots are thought of as naturally necessary and eternal categories, so are the forms of human interaction for the purposes of consumption, pleasure, and spiritual development conceived as eternal and unchangeable.

This chapter has attempted to show that there exists a constant dialectic between society in general and the bourgeois family in particular. In the family, character types are produced that, by following the father's example and by accepting the values of domination and subordination, strive to realize these same values in society by seeing their achievement of success within the parameters of the status quo and by opposing the tendencies that call for a change in the structure of the given order. And, the workings of society, its laws of production as well as the mores and reactions connected with it, encourage individuals continually to reproduce the family. This process of exchange maintains existing power relationships and acts in this capacity as a retarding factor, as a putty holding things together when the contradictions of this order begin to threaten the order itself. This relation of society to the family as a repository of social authority helps determine a considerable part of a person's destiny. Certainly, on the one hand, in a world of competitive battles between opposing profit interests, the family is the place of rest and emotional relaxation, where the individual may behave unencumbered by the laws of competition and can fulfill his own personal wishes. On the other hand, the influence of interests related to the preservation of the social order also has a negative effect in the family.

Because the economic factor plays a role in all relationships, it remains uncertain what form interpersonal relationships would take under social conditions where production and profit were not so closely related. Love between spouses, as well as that felt for children and between siblings, is subject in every detail to general social influences— e.g. the fundamental relationships of domination and subordination, the restrictions placed on women's self-realization, and the disciplining of adolescents in accordance with their later social functions in a society split according to competing classes. This obviously signifies a far-reaching curtailment and atrophy of the possibilities for human development. Just as the social forces of production are hampered by the special interests who control their means, similarly the force of production capable of forming every human individual is based on a constant restriction that the individual experiences as a basic fact of life through the authoritarian functions of the family.

When at the end of the nineteenth century certain progressive literary groups of the bourgeoisie became aware of the problematic of the family and its dubious significance for human happiness, the phenomena of oppression and the gradual atrophy of authentic life forms were expressed in literature. Ibsen's naturalistic dramas portray the tragedies of women and children who due to the economically conditioned authoritarian structure of their family life fail to find meaning in their personal existence. Strindberg's works reveal the enormous human cost of the machinations of authority that is paid by the emotional reactions of oppressed individuals: people become evil. Whether under different social conditions, where the family would no longer have the task of promoting an authority that supports a contradictory social order, the family would continue to fulfill some or all of its other functions is a question that must remain unanswered here.

Notes

1. Cf. besides Max Weber's well-known works on the sociology of religion, especially Levin L. Schücking, *Die Familie im Puritanismus* (Leipzig and Berlin, 1929).
2. W. H. Riehl, *Die Familie* (Stuttgart and Augsburg, 1865), pp. 124f.
3. Cf. Löwenthal, *Schriften,* vol. 2, pp. 349ff.
4. Cf. ibid., pp.193ff., 237ff.

Excursus

Draft Animals and Slavery

On Lefebvre des Noettes's book *L'attelage. Le cheval de selle à travers les âges* [Harnessing the saddle horse through the ages] (vol. 1, text; vol. 2, illustrations; Paris: A. Picard, 1931).

Although the Enlightenment, which gave the period its name, saw in the Middle Ages only the relapse of the human spirit into dullness and superstition, the Romantics glorified the period as the highest flowering of human culture. Lefebvre des Noettes (L.d.N.), a former French cavalry officer who during and after his service dedicated himself to studies on specific technologico-historical problems, has made significant contributions to a more realistic assessment.[1] He has succeeded in showing that in this "night" of human history civilizatory advances were realized that radically changed human life in all areas of culture.[2] Inventions of the time were of crucial significance for social development, for example, in the twelfth century, water and hand mills, mechanical sawing, the iron hammer and the bellows, window glass and wax candles, stone paving and the Gothic rib vault; in the thirteenth century, the wheeled plow, the movable rudder on boats' sternposts; and in the fourteenth century, the sluice and gunpowder, the pendulum clock and the carpenter's plane. Increasing division of labor and specialization of all artisanal and industrial trades due to this kind of newly opened-up technical possibilities, the higher development of a network of transportation, and the new sophistication in housing all helped to bring about social changes in the distribution of social wealth as well as in intellectual production, even in the individual's private emotional life. Without knowledge of the influence of technological innovations, one cannot hope to understand the period adequately. Our French scholar has provided medieval historical scholarship with important new stimuli.[3]

The dating of some of the achievements mentioned may be found in several specialized reference works. New, however, is L.d.N.'s discovery that already in the ninth century there was in use the type of saddle and harness for horses that is still being used today, and that in the tenth century the modern system of harnessing animals to pull plows or wagons was devised. The emphasis we place on the invention of this technical specialty may at first seem misplaced. What general historical and historiographical interests should be connected with the different composition of objects made of leather, wood, or rope that were used to harness horses or oxen to some sort of machinery, wagons, or plows? To a great extent, L.d.N. attempted to give the answer himself: in several essays, but above all in the work under review, which bears the subtitle—at first glance astonishing— "Contribution à l'histoire de l'esclavage," he shows what insights may be gained for history and sociology from the exact analysis and interpretation of one particular technological detail.[4]

We begin by describing and enumerating the technical facts. The harnessing of draft animals was known in the Orient in 4000 B.C.; in Europe, not before approximately 1000 B.C. In ancient times oxen were harnessed in approximately the same manner as today, but the harnessing of horses differed very considerably from contemporary practice. The ancient horse harness consisted of five main parts—horse collar, girth, yoke, shaft, and bit, that combined and connected in a very particular manner to accommodate the tasks of pulling, turning, braking, support of the wagon, and steering. The collar was a flexible strip of leather without mountings that was placed around the horse's neck right on the spot where the windpipe lies directly under the skin. It was fastened to the yoke above the withers and did not touch the horse's shoulders. The girth, also a flexible leather strip, was fastened around the horse's body close to the front legs, and was attached to the yoke at the same place as the collar. The yoke was a straight or bent wooden rod connected by a tenon and a copper mounting to the front part of the shaft. It rested on the winters of the horse and was tied at both ends to the collar and girth. The shaft was a long, elastic, straight or bent wooden rod that attached to the yoke on one end, and to the axle under the wheel casing on the other. The bit was for all practical purposes similar to the bit in use today. The team generally consisted of two horses harnessed side by side under one yoke. If more than two horses were used, they were also harnessed laterally, but in fact the pulling was done only by the two horses attached to the center shaft that were under the yoke. Attempts were always being made to produce a yoke for more than two horses, but they were unavailing.

The harnessing of oxen in ancient times differed from the modern system in that, just as with horses, oxen were never harnessed with the aid of a guide rope in a long line, one behind the other; only the lateral harnessing method was used. Another difference shared by horses and oxen was the lack of iron shoes to protect the hooves. Contemplating this detail, the nonspecialist will most likely begin to understand the great importance of the matter under consideration.[5] Clearly, animals' hooves were subject to considerable injury. Even more important, was the reduction in draft power caused by the gear described above. The work yield of harnessed animals depends not only on durable hooves but above all on the effort that the individual animal can expend and on the numerical size of the team.

Oxen teams were unsuitable for transport over long distances because their especially sensitive hooves could not endure the hard surfaces of ancient roads. When a horse pulled, the horse collar pressed against the animal's throat and hindered breathing, especially when the animal lowered its head; the relaxed and slack mucles were hence not able to protect the windpipe. The animal would involuntarily throw its head up and rear, the posture often seen in ancient representations of horses. It is precisely this posture that severely reduced the draft power because the animal thereby shifted its weight back and was unable to use its own weight in pulling forward. Consequently, the draft power of an individual horse was extraordinarily small in ancient times. It would have been possible to increase this power had the animals been harnessed in tandem rather than laterally, but this technological notion never occurred to the ancients. The three great technical deficiencies—the throat-constricting collar, the lack of iron shoes, and lateral harnessing—rendered the use value of animal draft power in ancient times surprisingly small. In fact, the maximum weight that the strongest wagon could carry did not even reach 500 kg.

At this point of our discourse it is not surprising if our specialist in the history and technology of harnessing, road material, and wagon construction asks. Why did slavery arise? What was its role in ancient times? Why were so many millions of human beings subjected to the most appalling suffering and regarded as mere machines? Why did the ancient world not do away with this atrocious sore that gnawed on it and that was equally degrading for slave and slaveholder? Why did even the church defend the principle of an institution whose last traces even today we have yet to eradicate totally?

The answers to these questions, according to L.d.N., must be that achievements of civilization such as houses, temples, pyramids, streets, plumbing, and other structural monuments demand the transport of heavy and bulky materials. This transport could not have been accomplished with the kind of animal harness apparatus known to the ancients, and thus necessarily entailed the use of a human work force. When the moving of, say, huge blocks from the quarry to the building site and the utilization of these blocks in the building process were to be carried out solely with human bodily strength, the work exceeded the amount of exertion and physical strain that humans will subject themselves to without being driven to do so by physical violence.

Another operation powered by human exertion in the ancient world was the milling of grain. In principal, windmills and watermills had been invented but the miserable state of the gear for draft animals made their use in the production of flour an impossibility, for the transport of sacks of grain and flour on a large scale would have been exceedingly laborious and costly. However, the hand mill's demands on the human body represent essentially the same amount of effort as does the transporting of these loads. It follows, then, that the reasons for slavery in ancient society may be found in the deficiencies of the harnessing apparatus used on draft animals.

This fact leads us to a sociological law: in every historical period where draft and work animals are not used or used only with very low efficiency, forced human labor will prevail. To ignore this connection between the role of animal power and the forms of social life in historical and social studies is as great an error as a description of modern society and its way of life without consideration of railroads, steamships, automobiles, and machines in general. The revolutions in the means of transport are a crucially important chapter in not only technology but history in general.

"Technology contains in itself man's active behavior towards nature and the direct processes of production of his life and similarly of his social relationships and the mental conceptions arising out of them. Even all history of religion which comes out of this substructure is— uncritical." It is as though L.d.N.'s description had taken this casual observation by Marx as a guiding principle. Indeed, his work represents an important contribution to a "critical history of technology." L.d.N. examines all of the ancient peoples from China to Rome, from the Elam Empire in the fourth millennium B.C. to the Byzantine Empire, then goes on to study the history of colonization from the opening up of American markets to the modern settlements in Madagascar and the Congo. We shall report only a few important points from these historical studies.

It appears that the higher the level of development present in an epoch and the more "cultural structures" it erected, the more severe was the treatment of the slaves.[6] The Arabs, who built almost nothing, the Japanese, whose building materials consisted of light and easy-to-move materials, and many barbaric tribes who were to a certain extent nomadic and thus did not manifest a developed style of living could afford a relatively patriarchal and mild handling of slaves. On the other hand, the building of huge structure such as Assyrian cities, Egyptian royal tombs, Grecian temples, and the various Roman structures of utilitarian or ostentatious nature demanded a particularly onerous fate for the forced laborers. One may counter that slavery was practically unknown in China and yet one finds there numerous great structures, most particularly the famous Great Wall. Despite this, the Chinese did not know the modern method of harnessing draft animals and furthermore, its introduction in modern times was of little use due to the poor state of Chinese roads. L.d.N. argues against this objection as follows: the principal reason that the Chinese, despite their faulty harnessing technique, knew forced labor only in exceptional cases may be explainable because, first, the most important building materials, namely brick and wood, were to be found on the spot; and second, because of their diet of rice, the Chinese did not need thousands of slaves for the operation of the hand mill.

When toward the end of the West Roman Empire the slave trade began to ebb, a long period of decay in public and private construction set in and lasted in Europe until Carolingian times, that is, until just after the revolutionary invention of the new method of harnessing draft animals. At the same time one witnesses the breakdown of serfdom and bondage, a modified form of ancient slavery that still was needed by agriculture as long as horses and oxen proved insufficient help in working the fields. But since the Carolingians an extremely brisk rate of building activity can be observed: monasteries, churches, royal castles, and fortified cities rose up in rapid succession. The history of technical procedures in the Middle Ages reports at length on artisans of all kinds but does not mention slaves at all. Their historical necessity had long passed; they no longer represented a productive economic force but rather a regressive factor that drove prices up in comparison to the efficient power of draft animals. Once that efficient source of power was introduced, there occurred the transformation of the Roman *coloni* and serfs into free peasants who retained their freedom until the social revolutions that began in the early fifteenth century.

The last word on slavery in history had not yet been spoken. The economic opening up of the New World from the sixteenth century until well into the ninteenth century is intimately connected with the slave trade. The treatment slaves were subjected to differed in no way from that of their Roman counterparts, and the social causes were identical. The European conquerors found neither horses nor oxen but needed considerable draft power for their economic enterprises, especially the cultivation of agrarian raw materials, the laying out of roads, and the construction of houses and storage facilities. Although the colonizers were doubtless acquainted with efficient methods of harnessing draft animals, imported beasts soon sickened and died in the new climate. European history was reversed, as it were. A substitute for the animals was sought in the indigenous populations, which were driven into forced labor. When the natives perished rapidly under this treatment, the African slave trade came into being.[7] After the Civil War in the United States, however, the defeated southern states were well able to do without slavery because the agriculturally advanced American Quakers became instrumental in introducing large numbers of draft animals and, hence, efficiently exploitable draft power.

Equally illuminating is the connection between the lack of adequate animal draft power and forced labor in Africa that L.d.N. points out.[8] There were, indeed, oxen in Madagascar, but neither the knowledge of the optimal way of harnessing nor the necessary machinery; moreover, in equatorial Africa the tse-tse fly was a deathly enemy of the ox. Until the introduction of usable oxcarts and the construction of railroads and highways, the economically necessary result of this deficiency—whether it is explained as culturally caused or as arising from natural conditions—was the bearer system, which L.d.N. rightly calls a euphemism for slavery.[9]

These examples give an idea of the richness of the subject matter and the stimulus for further study contained in L.d.N.'s research. Many more could be given. For instance, his research on the genesis of the wheel and the wagon (incidentally, he shows that the wheel had a long and differentiated history before it came to acquire the form as we now know it); on the exclusive use of two-wheeled carts in war, for a pivoted front axle that allowed for steering was invented only in the late Middle Ages (previously, turning a cart had been an extremely troublesome operation); on the deficiencies of ancient roads, including Roman ones, which because of exceedingly hard surfaces caused injury to animals' hooves—as we have seen—and rapidly developed cracks that could not be repaired properly; and on the many attempts—usually unsuccessful—at reforming methods of transportation that were undertaken in the course of the millennia.

All these investigations were carried out with exemplary methodological exactness.[10] L.d.N. took into account the modern criteria of evaluating source material. He never relies on secondhand descriptions or sources; everything is verifiably demonstrated from a study of primary literary and artifact sources. The 500 photographs in his main work present a wealth of depictions of transport and draft technology of animal or human power. Numerous texts are quoted literally and analyzed in detail. The most interesting text, long known to specialists, although its historical value was never appreciated, is Caesar Theodosius's "De cursu publico." This document sets down the maximum allowable payload weight for various commonly used Roman wagons. The top weight was once again only 500 kg., a weight that can easily be moved by a single person with a modern hand truck, thanks to its suspension and stability.

L.d.N. did not limit himself to the study of documents but also carried out practical experiments. In 1910 he used the ancient harnessing on a horse and wagon and was able to prove experimentally the correctness of both his technical theses and his interpretation of ancient documents. In this way he enriched significantly the source-critical apparatus of historical scholarship and contributed to the demolition of the legend that historical scholarship may have no pretensions to scientific exactitude because it does not have recourse to experimentation.

The destruction of legends is, in any case, the duty and characteristic of a progressive study of history. In this respect L.d.N.'s research has a very special significance. Sigmund Freud once said that the resistance that psychological insights encounter may to a great extent be traced to the fact that they offend human narcissism; it is difficult to accept that the most sublime achievements of the emotional apparatus, feelings of love, religion, and the like, have their foundation in the same drives that condition all other manifestations of life, including those not so esteemed by human consciousness. L.d.N.'s statement that slavery disappeared not under the influence of new moral or religious doctrines but exclusively out of technological change and economic necessity is, as it were, in the social sense a similar attack on human narcissism. He not only makes reference to the pitiless and inhuman attitude toward the slave question held by the finest minds of ancient philosophy but also shows how early Christianity and the church fathers, far from fighting slavery, actually exhorted the oppressed individuals to further obedience. He shows that when in the United States slavery became economically necessary for the reasons mentioned above, slaves were again exposed to the same backward moral views as before. The justification of slavery, whether it assumes the brutal features of Aristotelian philosophy or the exalted features of religious teachings, is nothing more than an ideology that serves to transfigure an economically necessary but humanly odious institution.

Passing reference must be made to other successful explanations of L.d.N.'s. The much-praised technical feats of the Roman Empire are revealed in their relative poverty; consequently, many previously held traditional historical conceptions fall apart, for example, on Roman roads,[11] or the alleged enormous transports executed using draft animals,[12] or the stories of breakneck chariot races on the Quadrigas.[13] Similarly, the myth of the technical backwardness of the Middle Ages[14] has been exposed, as has the error of art historians on the meaning of the rearing stance of the horse—previously explained on purely aesthetic grounds.

More essential, however, than these details is the underlying principle. L.d.N.'s studies represent an important theoretical contribution to the understanding of social laws, and in particular to inquiries into the process of man's struggle with nature. L.d.N. begins as a technical specialist, but the inner logic of his research causes him to go beyond this and to study the structure of social life as a whole by concentrating on one particularly illuminating aspect. The forces of production, i.e. that part of the human and the natural world that a society is capable of controlling, represent the fundamental basis on which human life rests. Animals are part of these forces. The extent and ways in which the "controllable" forces of nature are at man's disposal set forth the boundaries within which people must reproduce their lives.

The conditions of a mode of production in which, due to adverse climatic conditions, the animal does not represent a labor source or, due to the low level of technological knowledge, its labor output never reaches that high level required by a certain stratum of society are fundamentally different from those in which a rational technique allows newly discovered natural forces to be exploited in every way. The question of slavery is thus subject to critical historical treatment that goes back directly to the actual sources of social life,[15] and is no longer obliged to limit itself to political,[16] economic,[17] or moralistic[18] arguments. The history of the animal harnessing apparatus is certainly not sufficient to explain such a momentous and complicated historical problem as slavery; correctly recognizing this fact, L.d.N. himself calls his book only a "contribution" to the history of slavery. This historically significant technical detail must, rather, be fitted into the totality of the infrastructure of past epochs; it is one chapter in the organization of the forces of production, the whole natural and technical basis of a certain period. What is most important, however, is L.d.N.'s *method* of research.

In contemporary sociological literature there is a tendency to speak vaguely of a "social" conditioning of all historical events. But the shortcoming of positivism, to dispense of a coherent theory of all historical phenomena, is not overcome by an empty and vague formula that allows for arbitrary metaphysics of historical interpretations. On the contrary, legitimate historical theory comes about only when its methods are so concrete that the study of changes in the cultural sphere can refer to specific fundamental processes of social relevance. History is by no means a unified process in which an ontological "human nature" causes social groupings to be substituted and followed by other social hierarchies. Neither are class struggles irreducible unities of human history; rather, these struggles are rooted in the various stages in which man's relationship to nature is developing.

Historical materialism differs from every kind of "sociologism" precisely in this denial of the inner-human, meaning-giving, unity, as it is still manifested in the dogma of the autonomous dynamic of social groups as an ultimate interpretation of history, a dogma that pretends in vain to overcome another dogma—that of constructing history out of the idealistically conceived human sciences alone. According to the materialist view, the theory of the class struggle is neither merely a working hypothesis nor a schema of historical development that dodges scholarly evaluation; rather, this theory is a perspective constantly to be reviewed and verified by the historical consequences produced in the process of man's struggle with nature. By using a very specific chapter out of the history of technology to explain slavery, L.d.N. helped enrich the concept of social conditioning with an important chapter of scientifically verifiable data.

The cultural-historical results of L.d.N's approach are a good example for the meaning and the limits of division of labor in science. Constantly increasing specialization is doubtlessly legitimate and necessary in order to do justice to the growing multitude of phenomena perceived by man. But in the social sciences, just as in the natural sciences, meaningful results are reached only when a specific study is based on a theoretical image of a totality. In L.d.N's research the special significance of technology as an auxiliary discipline of historical science is once again confirmed. A "critical history of technology" may help to overcome the dogmatic separation of "science" from "humanities"; the technology of the animal draft-harnessing apparatus is on one hand applied physics, and on the other hand a requisite for a concrete sociology of human society. L.d.N. starts by describing the mechanics of the horse harness and ends his study with the conclusion that the theoreticians of the French Revolution were in error when they believed that it was possible to find an example of human solidarity in ancient Greece and Rome. Certain critics of L.d.N's work err no less when they see themselves obliged to conclude that just as the horse and oxen once freed humanity from slavery, now it must necessarily come that the high level of machine technology will automatically remove from human workers the burdens that, as a result of technical backwardness, still oppress them. Although technology is indeed an auxiliary discipline of social theory, it is not its key.

Notes

1. For a bibliography of his works, in particular the numerous scattered essays, see Georges Moulinier in *Bulletin de l'Association—Guillaume Budé*, no. 39 (April 1933): 33–52.
2. Cf. especially his essay "La 'Nuit' du moyen âge et son inventaire." *Mercure de France*, May 1, 1932.
3. In his *Histoire sincère de la nation française,* vol. 1 (Paris, 1958). Charles Seignobos writes, to be sure, without expressly referring to L.d.N.: "The admiration inspired in historians by the Renaissance has given rise to the

habit of considering the Middle Ages as a long period of sterile barbarity as regards inventions. However, the detailed study of labor-related technology has recently been able to show that several processes unknown to the ancients were in common use before the end of the fifteenth century, often even before the thirteenth, although the precise time and country of the invention cannot always be ascertained" (p. 249). (An enumeration of the inventions from L.d.N.'s article [see note 2 above] follows.)

4.   The report that we give on L.d.N.'s research is based essentially on this book but occasionally on his essay "L'esclavage antique devant l'histoire" (A historical view on ancient slavery). *Mercure de France,* February 1, 1933. We will dispense with continual page references to L.d.N.'s arguments.

5.   The French daily press has contributed substantially to making L.d.N.'s research accessible to a broader public by referring to some general perspectives revealed by it. From the Parisian *Temps* to the *Dépêche Tunisienne,* the book on l'*attelage* and the essay on the Middle Ages are considered among the most exciting of contemporary historical literature. For the insight into the numerous reviews in scientific and popular newspapers and magazines, we are indebted to Mr. Lefebvre des Noettes for his kind help.

6.   Gustav Schmoller also sensed this in his *Grundriss der allgemeinen Volkswirtschaftslehre* (Leipzig, 1908): "It was an institution which necessarily arose where large or even enormous projects needed to be carried out with simple technology; only with severe discipline and pitiless treatment could such well-trained workgangs be created out of what was usually the lowest racial elements. The aggravation of the laws of slavery was in many ways the prerequisite for the creation of something great, something technologically better than before" (p. 362).

7.   One of the most striking descriptions of slavery in the New World is Lucien Peytraud's book *L'esclavage aux Antilles Françaises avant 1789* (Paris, 1897).

8.   Cf. the following comment made by Ch. Letourneau, *L'évolution de l'esclavage dans les diverses races humaines* (Paris, 1897): "However, Barth did see, on the southern limits of the Sahara, three slaves tied to a plough and forced to work thus by their Tourareg master, exactly like beasts of burden" (p. 252). To be sure, no conclusions are drawn from this. Similarly Karl Bücher, *Die Entstehung der Volkswirtschaft* (Tübingen, 1908), does not attempt to evaluate the following observations: "Oxen are only to be found among some of the Malays and along a strip of territory, sometimes wider, sometimes narrower, of East Africa, which runs nearly the length of the continent. . . . But most of these peoples do not use the ox as a draught animal . . . here and there in equatorial Africa the ox is used as a riding or pack animal, in general, however, among the Negro peoples possession of oxen . . . is no more than a hobby" (p. 51).

9.   Cf. also Charles-J. Fayet, *Esclavage et travail obligatoire. La main d'œuvre non volontaire en Afrique* (thesis; Paris, 1931): "The greatest necessity in French Equatorial Africa, whose biggest fault is its immensity, was to completely abolish the bearer system by creating bold new access roads and introducing the means of modern communications" (p. 19).

10. This has also been recognized by specialists who—aside from very few exceptions—praise L.d.N.'s studies highly. Cf., for example, Roger Picard (in

Revue de l'histoire économique et sociale, no. 1, [1932]). Victor Chapot writes the following on the attempts to discredit the results of L.d.N.'s research (in *Journal des Savants* [May 1932]): "However, none [of these attempts] has succeeded in disproving the book's basic thesis since the first edition" (p. 209). Cf., also, *inter alia,* Paul Couissin (in *Revue des études anciennes* [1932]: 70). L. Levillain makes an ingenious contribution to the discussion (in: *Le Moyen Age,* no. 3, [1932]): "One could even hold the converse of this thesis to be true . . . that the scarcity of human slave material in the great rural exploitations of Frankish times caused by the drying up of what had been the principal source where the recruitment of slaves had been supplied from the interior, i.e. wars of enslavement, and by the practice of *franchisse-ments,* made it necessary to improve the economic apparatus, in particular the methods of transport and this improvement itself had the effect of favoring, to a certain extent, a social transformation whose roots reach back to the period well before the tenth century" (p. 225). This reference to the societal conditioning of the point in time when a certain invention occurs, and, above all, of its historical effectiveness, is an important supplement to L.d.N.'s thesis but could very well be merely an extrapolation along the line of his historical perspective. (More recently, in *The Structures of Everyday Life* [New York, 1981], Fernand Braudel criticizes L.d.N.'s thesis as an "over-simplification" and writes, "The mistake of Lefebvre des Noettes, still in many ways an admirable writer, was to reduce the history of technology to a simple-minded materialism" [p. 334].)

11. Among the specialized works we sampled: Eugène Campredon, *Le rôle économique et sociale des voies de communications* (Paris, 1899), who calls "the Roman roads . . . one of the glories of the Empire of the Caesars" while allegedly "the Middle Ages knew once more the rudimentary roads of the first centuries" (p. 10); similarly Curt Merckel, *Die Ingenieurstechnik im Altertum* (Berlin, 1899), p. 313; and Heinrich Nissen, *Italische Landeskunde,* vol. 2, first half (Berlin, 1902), "The admiration afforded Roman road con-struction is completely deserved" (p. 150).

12. L.d.N. himself points to Theodor Mommsen's and Karl Joachim Marquardt's uncritical statements on this point.

13. L.d.N. shows that such high speeds as are today [1934] portrayed in popular descriptions and in films could never have been reached.

14. P. Boissonade, *Le travail dans l'Europe chrétienne au moyen age,* new edi-tion (Paris, 1930), has the following to say: "[The Middle Ages were] one of the most brilliant and fecund periods of past history during which labor passed through one of the most decisive stages toward well-being, justice, and liberty" (p. 11).

15. L.d.N.'s views on the Ancient period are recognized and accepted in the newest edition of Gustave Fougères's *Les premières civilisations* (Paris, 1926), p. 404.

16. For example, Boissonnade, *Le travail dans l'Europe chrétienne au moyen âge,* p. 304, who sees in the release of peasants from bondage in the eleventh and following centuries "necessities of the social and economic order" because otherwise the landlords would have lost their serfs to the cities, princes, and ecclesiastic lords who opened their gates to them (p. 304). Strangely

enough, in this context, shortly before this passage he himself—probably without L.d.N.'s influence—observes: "Besides work with a hoe or spade from then on deep ploughing was practiced, repeated as many as seven or eight times, using a plough with an iron ploughshare; the plough was drawn by a powerful team of horses or oxen" (p. 290).

17.   In this vein Peytraud, *L'esclavage aux Antilles Françaises avant 1789*, writes: "As for the plough, for example, it had been imported to the Antilles by the first settlers. But it remained almost totally abandoned until the price of labor fell very low" (p. 451).

18.   Augustin Cochin, *L'abolition de l'esclavage*, 2 vols. (Paris, 1861), p. 456; similar views in H. Wallon, *Histoire de l'esclavage dans l'antiquité*, 3 vols. (Paris, 1879). Turgot pays homage to a humanitarian theory of "natural rights" in his famous treatise "Sur la formation et la distribution des richesses" (*Oeuvres*, vol. 1 [Paris, 1844]: "And though one may supplant human labor by that of animals, there comes a time when the fields can no longer be worked by slaves. Slave labor then survives only as servant work within the manor house and eventually disappears entirely because as nations become civilized they establish among themselves conventions for the exchange of prisoners of war" (p. 18).

Afterword

All the studies collected in this volume on the problems of authoritarianism and anti-Semitism are directly related to the sociopsychological investigations done by the Institute of Social Research in the 1930s and 1940s.

Part I, "Prophets of Deceit. A Study of the Techniques of the American Agitator," was first published in 1949 by Harper as volume 4 of *Studies in Prejudice,* carried out in the 1940s jointly by the Institute of Social Research and the American Jewish Committee.

Part II, "Terror's Dehumanizing Effects," written in 1945, analyzes the first reports given by former prisoners in concentration camps. This essay appeared originally in *Commentary* in 1946.

Part III, see Prefatory Note.

Part IV, the essay, "Toward a Psychology of Authoritarianism." was written in 1934. Both in its contents and in its genesis this essay belongs within the context of the discussions of the early Institute of Social Research. The *Studien über Authorität und Familie* (Studies on authority and family), published by Félix Alcan in Paris in 1936, discussed the historical and historico-theoretical place that the category "authority" assumed in these discussions. The essay was originally conceived as a contribution to the theoretical part of the *Studien,* but because of the diversity of philosophical, historical, and sociopsychological references that characterize it, it could not be incorporated into *Studien über Autorität und Familie*. It is published here in English for the first time.

Excursus, "Draft Animals and Slavery," appeared originally in the *Zeitschrift für Socialforschung* 2 (1933) as a review essay on Lefebvre de Noettes's *L'attelage. Le cheval de selle à travers les âges.* The review of an inherently technicohistorical study examines the historical role of technology in the transition period from the late ancient to early medieval social organization.

Helmut Dubiel

309